Disrupting Archaeology and Art

ALSO AVAILABLE FROM BLOOMSBURY

Curating Transcultural Spaces, Sarah Hegenbart

A Homeric Catalogue of Shapes, Charlayn von Solms

The Parthenon Marbles Dispute, Alexander Herman

Prehistoric Pictures and American Modernism, Elke Seibert

Women, Making, and Everyday Value in Contemporary Installation Art, Elyse Speaks

Disrupting Archaeology and Art

Excavation and Contemporary Painting

DOUG BAILEY AND SIMON CALLERY

BLOOMSBURY ACADEMIC
LONDON • NEW YORK • OXFORD • NEW DELHI • SYDNEY

BLOOMSBURY ACADEMIC
Bloomsbury Publishing Plc, 50 Bedford Square, London, WC1B 3DP, UK
Bloomsbury Publishing Inc, 1359 Broadway, New York, NY 10018, USA
Bloomsbury Publishing Ireland, 29 Earlsfort Terrace, Dublin 2, D02 AY28, Ireland

BLOOMSBURY, BLOOMSBURY ACADEMIC and the Diana logo are trademarks of Bloomsbury Publishing Plc

First published in Great Britain 2026

A catalogue record for this book is available from the British Library.

A catalog record for this book is available from the Library of Congress.

ISBN: HB: 978-1-3505-0751-7
       PB: 978-1-3505-0750-0
       ePDF: 978-1-3505-0752-4
       eBook: 978-1-3505-0753-1

Typeset by RefineCatch Limited, Bungay, Suffolk
Printed and bound in India

For product safety related questions contact productsafety@bloomsbury.com.

To find out more about our authors and books visit www.bloomsbury.com and sign up for our newsletters.

For Claudia
For Paola

Contents

Figures

Figure credits and copyrights

Preface

This book is a conversation between an artist and an archaeologist about what they do, how and why they do it, and how each has worked to perforate the boundaries of his discipline. It is an in-depth exploration, in their own voices, of two people's efforts to work in territories not normally visited by their colleagues and peers. It is a book for artists interested in making work that is archaeological, and for archaeologists interested in making work that is artistic. It is a book for the many members of the public who visit excavations and museums of history and archaeology, and who want to know more about those places and processes from the perspectives of an archaeologist with field- and research-experience. Equally, it is a book for those who visit art museums and galleries where art of an archaeological aesthetic is on display, and who want to look inside the processes of one artist who has made work of that type. Readers in search of detailed histories or theories of art or of archaeology are advised to look elsewhere.

Acknowledgements

Doug Bailey

None of the work that I include in this book would exist if I had not had the support, advice, critique, and encouragement of many people; this starts with my colleagues and students in the Anthropology Department of San Francisco State University. They are the foundation for what is possible. More specifically, as relates to each of the main works discussed, the following particular thanks are gratefully given.

The list of essential collaborators, friends, and allies without whose help *Twenty Minutes Inside Out* would not have come into being begins with colleagues in Romania at the Teleorman Regional Historical Museum (Pavel Mirea), at Cardiff University (Steve Mills), as well as at SF State (Peter Biella, whose guidance in making the film, but also in editing it for me, was invaluable). Many thanks to Ruth Van Dyke and Reinhard Bernbeck for their invitation to contribute to the session at the Sacramento meetings of the Society for American Archaeology and then their willingness to include the montage-chapter into the book that resulted. To make that montage I relied heavily on my co-author Melanie Simpkin.

Inspiration for *Which Ruins do we Valorize* came fully from the invitation by my friends and colleagues, Bjørnar Olsen and Þóra Pétursdóttir, who found conceptual space in their book for my unusual contribution. Without the support of the staff at the Hoover Institution Library and Archive, I would have struggled to identify and use the many items of image- and text-based material about mid-twentieth-century Romania.

Long is the list of people to whom I am in debt related to making *Releasing the Archive*, ranging from colleagues at SF State (Niccolo Caldararo, who brought me the original box of transparencies), to my cohort of research fellows at the Centre for Advanced Study of the Norwegian Academy of Sciences where I experimented with and developed that work (Elin Andreassen, Torgeir Bangstad, Hein Bjerck, Caitlin DeSilvey, Bjørnar Olsen, Þóra Pétursdóttir, Tim Lecain, Alfredo González-Ruibal, Chris Witmore), and to my never distant creative muse for that project (Michelle Jones). Colleagues who invited me to present workshops and lectures about *Releasing* as it developed in Oslo (at the Kulturhistorisk Museum; thanks to Silje Opdahl Mathisen and her colleagues), at the Centre for Advanced Study at the Academy of Sciences (thanks to Rune Flaten), in Gothenburg (at the Museum of Antiquities; thanks to Anita Synnestvedt), in Stockholm (at the Department of Archaeology and Classical Studies of the University of Stockholm; thanks to Mats Burström and his department colleagues), and in Copenhagen at the Saxo Institute (thanks to Tim Flor Sørensen and his students and colleagues), as well as to the engaged audiences at each of those public lectures.

The two exhibitions of *Releasing* in Portugal would never have occurred without the early connection with friend and sculptor Sara Navarro. Her invitation to collaborate led first to the show at Santo Tirso's International Museum of Contemporary Sculpture (and their incredible team [thanks to Álvaro Moreira, Tânia Pereira]), which, in turn led to the follow-up exhibition in Lisbon at Carpintarias de São Lázaro (thanks to their phenomenal group of colleagues: Fernando Bela, Alda Galsterer, Luís Leal, Ana Malta, Luísa Correia Silva). Support from an SF State Marcus Research Grant helped with shipping costs for the Santo Tirso show. Many thanks both to Morgan Collins and Mark Hanson at Hanson Digital in San Francisco and to Amélia Dias at Casa dos Reclamos in Santo Tirso for preparing the digital files and for printing and mounting the images for the Portuguese shows.

At a much more specific level, this book would never have emerged if Simon Callery had not accepted my invitation to participate in the *Ineligible* show in Santo Tirso. Meeting Simon (finally) in person at that opening in 2020 led to what has become a never-ending series of conversations and collaborations (and hours of Zooming during Covid) that is the guts of this book. I am grateful to him for his patience with my approaches to contemporary art (and his work), and I look forward to much future work with him.

On the most personal note, none of what I do would be possible without the quiet care, patience, and support of my wife, Claudia, and to her I dedicate this work.

Simon Callery

I would like to take this opportunity to thank archaeologist Gary Lock for the unrestricted access he has offered me into the world of field archaeology for over twenty-five years. I have been extremely fortunate and have received an education without parallel on his excavation sites. Thank you to my co-author archaeologist Doug Bailey for his determination and belief in the value of archaeology and art collaboration and for steering this book through multiple stages.

There are many people I wish to thank for their individual contributions. Some have assisted me with art-making or with the preparations for exhibitions. Others have dug the sites where I have worked or have been instrumental in organizing them. Each and every one has offered something valuable, directly or indirectly, for my painting. There are organizations and funding bodies to thank. Some of their names have changed over the time span of my projects so, here, I use the original names.

For the *Segsbury Project*. The University of Oxford, Ruskin School of Drawing and Fine Art (Paul Bonaventura). Paul initiated my art and archaeology collaboration and set it all in motion. The Institute of Archaeology (Gary Lock, Chris Gosden, Zena Kamash, Tyler Bell, Sheila Raven). The Henry Moore Foundation Contemporary Projects (David Thorp, Charu Vallabhbhai). English Heritage (David Miles, Miriam Levin). Art + Archaeology (Helen Wickstead). The Storey Gallery, Lancaster (John Angus). Fellow artist, photographer Andrew Watson and printer Gordon Bishop. For work on the realization of *Trench 10* (Artist Kabir Hussain, Michael Boffey, Phil Brown, Alex Dexter, Katie Dexter, Tom Slingsby, Anthony Sleesor, Matthew Roberts, Stephen Nelson, Andy Payne. Chris Callery, Jonathan Callery, Andreas Callery). Photographer John Riddy, designer Martin Brown, and AB Foundry.

For *Chromium Oxide Cut Pit Painting*. The Arts and Humanities Research Council Creative Fellowship. The University of the Arts London, Wimbledon School (Mark Fairnington, Anita Taylor). Oxford Archaeology (David Jennings, Ben Ford). Oxford Archaeology excavation team on A2 Site

(Alexa Stevenson, Anthony Morrin, Celine Beauchamp, Kieron Armitage, Sam Oates, Dan Millar, Rachel Bynoe, Dan Howells, Paul Clarke, Veronica Bisio, and colleague Graham Fawcett).

For *Country Register*. The University of Oxford, School of Archaeology (Gary Lock, John Pouncett). The University of Southampton (Paul Reilly). Denbighshire County Council (Fiona Gale). CADW (Will Davies). Fellow artist Stefan Gant. Excavation team (Jude Brown, Paula Levick, Simon Maddison, Pete Robertson, Christine Markussen, John Gibbs, Alice Bray, Eric Harkleroad, Richard Coe, Matthew Stevenson, Jon Humble, Guus Lange, Debs Young, Lisa Brown, Peter Davenport, Gary Shipp, Linda Richards, Sally Taylor, Shelagh Norton, Lorrae Campbell, Owen Kearn).

I dedicate this book to Paola Piccato. With heartfelt thanks for your support and help with the reading and re-reading of many draft texts.

Both of us (Doug and Simon) found in Lily Mac Mahon (Commissioning Editor for Archaeology and Ancient History at Bloomsbury) a true supporter with never faltering belief in this book project. We are in debt. To Sophie Beardsworth, we offer thanks for her careful and expert oversight of the book's production. Thanks, as well, to the anonymous reviewers of the original proposal and of the final manuscript; your comments made for a better final book.

1

Two journeys, three voices

This book brings together output and dialogue of a contemporary painter and an archaeologist. In their work, each has moved in unconventional directions: with his work on excavation sites and in exhibitions, Simon Callery rethinks what contemporary painting is and what it can be; with his art/ archaeology publications and exhibitions, Doug Bailey questions the primacy of archaeology as the best way to engage the past and its artefacts. Though their efforts sit within two distinct disciplines, Bailey and Callery share significant concerns and intentions. This common ground is seen most obviously in their shared attention to archaeological action, both as a field practice and as a means of relating our present to the past.

This book explores these common themes in two ways. First, six chapters examine Bailey and Callery's shared and individual takes on authorship, originality, time, and meaning within disciplines; those chapters also explore the potentials for innovative collaboration between art and archaeology. Second, six chapters present Doug and Simon's individual creative works. In an effort to register the mix of personal and shared perspective and output, these latter six chapters are written in the first person, while the former come from an anonymous third person: an amalgam of Bailey and Callery's voices. Intermingled, the chapters take the reader on deep dives into transformative work at the intersection of art and archaeology, led by the words and works of two people standing at the centre of those crossroads.

More than the usual academic, manifesto-making, and philosophical wondering about what might be possible, these twelve chapters explore art and archaeology from finished work (richly described) and from conversations about why those works were made, about their makers' intentions, about the consequences for both art and for archaeology, but also about how work can transcend both authors' disciplines. In format and tone, this book is not a research monograph in the standard tradition, heavy in jargon, theoretical positioning, diverted with references and footnotes. Instead, as with Doug and Simon's ways of working, the chapters flow freely as if a conversation, which, in fact, was how the book was created.

Simon Callery: a contemporary painter on excavation

An established artist who has shown internationally since the 1990s, Simon has built a position as one of the artists most fully engaged with archaeological work. His project-based collaborations with archaeology span a number of locations: Segsbury Project (Segsbury Camp and Alfred's Castle,

Oxfordshire, 1996–2003); Thames Gateway Project (London, Kent and Essex, 2006–09); Stonehenge Riverside Project (Wiltshire, 2008); and the Moel-y-Gaer, Bodfari and Nesscliffe Hill Camp excavations (North Wales and Shropshire, 2013–24). Simon worked with the School of Archaeology, University of Oxford on the Segsbury Project, the excavations of which were directed by Gary Lock and Chris Gosden. Also, at Bodfari and Nesscliffe Hill Camp, directed by Gary Lock, John Pouncett, and Paul Reilly. The Thames Gateway Project was an Arts and Humanities Research Council, Creative Fellowship in partnership with Oxford Archaeology hosted by Wimbledon College, University of the Arts London. The Stonehenge Riverside Project was an Art + Archaeology project organized by Helen Wickstead.

Simon's attention has always been on the process of excavation rather than artefacts, post-excavation analysis, or interpretation. For him, working with archaeology is about access to the landscape-based process of field archaeology. His work on site has been seasonal: intense periods of two or three weeks followed by long periods when he would be back in his London studio. The resulting works have included photography, large-scale sculpture, painting, and paper-based drawing.

When he was first invited to work with archaeologists in 1996, Simon initially saw it as an opportunity to immerse himself in landscape. He wanted to confront it as a subject for contemporary painting. His work at the time was rooted in the urban environment, but it was starting to lean towards a broader notion of landscape. This was a difficult period to be a painter. Negativity towards painting was the accepted position of fashionable curators, critics, and artists in London in the mid-1990s. There was a particular scorn reserved for the landscape painting. Simon was not immune to this criticism and knew it was the moment to question the function of painting and what it needed to remain a relevant art form.

From image to material

Simon first went on site at Segsbury Camp, an Iron Age hill fort on the chalk downlands of the Ridgeway in Oxfordshire. He immediately recognized similarities between the two disciplines, particularly in the management and treatment of surfaces. Simon was fascinated by the physical process of excavation, by the archaeological recording methods, and by the textures, colours, and spatial complexity of the excavated surfaces. As an artist concerned with finding ways to slow down the experience of looking at painting, he found the sense of temporality on the excavation site particularly compelling.

The primary focus of Simon's work has been to find ways to make artwork in response to the physical characteristics and features of excavation sites. His thinking has been informed by the excavation process and by aspects of archaeological thought. Stratigraphy was important in connecting a principle of excavation to painting through its geometry of intersecting vertical and horizontal line and expression of time. The concept of a continuity of use of a site or a landscape provoked new ways for Simon to think about place, not only to help him find his own place in the landscape, but also to think about a new place for painting and a new place for the viewer. All along, on all the sites he visited, Simon was quietly receiving an education of the senses. This was not an education on offer at any art school. The modern English word 'landscape' is derived from the Dutch word landschap, *a word used specifically to describe a genre of Dutch painting. From the very beginning, the northern European concept of landscape has been indivisible from visual appearance and closely related to painting itself. As soon as Simon began to relate to landscape in terms of materiality, it was impossible for him to continue with any of the established traditions of the picturesque. This education of the senses was the hidden subplot of the art and archaeology relationship. It was a balancing and a recalibration of the senses, and it was instrumental in encouraging the artist to develop a language of painting based in materiality.*

Being direct

The on-site art making process was part of Simon's ambition for a painting to be as direct as possible a register of the place. There was a precedent to this way of working, when he made a series of drawings on Kimolos, a Greek island in the Cyclades. Over a number of visits, he made a related group of nineteen drawings related to the geology of the island. To make them, the paper had to be wet, in order to absorb the marks made with coloured clays and earths, into the paper fibres. At the end of each session, the drawings were wrapped in polythene and taken back to London where they were stored in a desk. The following year, the drawings were unwrapped, the paper still damp, and ready to be worked into again immediately. At the core of this process, which has been carried through to his work on excavation, is an understanding that decisions and actions must be made on site and that this is perceivable in a finished work.

The artist as witness

There is quite a lot of artwork made in relation to archaeology. The danger is that it is easy for an artist to lean on the richness of the discipline and export the appearance or look of archaeology to the art gallery where it becomes exotic and different. This strategy can take a number of forms including presenting the look of the excavation site, the post-excavation laboratory, or a museum-style display of artefacts or objects. This way of working with archaeology as the subject of an artwork has links to the art history of the ready-made object, transformed by presentation within the context of the gallery. The word 'excavation' is used frequently as a metaphor in the art world for many reasons. For Simon, excavation is not a metaphor. For him it is a physical activity, and to be on site is to experience the full materiality of landscape and evidence of past and present human activity. Simon has made it clear that his work is not a representation of excavation sites or archaeology. It is about the impact of the excavation site on painting. The paintings, for example, are a register of a contact with the landscape and are not a visual record of it. His works are concerned with what can be done to advance a language of painting based in materiality rather than image. The excavation sites have shaped and informed this approach. Understood in this way, the diggers or field archaeologists provide the site for the artist to respond to. They create the ideal model for what the artist is looking for: a union of materiality and temporality, a collaborative work of past and present human activity.

Compression and decompression

Simon sees his role on site as a witness to the process of excavation and in a position to respond to what excavation produces. He has always resisted taking up a trowel; doing so would alter the perception of the purpose of an artist on site. At times it is not easy to be in residence in another discipline. Ideas take time to crystallize; there are no immediate results, and it is important to go through a period of acclimatizing, absorbing, and getting to know the diggers and the archaeology. Results can often take months to appear, often well after the dig has ended. There are parallel processes in archaeology and they cannot be short cut either. In step with the excavation process, Simon has to experience it layer by layer and find a way of translating this experience into information for an artwork. The excavation process opens the surface of the landscape which we could think of as a form of decompression. The art making process and the archaeological interpretation can be seen as a form of recompression. They are the ways we have found to compress an unmanageable amount of information and numerous possible questions back into a manageable form for communication. In this respect archaeological process and the process of making a painting operate in the same way.

Doug Bailey: an archaeologist breaking the past

An established archaeologist with experience both leading field projects and publishing analytical, synthesizing, and interpretive works, Doug has defined and developed an alternative to traditional archaeological approaches to the past which he has termed art/archaeology. Over the past twenty years, Doug's work has moved progressively away from the traditional study of the past and its material remains. This journey started with a break with tradition in the ways that we respond to prehistoric art (specifically in the form of anthropomorphic figurines) and has found most recent traction in a more radical repurposing of artefacts into raw materials with which artists and other creators make original artwork. In all of this, Doug's work has increasingly challenged the role that archaeology has occupied for the past century and a half, as the best (and often the only) way to encounter and manipulate the past.

Archaeologist and iconoclast

Doug's journey started with a traditional archaeological training and education, progressed through an early academic career of fieldwork, research, and publication, and then shifted towards a greater interest in graphic and physical artistic creation. Along this route, he has stepped into and out of his role as an archaeologist, asking increasingly difficult questions about how we shape our engagement with, and uses of, the physical remains of the past.

Having completed a PhD in Archaeology at Cambridge, Doug dove into collaboration with archaeologists from Bulgaria and Romania, directing excavation projects, writing introductions to the prehistory of the region, editing collections of papers by regional specialists. In 1993, he took up an academic post in the School of Archaeology at Cardiff University. There, Doug was drawn to the work of performance artist and researcher Mike Pearson who had been making provocative work in south Wales and abroad as one of the co-founders, and as Artistic Director of the theatre company Brith Gof. Mike had his own connections to archaeology, as a graduate of the same Cardiff University department, and when Doug started teaching at Cardiff, Mike was re-connecting to archaeology, in collaboration with archaeologists from St David's College, Lampeter: first with Neolithic specialist Julian Thomas and then with theoretician Michael Shanks.

In the mid- and late-1990s, Doug was gripped by exhibitions, events, and conversations at Cardiff's Chapter Arts Centre (where Brith Gof was based), increasingly finding exhilarating touchstones in works by local artists (such as Emma Lawton's 1994 wall excavation installation, Banquet). A series of collaborations started with Mike and Michael and other similarly engaged archaeologists in a sequence of conference sessions (at the annual meetings of the Theoretical Archaeology Group and the European Association of Archaeologists) and on lecture tours (most specifically in collaboration with the Swedish performance archaeologists Jonna Ulin and Fiona Campbell in 2003). In 2001, Pearson and Shanks published their ground-breaking book Theatre/ Archaeology, *which took advantage of Shanks' skills as intellectual provocateur and laid out Pearson's vision for the role of performative narrative within archaeological and historical work.*

As a result of these collaborations, Doug spent 2001 on an Arts and Humanities Research Council funded sabbatical at the Archaeology Center at Stanford University working on a book project about prehistoric figurines (published in 2005 as Prehistoric Figurines: Representation and Corporeality[1]*). By the end of that year, Doug had spent very little of his time in Palo Alto looking at figurines, and most of his time in the stacks of Stanford's art library, at the San Francisco Museum of Modern Art, and visiting the city's other major museums and art galleries. Originally planned as a way into new thinking about prehistoric statuettes, Doug read philosophies of art, art theory and criticism (especially about modern and contemporary sculpture). Increasingly, however, and more importantly, he took deep dives into art of late 1960s and 1970s America, especially Land Art and Minimalism: submerging into the works, notes, interviews, and memoirs of Carl Andre, Walter DeMaria, Dan Flavin, Michael Heizer, Donald Judd, Sol Lewitt, Richard Long, Gordon Matta-Clark, Robert Morris, Dennis Oppenheim, Charles Ross, Tony Smith, Robert Smithson, and Michelle Stuart.*

In both Minimalist and Land Art, Doug relished the turning away from meaning and the central place given to materials and the ground as medium, method, and work. So much archaeology of the 1980s (the decade of Doug's educational grounding) had turned to other disciplines of fieldwork (geography, ethnography, phenomenology) and social sciences (sociology, critical theory, semiotics, structuralism) in order to find the interpretational analogies, intellectual approaches, and technical methods that could be borrowed and mapped onto the archaeological search for meaning, motive, and intent. In the works of Minimalist and Land Artists, Doug found freedom from the requirement to explain that dominated archaeology. The potential for anti-meaning, or at least for alternatives to meaning took hold in the ways that Doug chose to devote his thinking and output.

At the same time and in the same Stanford libraries, Doug found the time and the resources to explore other interests in twentieth-century art: Dada and Surrealism. For Doug's emerging thinking on the past, these two areas of work delivered examples of, and validations for, the nonsensical and the intentionally provocative. Here were creators who had explored new ranges of impact for making graphic, performative, and textual works. Also, and for Dada perhaps more centrally, these people had worked explicitly to insert political intent to function as a medium of social critique: creative work outside of the expectations of society or the artistic and intellectual communities, confronting political agendas, as well as rejecting the need for rationality and reason. A passing interest in Marcel Duchamp led Doug into Dada, to the Cabaret Voltaire *(1916), to Hugo Ball and Kurt Schwitters. Dada also led Doug to political collage, photo-collage, and montage, and the works of Hannah Höch, as well as of Hausmann, Heartfield, and Grosz, an influence that appears in his montage chapters, as discussed in Chapter 8.*

Dada also led Doug to the Surrealists, who he had encountered some years earlier while reading James Clifford's classic 1981 essay on ethnographic surrealism.[2] In turn, re-reading Clifford's article led Doug to the 1929/30 French surrealist journal Documents, *edited by Georges Bataille.* Documents *led Doug to the work of Michel Leiris (and his 1934* L'Afrique Fantôm *[Phantom Africa][3]), to Hans Bellmer, André Breton, Luis Buñuel, Marcel Duchamp, Paul Éluard, Max Ernst, André Masson, Yves Tanguy, and Tristan Tzara. As importantly (perhaps more so), these artists led Doug to other surrealist magazines of the first half of the twentieth century:* Littérature *(1919–21),* La Révolution Surréaliste *(1924–29),* Minotaure *(1933–39),* Acéphale *(1936–39). Here Doug found a medium for creative output that would provide a means to invade traditional academic publication.*

An initial result from his deep dive into Minimalism, Land Art, Dada, and Surrealism was a shift in Doug's fieldwork in Romania, and the ways that he thought about what we should or could say about the past: a shift from explanation to stimulation, from recording, reconstructing, and interpreting traces of past human behaviour, to an abandonment of searches for meaning and intention. The shift can be seen in the structure and contents of Doug's 2005 book Prehistoric Figurines: Representation and Corporeality *reaching outside of archaeology for inspiration, but more importantly turning away from the explicit acceptance of false securities implicitly assumed for most archaeological explanation and interpretation. Results are also seen in the types of essays and reports that Doug started to write, as well as how he titled those articles and book chapters: the word 'beyond' started to occupy a central place.*

Doug felt that there was further to go. Both the Minimalists and the Land Artists had had clear appeal to archaeology and archaeologists; see the attention given especially to Richard Long and to Michael Heizer by many archaeologists in their own writings, especially the latter's scientific studies of prehistoric monuments and landscapes. These academic interpretations sat comfortably within archaeology's long-running search for analogies as an inspiration for better understanding the past and explaining what had happened during it. Doug wanted to break that connection with the past.

In 2007, Doug benefitted from the focus on art and archaeology at the Dublin meetings of the World Archaeological Congress and an invitation to record a podcast[4] and present a conference paper challenging colleagues (and himself) to go beyond the accepted boundaries of what archaeologists could do with creative arts practices. The resulting publication 'Art//archaeology//art: letting go beyond' appeared in 2014.[5] Early attempts to 'go beyond' included Doug's European Union funded project that took artists into the field in 2010, as discussed in detail in Chapter 4. For that 'Art – Landscape – Transformations' project Doug took a dozen artists into the southern Romanian community where he was coordinating excavation of a Neolithic site, and asked them to apply their particular creative skills sets and experiences to create work that evoked that place. In the same year, Doug curated an exhibition at the Sainsbury Centre for Visual Arts in Norwich in the UK, and wrote the accompanying 'anti-catalogue' in attempts to disrupt standard presentations of archaeology and art (a fuller discussion can be found on pp. 105–7).[6]

During this period, Doug started to take whatever opportunities and invitations presented themselves to produce graphic work that could be inserted in otherwise traditional academic publications. These included a series of five montage-chapters offering non-narrative graphic provocations in discussions of archaeological topics (chronology;[7] landscape and excavation;[8] the human body;[9] why the past intrigues people;[10] and the valorization of cultural periods[11] – see Chapter 8 for a discussion of the last example).

Most recently, Doug has turned his attention to defining and putting into practice what he has termed art/archaeology: a trans-discipline that invites artists, designers, archaeologists, and other creators to disarticulate artefacts from their chronological, cultural, and functional pasts, and then to re-use them as raw materials to make new creative work that provokes thought and discussion about challenges facing the modern world (environmental, economic, social, political) or the individual makers. Art/archaeology asks uncomfortable questions about deeply held assumptions of how (and why) we value the past and the objects from that past which we have come to fetishize. Projects have included exhibitions (in 2020 and 2021 in Portugal) as well as colloquia and subsequent publications.

Painting and archaeology: beyond analogies and parallels

Much work that brings together art and archaeology is founded on the belief in the existence of an analogy between the two practices: of a parallel between them as physical practices that use the ground and the material to explore what it means to be human. Thus, the title (and content) of Colin Renfrew's 2003 book Figuring It Out: The Parallel Visions of Artists and Archaeologists[12] *and the premise of many archaeological forays into contemporary and modern art. The book before you holds a different position. In their joint vision, Doug and Simon see a much broader horizon for the potential for collaboration and co-production of work. If there is an analogy to be drawn, then it is not between art practice (or painting, in Simon's specific position) and archaeology (the latter understood broadly), but between excavation (and its actions) and art creation (and its actions). In examining these connections, Simon and Doug explore the ways in which their specific creative works argue for change in their respective disciplines.*

In order to maintain the sense both of the original dialogue that produced this book, as well as to offer a joint perspective on Doug and Simon's work and its engagement with painting and with archaeology, the chapters that follow are written either in the first person, formatted in normal font *(thus letting Simon or Doug to speak directly about their work and how and why they made it), or in an unnamed third person, formatted in italics (in order combine Doug and Simon's thinking as it addresses significant themes such as authorship, originality, time).*

2

Segsbury Project (Simon Callery, 1996–2003)

Early paintings: London Docklands

My early paintings were based on what I could see around me where I lived and worked in east London. The studio was on the sixth floor of a block of flats overlooking Limehouse Basin and across the water from the massive construction projects that were taking place in the docklands around Canary Wharf on the Isle of Dogs. It was a period of great change with an enormous amount of building and development instigated by Margaret Thatcher's urban regeneration policies of the 1980s. I was captivated by the scale and energy of all this activity and by the atmospheric complexity of London's historic docklands. I centred my work on this place, but I did not want to depict it. I restricted the use of colour to whites and greys and developed a language of mark-making derived from the architectural form of the construction site: lines drawn with oil pastel into wet oil paint on canvas. I did not want these paintings to represent architecture, I wanted them to be architectural in character.

I was gravitating towards landscape, and the paintings were becoming very reductive, drained of colour and quiet. Showing an interest in landscape as a subject for painting in the early 1990s was virtually a career suicide. The attention of the contemporary art world was fixed on new media, film and video, certainly in London, and a lot of work of the emerging YBAs (Young British Artists) set out to be attention-grabbing and controversial. I had doubts about the direction my work should take. I needed to understand if my growing involvement with landscape, albeit the urban landscape, was an irrepressible aspect of my character revealing itself, or was a reaction against the latest trend in contemporary art. Either way, I needed to confront the issue to understand it better.

My chance to do this came through an invitation from Paul Bonaventura, independent curator and producer, who at the time was the Senior Research Fellow in Fine Art Studies at the University of Oxford. Paul was bringing artists to Oxford to develop their work in cross-disciplinary contexts. He had spoken with archaeologists Gary Lock and Chris Gosden from the Institute of Archaeology, as it was called then, to see if they were interested in involving an artist in their Hillforts of the Ridgeway Project. Before he went to Oxford, Paul had been the Senior Exhibitions Organizer at the Whitechapel Art Gallery in east London, where I had freelance work with the education department, running practical workshops for schools and community groups and giving talks based around the

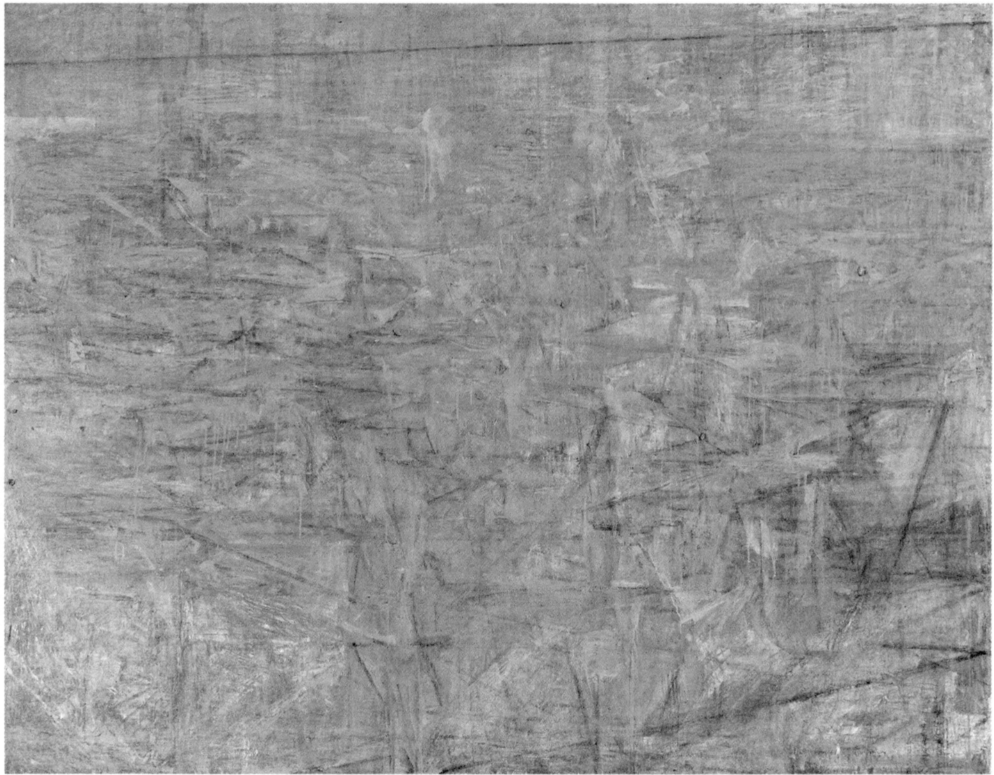

2.1 *Simon Callery.* City Painting. *1991. Oil on canvas. 123 x 153 cm.*

exhibition programme. He was aware of the developments in my work in the period leading up to my first solo show in London in 1993. The show caught the attention of the media, after Charles Saatchi bought all the paintings the day before it opened.

When I was offered the opportunity to work alongside archaeologists during the upcoming excavation at Segsbury Camp, I leapt at it. With support from Southern Arts for a year-long residency, I would be able continue to develop the work in my studio after the excavation period itself had ended. This was what I needed to confront landscape head-on as a subject for painting. There were no restrictions. This project was open and experimental. I was a London-based artist with a focus on the urban landscape placed in an environment that could be easily understood as a paradigm of English landscape: an Iron Age hill fort on the chalk downlands of central south England. Certainly, from an artworld point of view, this was exactly where I should not be.

Segsbury Camp

Segsbury Camp is located on the Ridgeway on the Oxfordshire border with the Berkshire Downs, close to Wantage. I found the excavation site extraordinary. The largest trench was 20 x 40 metres. It revealed a mass of evidence of an Iron Age settlement: roundhouse gullies, dense clusters of pits of all sizes, shapes and depths, post and stake-holes, all clearly defined in the white chalk

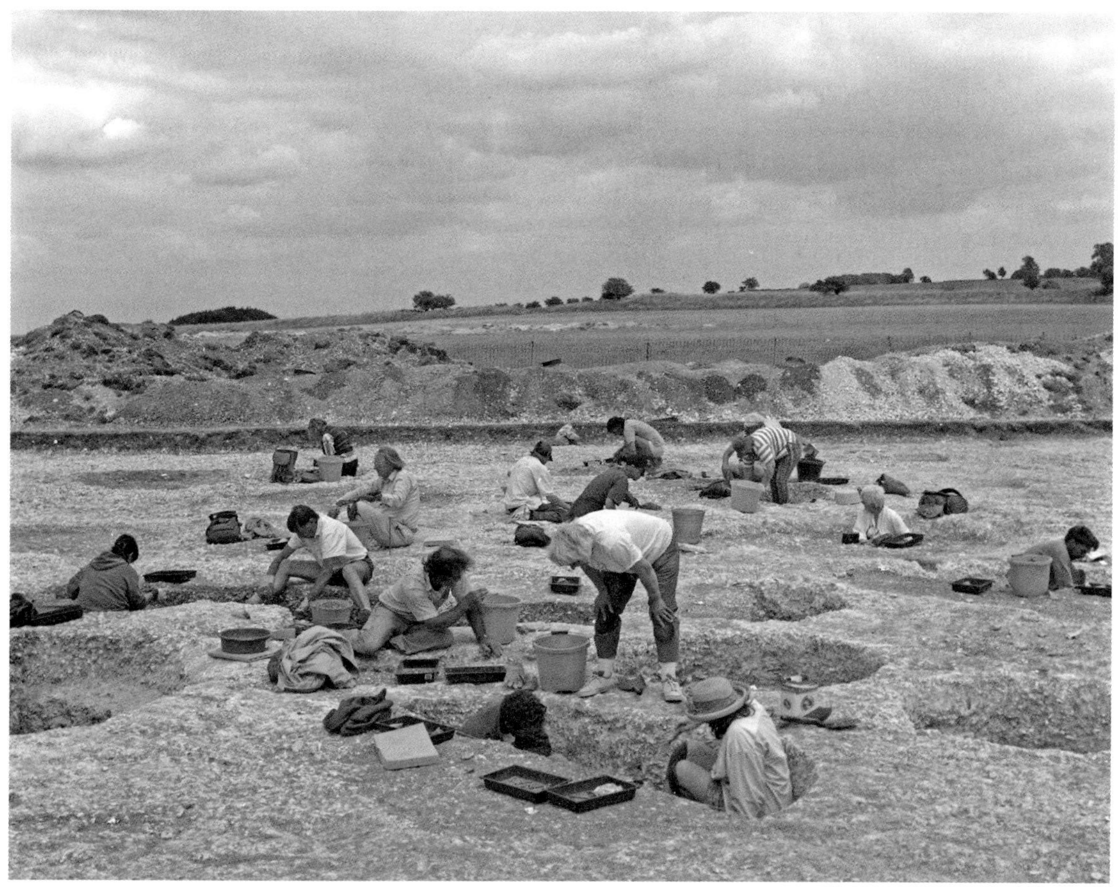

2.2 *Excavation at Segsbury Camp. Oxfordshire. 1996.*

bedrock. It was a very busy site with students and volunteer diggers and lots of conversation and discussion. Almost immediately I could see parallels in the excavation process with my painting process, particularly in the treatment of surfaces. I was fascinated by the archaeological recording methods, the field drawing and the texture, colour and spatial complexity of the excavated chalk bedrock. In terms of colour, I could see a relationship between the paleness of the chalk and the large-scale, lead white paintings in progress in my London studio. I could relate to the attention given to detail, with the physical work of trowelling away the layers of material and with the way the diggers cleaned and presented the fully excavated surfaces and sections. It seemed things were falling into place effortlessly and there was a clear interchange between the two disciplines.

Although there was a familiarity with the physical aspects of excavation process, I was starting to understand that its function was entirely different from painting, and this was new and unfamiliar territory. As I began to think seriously about what I could do at Segsbury, the real challenge emerged. I did not want to paint the site or the surrounding landscape in an image-based way. I was not concerned with its appearance for any pictorial purpose. I wanted to avoid bringing my established studio-based methods and materials up on site. I needed to establish a dialogue with the hill fort, its landscape, and the excavation process. I needed to take a risk and see where that took me. It was quite a drama at the beginning as I had to avoid any preconceived ideas. I put myself under pressure to produce new work in order to show the hardworking archaeologists that I, too, was working hard.

Segsbury photography project

Early on in the dig, the photographer Andrew Watson came up to Segsbury to see Gary Lock. Andrew had carried out aerial photography of historic sites in the area, including White Horse Hill, from light aircraft. We began to talk and quickly got to a point where we decided to make a collaborative photographic work. Recording an archaeological site from the air is not unusual, so we decided to record the surface of Trench 1, the largest trench, in detail from a very low level of 2.25 metres above the surface. We drew a grid over a plan of the entire trench, which gave us 378 plots, each measuring 1.5 metres square. Each plot needed to be recorded individually. Our intention was to be as informational as possible, to carry out the work as an objective survey and to suppress any desire to make any selections or aestheticize the images in any way. We rejected colour in favour of black-and-white negative film and a medium format camera. With spirit levels and tape measures attached to a pole and the camera mounted on the top, we established a consistent height and level for each image. A plumb line was hung off the bottom of the camera lens to locate it precisely over the centre of the square plots. We accommodated a slight overlap on all four sides of the square frame, so we would not miss even the smallest part of the surface.

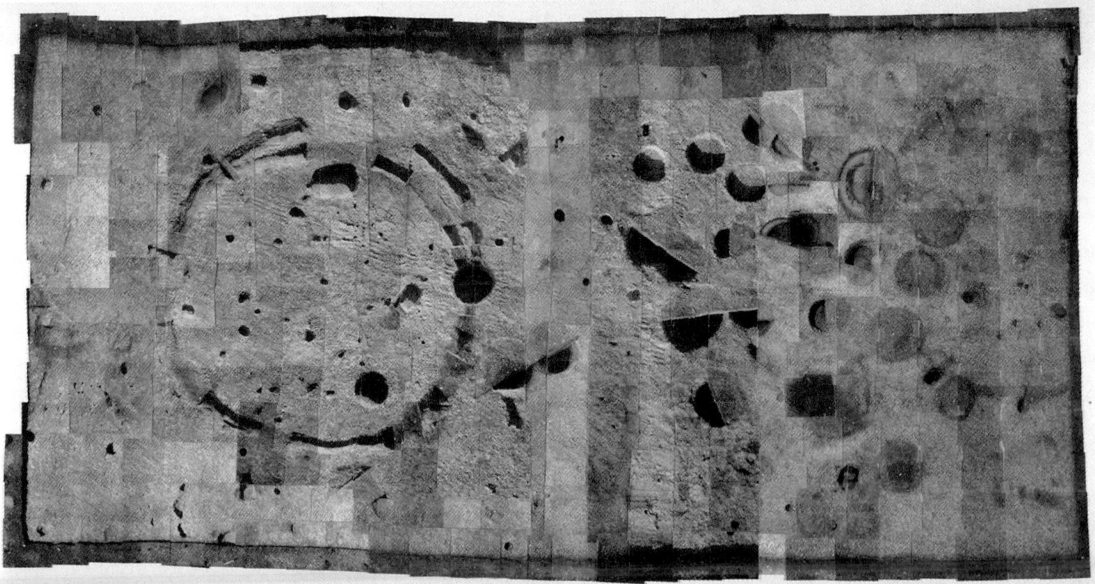

2.3 *Simon Callery and Andrew Watson.* Segsbury Project *overview. 1996–97. Joined black and white photographic contact prints. 86 x 144.5 cm.*

We recorded the whole site over a two-day period, going onto the trench with our gear the minute the diggers went off it for their breaks and then back on again at the end of the day. We moved methodically, without stopping, in changing light, across the surface according to our grid. It was photographed at a point where some archaeological features were fully excavated, labelled and recorded, while some others were still being dug, complete with the measuring strings and nails. It was a photographic survey of the surface detail of an excavation site and a record of the process of excavation.

The films were developed and contact prints made from all the negatives. There were so many images containing an overwhelming mass of visual information. We wanted to find a way to present them so that all the images were accessible to a viewer. The idea of sampling emerged as a possible method. An archaeological trench is itself a sample of a site or of the landscape in which it is situated. We decided that a set of cabinets containing all the images in drawers could mirror the idea of sampling. The negatives were printed up on high gloss paper at 60 x 60 cm, a scale close to 2:1, by a specialist in printing aerial photography. The resulting 378 black-and-white prints were an incredible record of surface detail. The cabinets were designed to take two images to a drawer, 27 drawers to each cabinet, and seven cabinets, adding up to a total of 189 drawers. The overall dimensions of all the cabinets lined up was 931 x 165.5 x 70 cm.

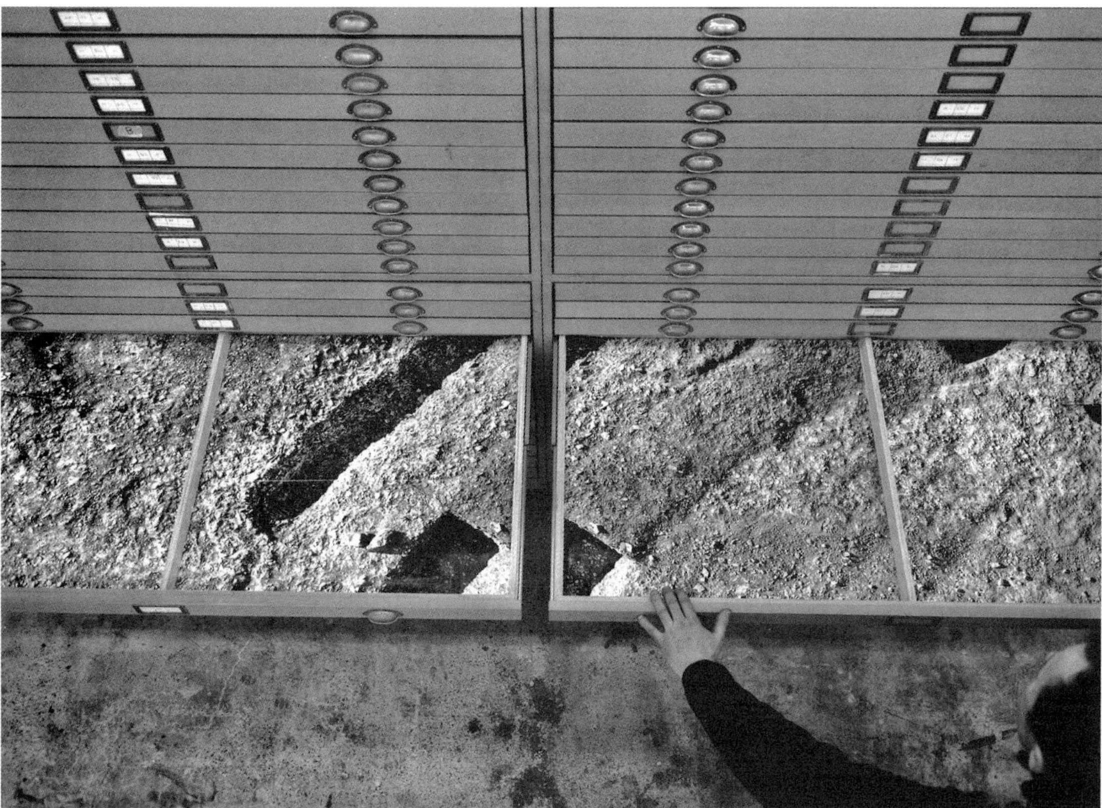

2.4 *Simon Callery and Andrew Watson.* Segsbury Project *plan chest (detail). 1996–97. Seven plan-chests, 378 silver gelatin prints (60 x 60 cm each). 165.5 x 931 x 70 cm.*

No one would go through all the drawers. That would be too much to expect. A viewer could study individual images and then move to the adjacent drawer in the next cabinet to travel across the surface. The archaeological features, such as the gully of the roundhouse, could be tracked across the plan chests by opening numerous consecutive drawers in the adjacent cabinets. This would swing you across the full width of the chest as well as taking you up and down it. Some of the images are very dense in terms of excavated archaeological features while other areas reveal long stretches of chalk bedrock devoid of any archaeology at all. All of them communicate the physicality and spatial complexity of the site. Moving from drawer to drawer makes increasingly tangible a grasp of the materiality of the excavated chalk bedrock and the texture of its pitted surface.

This work was called the *Segsbury Project*. It was first shown at Great Coxwell Barn, 20 miles from Segsbury Camp, the following year in 1997. The plan chests were presented as a block of four-by-three chests placed back-to-back, placed at the centre of the unlit stone barn. We intentionally provided no single image overview of the trench. This medieval tithe barn was an extraordinary place to show this work.

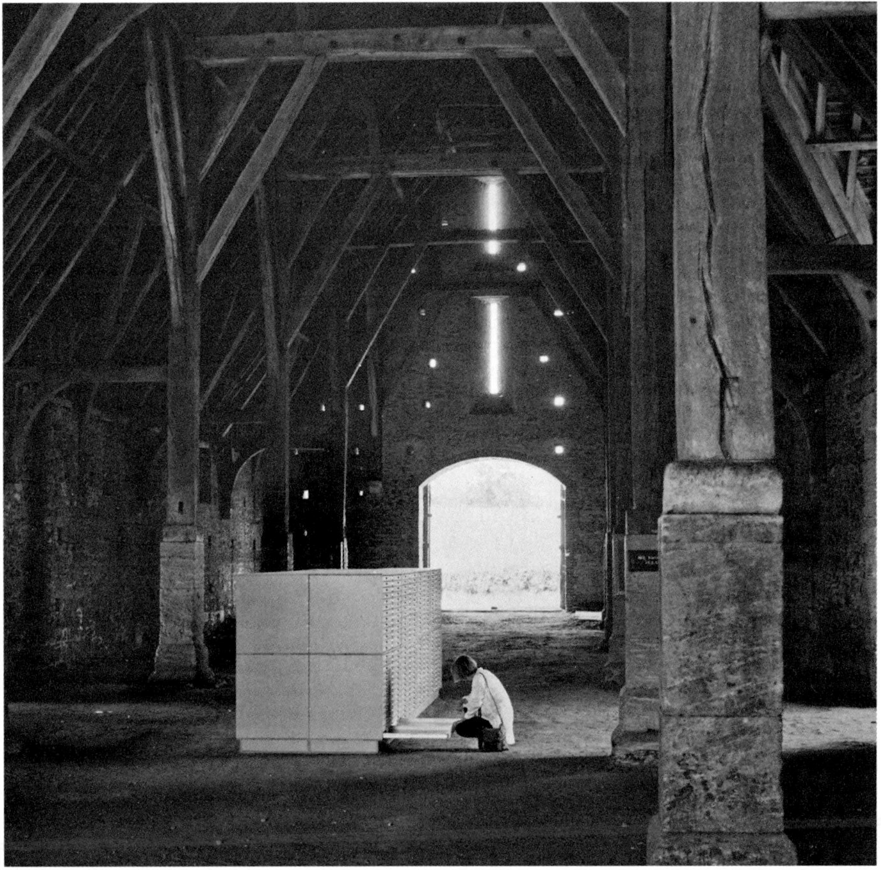

2.5 *Simon Callery and Andrew Watson.* Segsbury Project *exhibition at Great Coxwell Barn. Oxfordshire. 1997.*

Towards materiality in painting

Although this was a photographic work and it communicated entirely in visual form, it was nudging me incrementally towards materiality. I had managed to resist working at Segsbury in the same way I worked in my painting studio in London. It was agitating to be so uncertain about how to make paintings. People were questioning me: 'you're a painter, so where are the paintings?'. The first signs of progress in the painting were beginning to appear, informed by stratigraphy, one of the key principles of the excavation process. I had learnt how stratigraphy functions when it was explained to the students or volunteer diggers on site. The representation of material deposits on horizontal lines positioned on a vertical timeline was a graphic language I understood. Stratigraphy very clearly connected the two most important elements of my painting with the excavation process. I was beginning to make connections between time and material and to recognise this landscape as a temporal environment.

On site, I was thinking carefully about how to make paintings in response to a place or a landscape without resorting to depiction. In the studio, I had been making paintings with an emphasis on horizontality. I would draw horizontal lines through the wet oil paint with oil pastel causing it to bleed into the paint. These lines would be adjusted with a scalpel with a curved blade. The metal blade would burnish the metal content in the lead-based white paint resulting in a surface with luminous and subtle reflective qualities. These horizontal lines originated in the earlier city paintings and related to architectural form and the urban environment. In these new works the horizontal line became increasingly dominant as I looked for ways of controlling the pace of a painting. Some paintings were covered in hundreds of lines traversing the full width of the canvas. Some of the lines were black, while others were coloured red or green, in order to move the eye about the painting at different speeds. I was searching for ways to slow down the experience of looking at painting. Inevitably, the emphasis on horizontality generated a sense of depth, an illusion of deep space, which tied them to the image-based pictorial tradition. Although an image of landscape was not present in the painting, the illusion of depth, one of its most important constituent elements, was still there. I was trying to loosen the connections to picture making but they were not that easy to shake off.

When I finally arrived at it, the solution was actually very straightforward. The clue was in a painting left lying on its side in the studio. Optically, vertical lines operate in a completely different way to horizontal ones. They block a reading of depth, and they draw attention to what is happening on the surface. Curiously, the big step I wanted to take did not mean I had to throw everything out of the window and start again. In this case it was as simple as changing the orientation of the line. The next group of paintings I made (*Fabrik*, 2000; *White Flake Entasis*, 2001; and *Porch*, 2003) were all results of the shift in orientation of the line.

Flake White Entasis

Flake White Entasis is a 3.2-metre tall rectangular painting, with many vertical lines running down the full length of the canvas. The title also refers to the paint I was using. Flake white is lead white. I made my own paint by grinding the lead white powder into linseed oil. Not only was it a lot cheaper to buy large quantities of raw pigment, but it also meant I was starting to think about the material qualities of the painting very early on in the painting process. Lead white oil paint has a

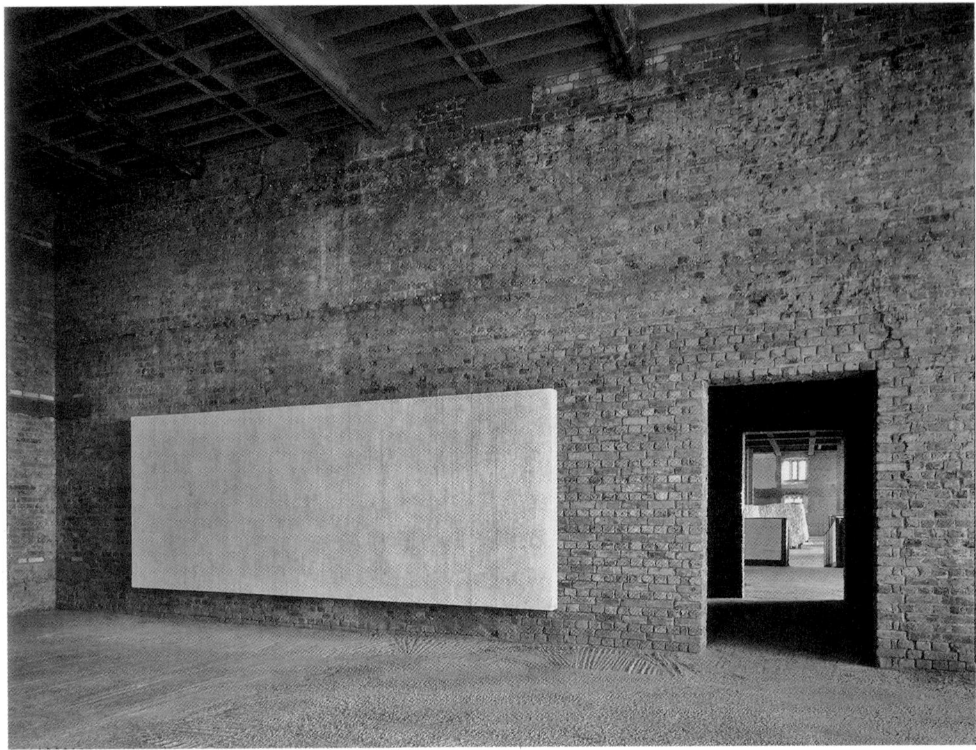

2.6 *Simon Callery. Fabrik. 2000. Oil and pencil on canvas. 208.5 x 540 cm. Officers Mess. Dover Castle. Kent. 2003.*

density that sets it apart from titanium white or zinc white. It can be worked without breaking down into a liquid and retains its body. This is important as the painting process involved a lot of scraping back of wet or dry surfaces with the scalpel, of overpainting with many layers of oil paint thinned down with turpentine and altering and adjusting the position of the lines, which are drawn and redrawn many times before finding their final position, their previous positions remaining as traces under the thin layers of paint.

While I was working on these new paintings, architecture and architectural principles continued to interest me. Entasis is the term for the classical Greek device of incorporating a slight bulge in an upright column and tapering it slightly inwards at the top. The Doric columns of the Parthenon in Athens are the best-known examples. When you stand in front of the building you are convinced about the form of the structure. The columns do what you expect them to do; they obey the visual logic that an object gets smaller as it gets further away from the eye. You understand the building physically as well as visually. There are many neoclassical buildings that appear top heavy and are not convincing because although they have columns, they lack entasis. The same applies to tall rectangular paintings. They appear top heavy without this subtle intervention and lack formal accuracy. *Flake White Entasis* is 5 cm narrower at the top than it is at the bottom. This tapering occurs at 5/8s of the height in line with the Greek order. My approach to painting was evolving. What seemed to be important now was to think of a painting as a physical structure and what that might imply for the viewer.

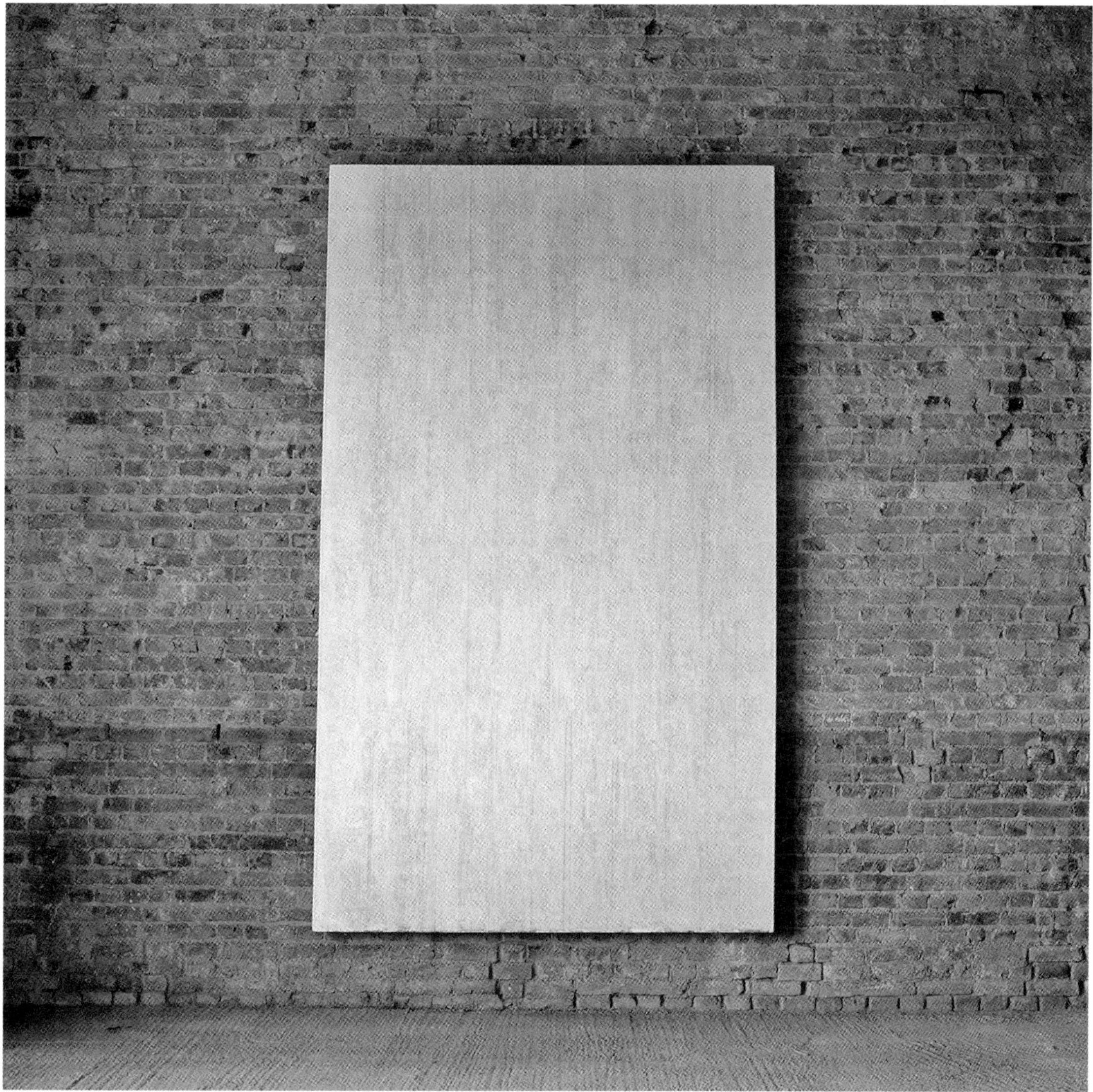

2.7 *Simon Callery.* Flake White Entasis. *2001. Oil and pencil on canvas. 192 x 329 cm. Officers Mess. Dover Castle. Kent. 2003.*

Alfred's Castle

The collaboration with the archaeologists at Segsbury Camp had been fruitful and I was invited back to work alongside them again at their next excavation, at Alfred's Castle on the Oxfordshire/ Wiltshire borders. The formal residency had come to an end with the show at Great Coxwell Barn. I was now an independent artist with access to all aspects of the excavation process and free to respond to the site. Alfred's Castle was a remarkable place. It was an Iron Age hill fort, much

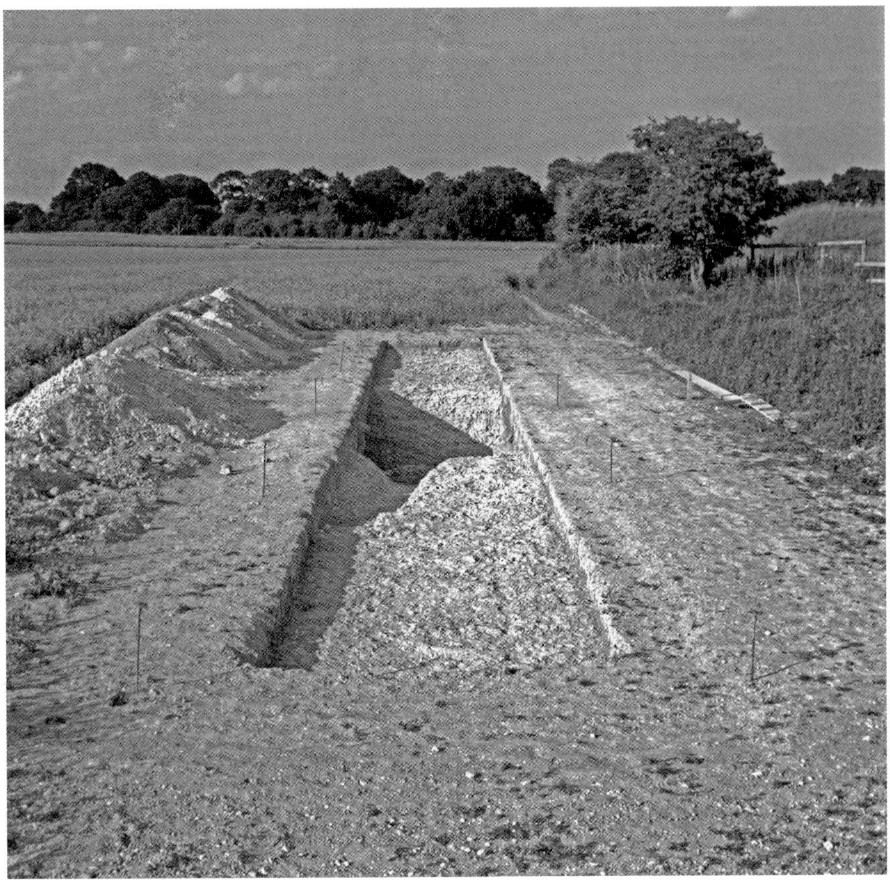

2.8 *Trench 10 fully excavated. Alfred's Castle. Oxfordshire. 2000.*

smaller than Segsbury Camp, situated in a wide and open bowl-shaped landscape. It was surrounded by agricultural land as far as you could see to the horizon in one direction and woodland to the other.

The excavation team camped on site. In the evening everyone would sit out, so there was plenty of opportunity to discuss the day's work and the progress of the excavation. The remains of a Roman villa lay in the centre of the hill fort. The characteristic circularity of the Iron Age structure enclosed the right angles and linear geometry of the Romano-British structure. I was interested in this language of form and what it can express. This was a vivid example of the differences, one laid directly over another. There were a number of trenches dug outside the ramparts, and I was drawn to one called Trench 10. This trench was 20 metres long and 2 metres wide. It had been laid out over a ditch that ran off the rampart and into the adjoining fields to the northwest. I would spend hours sitting watching the excavation of this trench. The long rectangular form was familiar. It reminded me of the long rectangular shape of *Fabrik*, a painting I was working on at that time in the studio. What was most exciting, though, was that at the mid-point the trench suddenly dropped three metres into the bottom of the excavated ditch before rising again on the other side to continue as flat chalk bedrock once more. Once it had been fully excavated and recorded, I asked Gary if I could work with this trench before it was backfilled. Up to this point I had worked with photography and had a group of paintings in progress but now I wanted to find a way to use the actual physical material of the excavation site.

Trench 10

Back in London for a weekend break, I went to visit a friend from college days, the sculptor Kabir Hussain, who also worked as a mould maker at AB Foundry in east London. AB is an established bronze casting foundry used by international artists, and over the years the floors and walls of the workshops had accumulated layer upon layer of plaster. There were no longer any flat surfaces or straight lines. Kabir and I began to experiment by pouring plaster directly onto these floors in discrete patches to see how much of the debris we threw down first would stick. I was thinking that I could use plaster panels to pick up the chalk loose laying on the surface of the trench. I wanted to see if we could apply this method and make a large-scale work from the full length of the excavated trench.

I got a small team together: Kabir, myself and Michael Boffey, another artist from the foundry. When we went up to start our work, the dig was in its final phase. There were still some trenches open inside the hill fort and others outside it in a field to the north. We stacked the bags of casting plaster up along the side of Trench 10, opposite the spoil heaps. In order to make the individual plaster panels a manageable size and weight, each one was designed to be one metre wide and two metres long. The panels in the ditch and gully would be idiosyncratically shaped and dealt with when we got to those points. Kabir and I had the job of flicking the plaster and Mick would keep us supplied with a constant stream of it. I did some very rudimentary clearing of the surface in advance, brushing out topsoil if it had fallen in, but mostly left it in the condition I found it. The wet plaster had to be flicked onto the surface by hand to make sure that it made complete contact with the chalk surface. It could not be poured on to avoid air pockets. We constructed a wood frame, bound together with jute scrim, for each panel as we made our way across the surface. We laid more scrim over the whole surface of each panel once we had built up a reasonable depth of plaster and then added more plaster to that for rigidity. We painted a grey clay slip on the sides of each section to act as a release for the next one.

Once we were all set up and running, the dig came to an end. The archaeologists all left the site and we were there to focus completely on this labour-intensive part of making the work. We were lucky with the weather. There was sun so it was warm but often a lot of cloud cover, so the exposed chalk bedrock did not dry out and it remained relatively damp. This was perfect for the plaster, as it would allow it to dry out slowly and the chances of it grabbing the loose chalk firmly was high. We gradually made our way over the surface of the flat top section of the trench and then down into the ditch. Each of these sections was made to take into account the complexity of that surface and the awkwardness of the angles. Coming up the other side of the ditch and back onto the flat again was a relief. By this point we were walking over the plaster panels already drying in the ground. This process took just under a week. When it was completed, we covered the whole trench in sheets of polythene to protect it and to keep moisture in. We left it like this in the ground for three days.

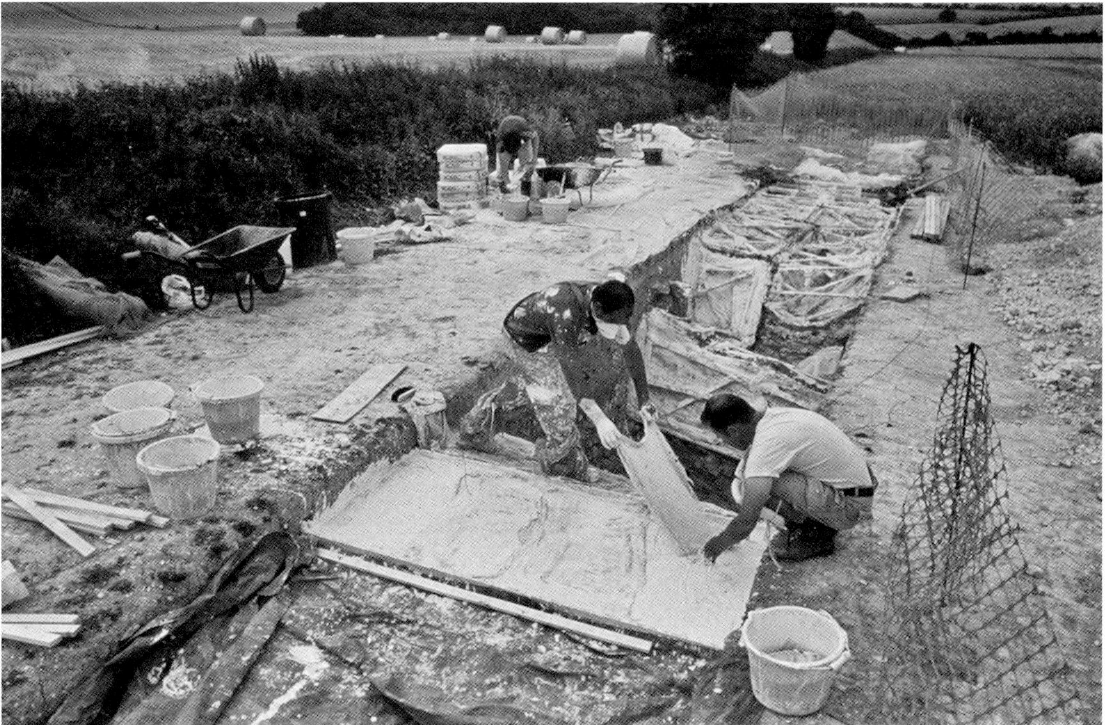

2.9 *Work in progress. Alfred's Castle. Oxfordshire. 2000.*

Lifting the panels

Back on site, we began to lift the plasters with an iron bar with a rag tied round it to avoid damaging the edges. We levered off the sections from the flat part of the trench at first. They were very heavy and still full of water. It was a moment of truth when we got the first section out and turned it over. The surface was encrusted with chalk. The plaster had grabbed not just the loose chalk but also a layer of the top surface of the bedrock. This was the mould-making element of the casting process done badly on purpose; a good plaster mould takes only the negative form of the object and nothing more. My aim was to allow the plaster to take as much of the object as it could, in this case, the chalk surface of the trench. The flat panels on both sides of the ditch came out without too much struggle. Each one was then moved up the hill to be laid out flat under polythene sheets, face up, to slowly dry out and made ready for transport to my studio in London.

Getting the irregular parts out of the bottom of the ditch posed all kinds of problems. The ditch sides held the plasters in place like a clamp and there was nowhere to get a bar in to lever them out. I got in contact with a local JCB driver and he agreed to dig around the plasters at the bottom of the ditch in order to make enough space to prise them off the chalk. With great delicacy he was able to use the forks on the front of the bucket to gently pick the plasters away from the bottom of the ditch and then to lift them carefully to ground level where we could barrow them away to the field at the top of the hill. The whole process made me very nervous. I knew the surfaces of the plasters were rich with compacted chalk and fragments of bedrock embedded into them. I also knew they were extremely delicate, very heavy and full of moisture. The hole around the ditch was quite large, when a Land Rover drove over the field and a furious farmer jumped out shouting why was there a JCB on his field. I don't know how many times I apologized and offered compensation. I would do anything at this stage to buy a couple more hours to get those plasters safely out and eventually into my studio. We did manage to get them all out of the ditch and finished that day back filling the entire site. After all the work involved (archaeological, artistic and that of the original Bronze Age ditch diggers), it was a very poignant moment to see this hole filled in and the ground levelled off.

The plaster panels were all loaded onto trucks, strapped down and transported off the hill and back to my studio in Haggerston in London. I could just about manage to move individual panels on my own and I set them all on blocks and lined them up all around the walls. The plaster and chalk were slowly drying to a subtle greyish white. They were pale and dusty. The awkward irregular sections that came out of the ditch and gully lay on the floor. The surfaces ranged from flat, compressed, and compacted chalk powder, all the way through to angular, studded clusters of bedrock. Although the plaster casting process had resulted in capturing the overall negative form of the trench, the surface detail was not a cast negative form. It was the actual underside of the top layer of the trench, an inversion of the material surface of the landscape.

Dover Castle exhibition

I started to think where to show this work and how it should be presented. I would lie in bed at night turning the image of the trench over and over in my mind, trying to decide what would work best. Should I return it to its original horizontal position as it was in the landscape, or should it be oriented another way? In the end, I decided to tip the entire form 90-degrees and reassemble all the parts, in their original place as they were in the ground, standing upright along one edge. Not unlike the solution to the painting problem, the answer was not going to be found by coming up with something completely new. It was solved by seeing what I already had more objectively, enabling me to present it in a new way. I approached Phil Brown, an artist and highly skilled technician, to see if he could work on this project of reassembly. He was fearless about the weight of the panels and was used to dealing with delicate and vulnerable surfaces. I hired another studio space especially for this job and moved all the plasters in there to be worked on.

At the same time, I had been writing letters to try and find somewhere to show the work. One of the people I wrote to was David Miles, at the time Chief Archaeologist at English Heritage, asking if he could help. I received a fantastic and positive reply. English Heritage had a large historic building called the Officers Mess within the grounds of Dover Castle, literally above the chalk cliffs. It was empty and English Heritage wanted to see if it could be put back into use; David Miles asked if I would like to come down and see if it was suitable.

The interior of the Officers Mess had been completely stripped back to brick and all the upper floors and staircases taken out. Traces of original features, patches of plaster-work or fireplaces were still evident stranded high up in the exposed walls. The whole space had been opened up to the wood rafters of the roof and a sawn concrete floor had been installed on ground level. It was a very raw and physical space and could not be a better context for the presentation of *Trench 10*. An exhibition was planned with the support of Oxford University, the Henry Moore Foundation, and English Heritage. It included the Segsbury Project plan chests, a joined contact print overview from Segsbury, three large-scale white paintings, *Trench 10*, and supporting archaeological field drawings and historic aerial photography alongside Andrew Watson's aerial photograph of Alfred's Castle. The supporting material had its own dedicated room with all the drawings and images presented on a single, custom-made long shelf that ran around the room. The two largest paintings; *Fabrik* and *Porch*, each had a dedicated room. *Trench 10* and the *Segsbury Project* chests and *Flake White Entasis* occupied the main hall. *Trench 10* was presented standing up at 90-degrees, running straight down the centre of this open space.

The wood structure that held all the sections of *Trench 10* in place was visible and an element of the work. Each plaster panel had an individual wooden frame holding it precisely in position in relation to the adjoining panels. The ditch section was supported on a set of complex frames that

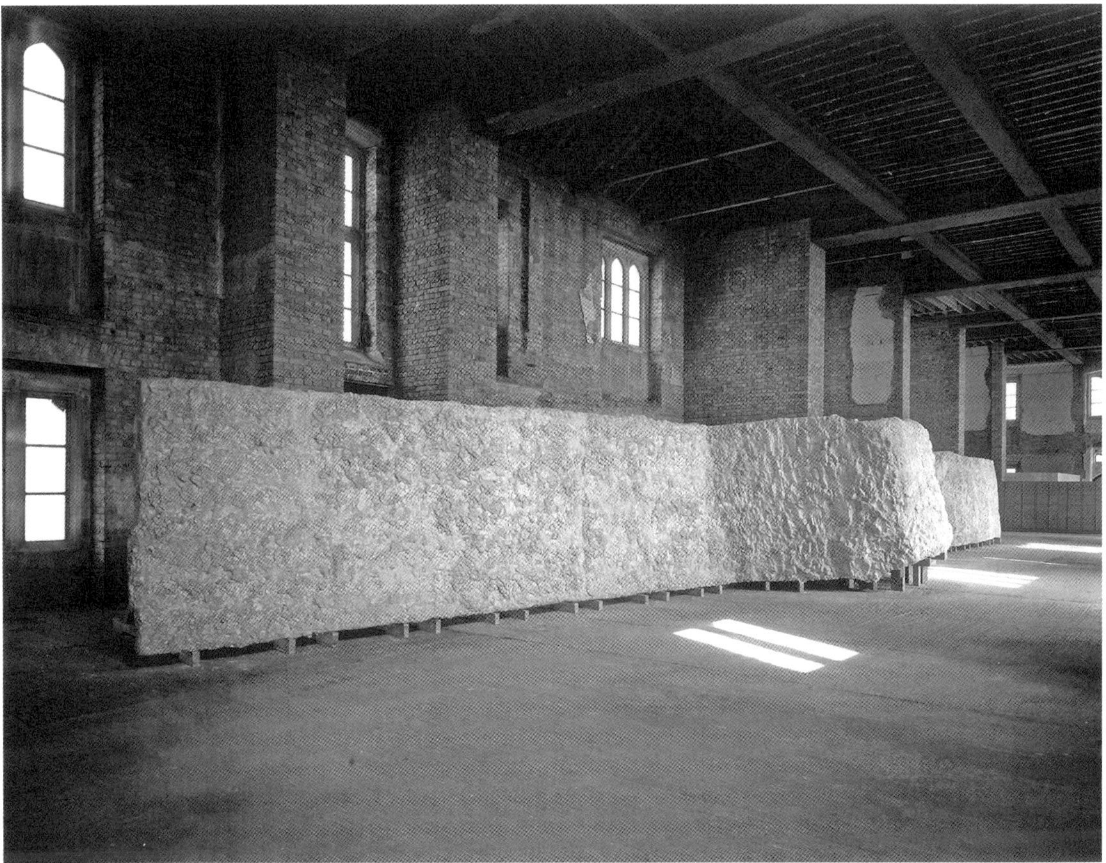

2.10 *Simon Callery.* Trench 10. *Plaster, chalk, and wood. 224 x 1919 x 513.5 cm. 2000–03. Officers Mess. Dover Castle. Kent. 2003.*

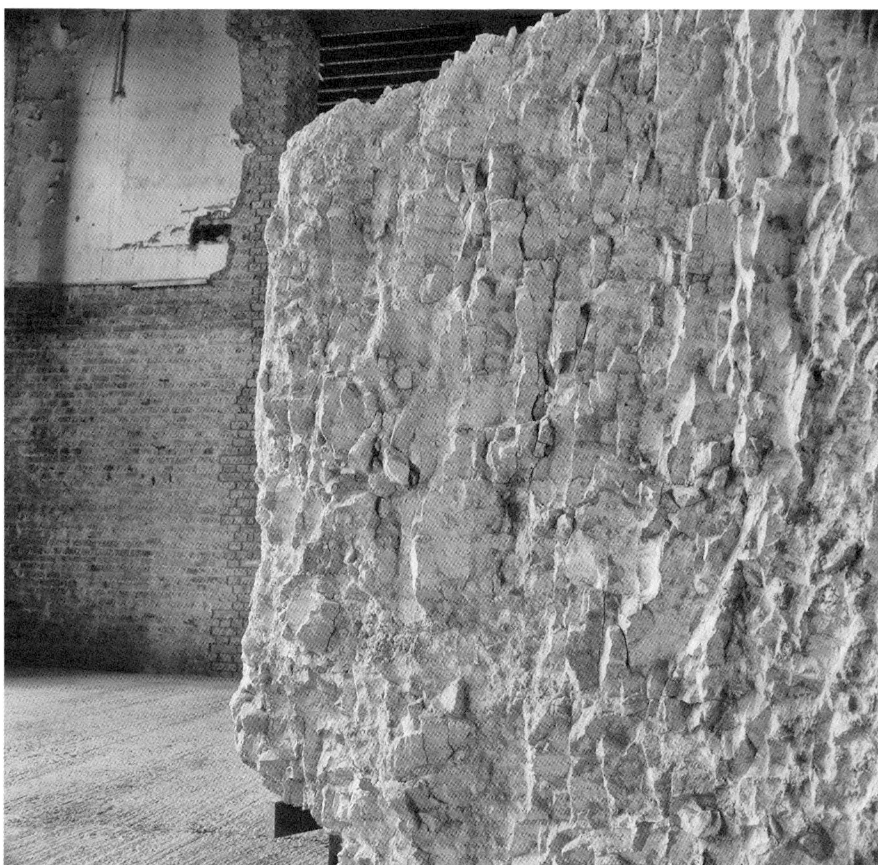

2.11 *Simon Callery.* Trench 10 *(detail). Officers Mess. Dover Castle. Kent. 2003.*

connected all those parts together. The entire twenty-metre work was held just above the floor, rising to a height of one metre only at the central point where the bottom panel of the ditch projected out three metres from the flat sides. The surfaces ranged from compacted and compressed dusty chalk while others were encrusted and studded with large chalk fragments. There were strong connections to be made between *Trench 10* and the large-scale white paintings. I wanted to suggest that the way of encountering the physicality of *Trench 10*, walking its length, or stopping to move in close to study the material qualities, was in fact also a legitimate way to experience the paintings.

What I had learnt on site was now evident in the work. The emphasis was on materiality, whether it was the massive weight and physical presence of the chalk and plaster of *Trench 10*, the overwhelming mass of visual information in the *Segsbury Project* photographs, or the austerity of the stripped back surfaces of the white oil paintings. The function of all this materiality was to call the attention of the body and to offer a counterbalance to our increasingly image-driven culture. What was especially important for me was the emergence of a temporal quality, a tangible slowing down of the process of looking and a physical awareness of oneself in relation to an artwork as the intention of the artwork.

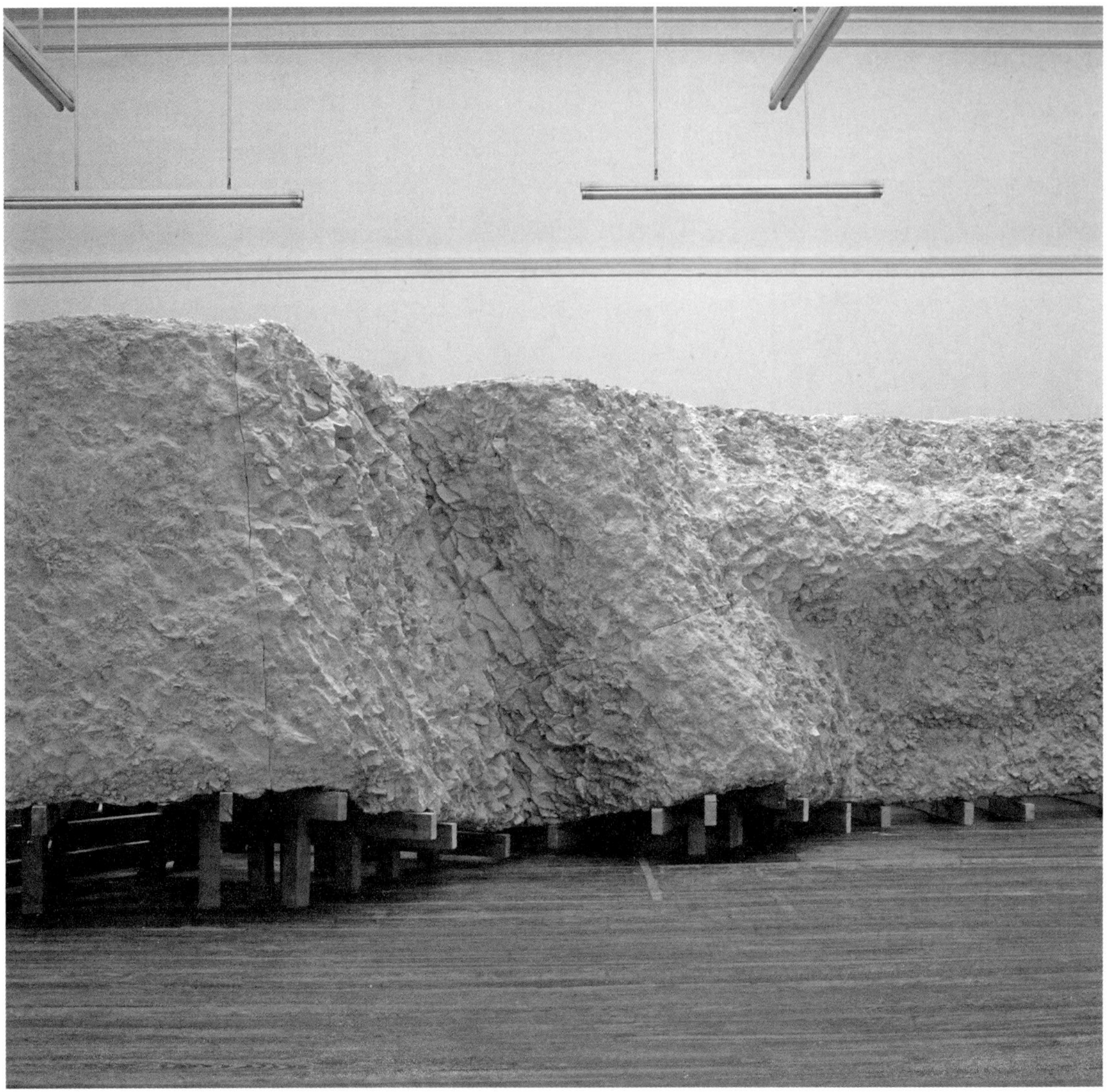

2.12 *Simon Callery.* Trench 10 *(detail). Storey Gallery. Lancaster. 2003.*

3

Authorship

Who makes it?

How do individual artists or archaeologists create art or archaeological knowledge, and what differences are there between the two processes? How visible is the individual in the final artwork, publication, or museum display? What part does collaboration or group work play in the two activities?

Artists as individuals and in groups

In 1997 Simon was included in Sensation: Young British Artists from the Saatchi Collection *at the Royal Academy of Arts, London. This exhibition brought together a number of artists under the label of Young British Artists. The show was controversial and was seen to define British art in the 1990s. From this point of view, success seems more possible if a number of individual artists, with shared attitudes to making art, are presented as a cohesive group. The artworks on show at the Royal Academy were all from the collection of Charles Saatchi, who before turning his attention to contemporary art had co-founded a highly successful advertising agency. In reality, the artists in the Royal Academy show were not a tight knit group of artists who knew each other and shared common ambitions and working methods. That was a fabrication. Sensation is a good example of how, if you create a group, it is easier to promote and to market. The YBA brand was in fact constructed around a small number of artists who had been at art college together at Goldsmiths, University of London in the late 1980s. When it made sense from the perspective of a collector, gallerist, or curator, other artists have been added to or subtracted from the YBA enterprise.*

From the beginning of his time on excavations, one of the things that Simon admired most about archaeology was the way that people worked together. While there was almost always discussion, debate, and argument on site, it was always for the benefit of the discipline. The way a contemporary artist works is different. Whereas an archaeologist will look for agreement to move forward, artists chose to disagree as a strategy to move ahead. A young artist will seek to overthrow what has been established by the previous generation in order to be noticed and taken seriously and reflect their times. There is a stress on the new, on originality; this is supported by the commercial art world of galleries and salerooms, which promotes the idea of the exclusive individual genius in the market place. In truth, artists build on the past achievements of other artists either by working with or against them. The past cannot be avoided, but its influence on contemporary art can be masked.

On excavation, Simon noticed something different taking place: dialogue and an almost constant collaboration among archaeologists that opened the perspectives of the people involved, and which then resulted in better work. While it also helps to prevent mistakes (as people comment on and check the work of their colleagues), more importantly, the collaborative dialogue invites a multitude of voices, opinions, and experiences into decisions as they are made across all parts of the process.

Archaeology as collaborative group work

Archaeology is a collaborative process; it is group work. In its collaborative character, it is distinct not only from art and art practice, but also from many other academic disciplines. When Doug worked at Cardiff University (1993–2007), he was part of the Archaeology Department (at the time it was formally called a 'Section') in what was then a larger administrative unit: the School of History and Archaeology. The School consisted of three different sections: archaeology, ancient history, and history. Archaeology is not history and is not ancient history, though there are some commonalities. Each area focuses on the study of the past, though the methods, outputs, and, in some places, the philosophy of the work undertaken differs. For most of the time that Doug was in Cardiff, the five or ten or fifteen members of each of those three sections worked independently as small self-contained groups: formulating their own section-based plans for what to teach, how to teach it, who to hire, and so on. To do this, the individual sections would meet every couple of weeks to manage their own affairs, and then the School would meet once a month or so as a larger group to receive reports from the different sections and to formulate overall school policy, particularly the distribution (to each section) of the University's funding allocation to the School.

In important ways, however, each section was very different from the others. While each studied the past in its own particular way, each section followed different implicit patterns of behaviour that had developed (most probably organically) over the longer histories of the three different disciplines. For example, if you compared the Cardiff sections in terms of published output, intellectual and social impact, and grant-winning (at the time these were the variables with which academic departments in the UK were evaluated and awarded different amounts of government funding), then each department performed with different levels of success. In many ways, the archaeologists outperformed the other two groups: they responded more quickly and effectively to centralized calls for funding applications; they won more and larger grants; produced more publications in the most significant journals and publishing houses; and ran larger research projects.

From Doug's perspective, the work of the archaeologists (and the ways that they worked and the successes that they had in securing funding and national recognition) was distinct from that of the historians and the ancient historians. One factor of this difference is that archaeological work (especially field and laboratory work) is often intense and specific and requires groups of individuals working together on a common research problem or project. To do their work, archaeologists (whether excavators or materials analysts or conservators) almost always have to go to specific places (a laboratory or a field site) in order to access equipment or a landscape that is usually highly regulated and the use of which requires precise budgeting (of both time and financial costs). All of that happens at a specific and relatively short period of time. Archaeological projects require clear-cut and intricate planning, procurement of funding, and management of various egos and skill sets. There are lots of moving parts and lots of people moving in and out of the process. Because of this, archaeology is a very social activity.

Related to what Doug experienced while working in Cardiff are Simon's observations of what was happening around him while he was making work at excavation sites. He recognized that most archaeological projects are collaborative efforts: individuals working together in teams, with each person bringing to a common project their own specialist knowledge or experience. In this sense, there are very few (if any) archaeologists who work on their own. Maybe at one time at the origins of European interests in the past (from the sixteenth to the nineteenth centuries), antiquarian scholars may have operated on their own: a member of the landed aristocracy collecting objects and keeping them in his (and it was almost always a 'his') gallery on his estate. With that earlier exception, however, archaeology is fundamentally a group activity. Doug's experience with the historians and ancient historians in the School of History and Archaeology at Cardiff showed him that while those non-archaeological colleagues were excellent at working on their own (one person exploring a complex and intricate topic, period, or text and then presenting their work to others), those scholars often lacked the experience, incentive, or desire to work in larger groups when they carried out their research and writing.

In these senses, archaeology (in the sense of a field science) is very different from many other research or academic disciplines; it is impossible for a single person to undertake every task that an excavation project requires. Because of this, there are always many people and many conversations taking place in the 'doing' of archaeology. Every well-run excavation, for example, functions with regular (planned as well as more spontaneous) conversations on site, whether it is at the end of each day's work (or before the day's work starts), or at the end of the week, or whether it is the constant discussion about what one is doing over here and how one is doing it, or what should happen next in that trench over there. This ongoing dialogue is at the core of fieldwork; it makes archaeology (especially fieldwork) a collaborative process.

It is not only at the academic end of archaeological research and excavation that the significance of group-work emerges. One of the attractions of working on an excavation (particularly for volunteers or students) is the sense of community cohesion that comes from doing analytical or physical work, day-in-and-day-out within a team. There is something especially comforting about being a member of a group of like-minded archaeologists. Furthermore, and less obvious perhaps, is that it is especially comforting if, in their non-fieldwork life, the individuals doing the digging see themselves on the periphery of the regular activities of life in Western industrial society: going to an office, having a 9-to-5-Monday-to-Friday work schedule, and perhaps sitting at a desk (the same desk) day after day. Excavation life and work are different, and a visit to almost any excavation will find (mostly) happy people, working incredibly hard, getting dirty, for little or no pay.

Furthermore, it is only partly a caricature to generalize that archaeologists (especially those working on site) do not come from elevated financial or socio-economic backgrounds, or may not have found success (or personal satisfaction) in jobs which would have put them in a corporate office or a bank building or lawyer's office. On the contrary, most excavators willingly make otherwise unnecessary personal sacrifices of living conditions, sustenance, and general physical comfort in order to do what they do. Most working adults do not normally end up with a trowel in their hand, on their knees, scrapping a pebble surface, as the rain drizzles.

Regardless of the accuracy of these caricatures of the field archaeologist, it is difficult to argue against the pleasures that people find in spending their time working on archaeological field projects. These are like-minded people who value, and put effort into, particular parts of their lives and surroundings and not into others. They are people who don't mind (or judge you for) smoking roll-up cigarettes, who don't care where you buy your clothes (or, commonly, how often you wash them), who like doing their work out-of-doors (regardless of the weather or the temperature), who don't mind living on Marmite-and-cheddar-cheese sandwiches for three weeks, and have no problem bedding down on the ground in tents each night after a day of heavy manual labour. When diggers go to work on an excavation, they find themselves among like-minded people.

Whose work is it?

If we agree that the practice of field archaeology (in distinction from art-making) is a collaborative process among like-minded people, and part of its success results from the shared conversations and group work, then an important question emerges: who is the author of the output that the excavation creates? Whose work is it? Also, if we agree that the production of an artwork is different (and much less collaborative) than archaeology, especially in the way that Simon works, then what are these differences and what are consequences that result?

*When Simon thinks about the work he has made resulting from his interaction with archaeological excavation (*Trench 10 *or* Segsbury Project, *discussed in Chapter 2, for example, or* Chromium Oxide Cut Pit Painting, *detailed in Chapter 6, or* Country Register, *in Chapter 10), he is aware that the excavation site itself is the product of the labour of other people: most directly, the excavators whose physical efforts removed the overburden and uncovered the archaeological surface; also, more indirectly, other project members who set the stage for the physical process of excavation. This latter group includes almost everyone from site director, to the geophysics specialist, to surveyor, and on and on, in fact to include everyone who supported that action of excavation, from the project cook to a driver or site guard.*

At the excavations where Simon worked, he was part of a team. Those places were not places that he found on his own. He was invited to participate by the projects' directors. Furthermore, he was only able to make his painting because other people had completed a lot of strenuous and detailed work excavating trenches and revealing the archaeological surfaces that Simon engaged with. Simon's paintings are just one output (of many) from that group-fuelled excavation project. Simon, as well as others, have been able to make their work (whether it is his paintings or, for example, a graduate student's PhD dissertation on the pottery or mollusk remains from the site) only because a team of other people had put a lot of work into creating and sustaining the project.

Simon makes much of his work directly from the material object that the excavators have created: the exposed site surface. Because of this, he recognizes that he has an ethical responsibility to acknowledge the people who produced that material object from which he creates his work. In other parts of his creative process, however, Simon sees a different relationship with the fabricators of the raw materials he uses. For example, someone has made the canvas that Simon puts the paint onto, and someone else has made the pigment that Simon applies to those canvases. No one (Simon included) formally recognizes those makers (of canvas and pigment) for the labour they expend. On the other hand, the excavated archaeological surfaces that Simon uses in his paintings have a different value from that of canvas and pigment. Simon feels a connection with the excavators who create the excavated surface, but not with the canvas and paint fabricators, whose work is distant from Simon's use of the materials they produce. Perhaps this disarticulation from the fabricators is manifest in the artists' acts of purchasing those materials. Simon doesn't pay the diggers, or the project directors, and he works (in his process of witnessing) at their side (or at the side of the trench).

The question emerges, therefore, whose work is a painting by Simon Callery? Similarly, whose work is the finished excavation report? When people purchase one of Simon's paintings, for example, they understand that Simon Callery (as artist) made that work. When someone sees the work in a gallery or a collector's home and asks 'whose work is that?', the answer is Simon Callery. While it is no surprise to us that the canvas and pigment makers do not factor in the authorship of the artwork, it is worthwhile to ask why there is little or no note of authorship given to the volunteers and students who trowelled and scraped and swept and sweated over that original archaeological surface.

In the corresponding case, archaeology also fails to credit those fieldworkers in the output that results from an excavation. When the final report of a project is published as a book, or when preliminary reports appear in journals or online, the standard practice is to list one or two authors (normally the project directors). In the larger book format (and increasingly online), it is common to find a list of the names of diggers and volunteers who worked on the site, and often there is a group photograph of the project team from each season of work. Also, there may be a list of the university students who took part for a summer or so, there may be a second list identifying who were the trench or site supervisors, and there may be yet another list for the funders or the people who worked in the lab during post-excavation analyses. Often, the excavation report includes individual chapters or sections authored by the relevant specialists who performed particular analytic tasks (e.g., absolute dating, pollen analysis, ceramic typology).

The site report as a whole, however, remains authored by the site director(s), and subsequent publications about the excavation refer to that report (and thus that excavation) with those few names. One realizes, therefore, that the listing of the names of excavators or individual specialists hides the absence of a recognition of the people who did the essential work in the field. This is a problem, because the individuals in the trench, at the lab benches, and at the pottery washing table are the people who made it all happen. Without them there would be no project and no final output. Is there also here, then, a similar break as seen in Simon's disarticulation from the canvas weavers and pigment grinders? Does a commercial (or other) transaction (such as academic credit for students, or access to the project for volunteers) justify the lack of adequate acknowledgement and appreciation for the people with their hands in the dirt? In this sense, archaeology, as a collaborative practice (especially as a field-based practice), is not all that dissimilar from art practice in the way that many (most, more likely) of the people who do essential creative work do not feature in formal statements of authorship of what results from that work. Textile mills or pigment manufacturers are industrial businesses, not a part of the essential creative work.

There are exceptions to this erasure of the labour providers in excavation projects and reports, of course. Some projects have given voice to the excavators and the other participants in a project, regardless of their position in the project's hierarchy. Barbara Bender, Sue Hamilton, and Chris

Tilley worked towards this in the book that came out of their project at Bodmin Moor in the UK (Stone Worlds[1]) which included student-scripted texts. In Turkey, the Çatalhöyuk project had a similar attitude: Sadrettin Dural, one of the site guards, published Protecting Çatalhöyük: Memoir of an Archaeological Site Guard[2] *in which he told his own story. There are other projects that similarly recognize the role of non-site directors in final publications, but, in general, the rule holds: the hands that do the manual labour are seldom acknowledged or even visible in the final product. It may be that the scale of collaborative group-work on site is one cause of this: there are so many hands and so many voices that it is not possible to efficiently or fully represent them in authorship. It may also be the case that one (or two or three) individuals (the site or project directors) undertook the writing of the final report or book.*

The failure to include in archaeological reports or the final artwork explicit reference to those many hands and voices necessary for either type of work actively disappears the individual inputs made to the archaeological project and the artwork. The significance is greater than merely a failure to acknowledge labour expended. Each individual involved in the works of archaeology or of art has her or his own socio-economic, racial, religious, historical, political, and gendered background: where they come from, why they are on site, why they decided to be an archaeologist (and not a banker or historian or a photographer or any other vocation); and how they ended up working at the foundry, or sitting at a loom weaving cotton into canvas. All of the different (unique, one could argue) positions that each excavator and fabricator occupies comes with those individuals' life experiences. Those personal positions affect what happens on site and in the making of art materials and completion of artist's instructions. In many ways we have developed and pursued a system of training, education, and validation which has removed these elements of individuality.

If we think about archaeology in this way, then we recognize the consequences of these absences and disappearances: those invisible workers and their repeated actions are at the core of the work made. The presence (acknowledged or not) of those formally invisible efforts of individual hands and muscles raises questions about the status of archaeology as a scientific, objective practice. In fact, the practice of archaeology (though less commonly understood as with the making of art) is a fully human and subjective process. Both are made from personal emotion, histories, hang-ups, worries, satisfactions, agendas, and disappointments.

The comparison is not equal, however, and the dissimilarities are noteworthy. For the most part, artistic production follows a different course from that of archaeological fieldwork; in most cases, it is a non-collaborative activity. Artists make work from their individual personal position; on their own, in private and out of sight in rented studio spaces. Most materials that artists use, were not specifically fabricated for the purpose of making art. They are raw materials with many applications. The painters' cotton duck canvas or linen is primarily produced for the textile or fashion industry, not for artists. The artists either buy it in bulk from textile merchants at market prices for cotton or at inflated prices at art material supply shops. Pigments are industrially produced in bulk for the paint and coatings industry, a subsidiary of the international chemical industry. Tiny quantities of what is produced make it into art shops, packaged as a specialist commodity, and sold at prices that do not directly reflect actual manufacturing costs. You cannot buy dry pigments directly from the manufacturers. It is a closed market. By the time any of these materials get to an artist they have already passed through many hands. They have, of course, all been paid for their work, unlike the majority of artists, many of whom struggle to sell theirs. The pigment makers or the linen weavers (paid a fee for their labour), and the volunteer excavators (paid a course credit for their effort), have all been removed from the position of authorship.

If we were to carry out an ethnography of archaeology, and study not the past but the real-time, day-to-day, hands-on-the-trowel-and-in-the-ground, ways in which objects and traces of the past are recovered, and the workers who carry out the work required for that recovery, then we would observe excavation as the anthropological object. Such a study wouldn't be so much about a recovered past, as it would be about focusing on what happens at the excavation: what are the power relationships on site (who is telling whom what to do and when); who is digging in this part of the landscape and not another (perhaps of less historical potential); and who is assigned to excavate in one particular (perhaps more interesting) part of the site and not another; how are some volunteers and students chosen to participate (and who are not selected); why do the trench supervisors wear one type of hat or shirt, with the site director another; why do they smoke the cigarettes that they do; why do they drink what they drink where they drink it; why do they eat what they eat; and on and so on. These questions focus not on the past that is being recovered (though few critical archaeologists would deny that the past is only ever constructed; it does not exist out there as static thing that can be discovered, described, and displayed), but on the real-time activity, behaviour, decisions, and life of the excavation. Because Simon's work is excavation-based (and not past-based), these questions are the relevant ones to ask: not questions about the chronology or function of the projects where Simon makes his work.

This perspective brings into focus Simon's position as an artist, making creative work, and the site director's position as author and authority. It also reveals the excavators as the labourers who produce the materials that both the artist and the site director then use to create their work. The diggers make the archaeological surface that Simon uses as a raw material for his painting and make (visible) the objects and data that the site director uses as raw material to make their published interpretations of dating, function, and human behaviour at the site. The final product that Simon makes (Country Register, for example) bears his name as artist and makes no reference to the many individuals who created the archaeological surface from which the painting derives. The original prehistoric pit was not dug in the Iron Age for the archaeologist to study, and the modern archaeologist did not dig it for the artist to use it in make his or her painting. What is interesting to figure out, however, is what these individuals (unintentionally connected by that pit) have in common, and what brings them to the site. This is an equation based on interdependency where the motives of the characters involved are entirely different.

That is not the whole story, however, as there is a strong connection between Simon and excavator. His work as an artist is similar to the work and position of digger on site. Both work at the same physical level in the same place. Both work with their hands: at the excavation site on and in the ground; in the studio on and in the canvas and the pigment. Both excavator and artist share a common manner of activity and work. Their work is repeated physical activity that might best be thought of as metaphysical. The work is less about answering grand research questions (such as when people shifted from a mobile to a sedentary lifestyle). It is something more than that, and it is something difficult to explain: perhaps impossible to define logically. In the end, it may not be something that we can understand from the rational perspective of objectified rationalist academic science.

4

Twenty Minutes Inside Out
(Doug Bailey, 2010)

In 2010, I made a film in the village of Măgura in southern Romania.[1] It is twenty minutes long, though I edited it so that it loops continuously. To make the film I set up a camera on a side street in the village, and I ran the camera for half an hour at four different times of one day. I just let the camera run and record whatever happened on that street. There was no plan beyond that. No script. No direction. No instructions to people walking by or living there. I had no real idea what would happen and what might result from the filming.

I asked my San Francisco State University colleague, Peter Biella, to arrange the videos on a single screen in a four-framed grid so that the viewer would see all of the film's running at the same time. The result was as if the four twenty-minute portions of the same day on the same street at the same time have been collapsed onto each other. At a point in each of the videos, I inserted one of three words: art, landscape, transformation. As each word appeared, it faded-in from a black background and then back out again into the sequence of the video.

When a viewer watches the four-framed video, it seems as if nothing is happening. There is very little movement in any of the frames; each presents the same bit of unpaved road: a stuccoed

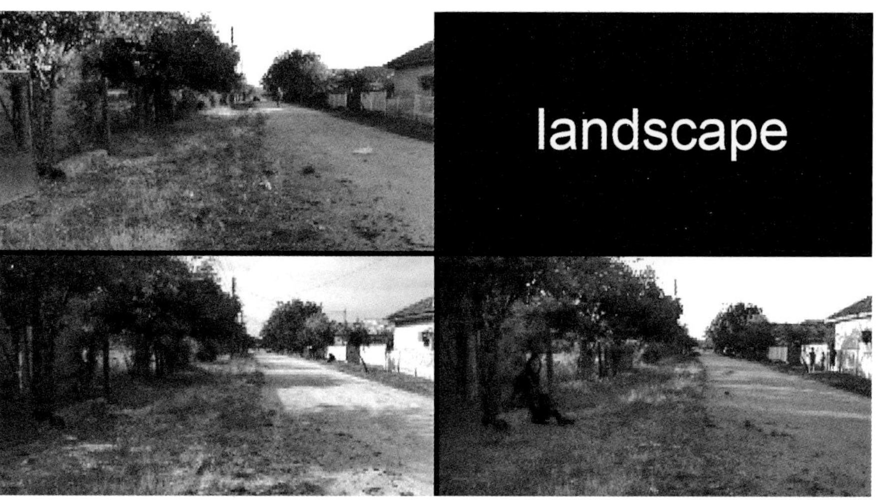

4.1 *Screengrab:* Twenty Minutes Inside Out: Landscape Transformation in Neolithic Southcentral Romania *(2010).*

building behind a fence to the right: trees hanging over a fence on the left. Frame to frame, shadows and sunlight differ: full sun at noon in the film in the upper right quadrant of the grid; deep shadows of late afternoon in the lower right; late morning in the upper left; early afternoon in the lower left. A soundtrack runs in the background: a man talking Romanian, cockerels crowing, a chaos of birds, my voice softened in whisper, the sound of a tractor's motor. A man, dressed in black, walks into one frame, up the street, and out of the shot. Another man rides away from us on his bicycle, with a plastic bag hanging from the handlebars, passing the man in black. The frames come to life: more men walk through the frames: one towards us and one away. Dogs bark. An ATV speeds past us chased by another barking dog, sprinting.

Then, the barest of movements in the left hand corner of one of the frames. In the dark shade under a tree, an elderly woman raises her arm. We realize that she has been in the shot all the time. She blends into the shadows. We look at the other frames. She is in one of the others. In the other two grids, however, she is gone; in each we see the low stone slab-bench where she had been sitting. She remains in the two other grids for the rest of the video, not speaking, barely moving.

Art Landscape Transformations EC project 2007-4230

The four-grid movie was one part of a larger project which I had been invited to join in 2008. I remember being in my office at Cardiff University. The phone rang. I picked it up. It was an archaeologist from Tomar in Portugal. His name was Gonçalo Leite Velho. He said that he knew about my work, though I'm not sure what part of it he knew about. It might have been the excavation of a Neolithic landscape that I had been directing at the time on the outskirts of the Măgura village. I would like to think that he had contacted me because he knew of my interest in an unrestrained combination of art and archaeology.

Gonçalo asked me to join a big European Union project about archaeology, the transformation of landscape, and art. I asked Gonçalo for more information about the objectives for the larger project, about what he would need from me in terms of application text, budgets, methodology, and about all of the other sections that a large application would require. I wasn't sure that I had the time. Gonçalo said that all I needed to do was to send him a couple of paragraphs by the end of the following week. I was in.

Looking back, Gonçalo's call came at a perfect time. I was in the middle phase of an excavation project in Romania, and I had established many of the delicate connections that such a project required: Romanian colleagues to work with, a local museum for collaboration. The people on the ground knew me and, together, we had established a trustful working relationship. On the Cardiff side, the University was eager for faculty to win large grants and to be a part of international projects, and they had a dedicated administrative team experienced in winning EU grants; they would be able to put together all of the financial numbers that Gonçalo would need very soon.

At a conceptual level, Gonçalo's project made sense. Archaeologists spend a lot of time working at landscape-scale, trying to recover and interpret long-term patterns of change in vegetation or soil fertility or river activity or settlement densities. This was classic modern archaeology as it had developed over the past fifty years. More than this, though, Gonçalo's project attracted me because it aimed to insert artists into more traditional approaches to people and the past. I wasn't sure what I would do with the funding if the application succeeded, but I was excited by the possibilities that it offered for doing something new and different.

It was probably the easiest project funding that I have ever received. The downside of this ease, however, was that I had not done any of the regular, detailed planning and project design, and because of that I had no idea what we were going to do with the money. I was left free to fashion the shape of the project and to select collaborators. In the end, I decided to take eight or maybe nine artists and archaeologists (archaeologists who were interested in art and archaeology) to Măgura where we had been excavating Neolithic sites for the previous five or six years.

Măgura Past and Present

In archaeology of the 1990s and early 2000s, there were many projects and much funding for work on landscape. I wanted to do something different, and so my only instructions to the project participants were that they should make work about the place, about the village of Măgura, to use their skills, knowledge, and experiences to evoke the place in their media. Each participant had particular skills and experiences, and I trusted them to proceed as they saw fit, to follow their creative senses and respond to the place in whatever way they could.[2]

Setting up a traditional archaeological fieldwork project is a different process, compared to what I was doing for the EU project;[3] the former includes detailed sets of aims, objectives, methods, and outcomes. Everything nests within a clearly stated and shared, explicit programme of work. It's strange, but in many ways archaeology is not about discovery; it is about having a clear idea about what you are going to find and then developing a research strategy to find it. While there are surprises, the best project designs are rational step-by-step methods and expertise applied to a problem in a place, in order to produce an expected result. This EU project was wholly different, and it allowed us to move away from that rational, predictive model for making work. If we had a clear goal, it was to release people from the normal constraints of what was possible (and particularly of what was allowed or expected) on archaeological field projects.

Risky work

Many of the participating artists responded to the project's call to experiment with dynamic results. In the aftermath of an earlier symposium at the Courtauld Institute in London, I had been in touch with the British artist Claude Heath. I became intrigued by Claude's 'sighted drawing' process: having been blindfolded, he would take an object in one hand, a pen in the other, and then using only his tactile understanding of the unseen object, would make a drawing of it. In a 2010 exhibition at the Sainsbury Museum in the UK and the corresponding book,[4] I had included Heath's sighted drawing of the Venus of Willendorf. I had a sense that Claude would enjoy the opportunities to experiment that the Măgura project would offer. He did not disappoint.

Claude set up a drawing space in one of the work rooms of the Teleorman Regional Historical Museum (MJT), with paper taped to a wall, a blindfold around his head, and a set of (sight-unseen) objects handed to him by museum colleagues. First, they handed him a wooden three-legged stool made by local Roma; he produced his unsighted graphic understanding of it. We put his hand

4.2 *Claude Heath*. Silex Drag Right *(2010)*.

on the plaster statue of the deposed and executed Romania totalitarian leader Nicolae Ceauşescu. Claude drew that. We even handed him a desiccated loaf-shaped piece of cow dung, and he drew that. Other objects stimulated Claude in increasingly transformative ways. His response to being handed a hafted Neolithic flint axe-adze was not to make a traditional descriptive drawing of it, but to use the axe-adze as the instrument of artistic creation. For him, the edge of the blade became an artist's tool to make a series of incisions into his art paper. When handed a 7,000-year-old flint blade-core from the museum archives, Claude dipped it into blue India ink and then used the inked-core to draw onto art paper. The results of these two works were unexpected and provocative; Claude used artefacts without any respect for (or perhaps even knowledge of) their original function or meaning, or of any modern, local heritage-based valorization of them as historically valuable remnants of a vital period of European history.[5]

Claude's bold experiments fit in with the thoughts starting to come to me about creative work that was related to archaeology, but also that broke the assumed rules of preservation and conservation. Claude's work ventured into the unexplored territories beyond the boundaries of archaeology and of art as normally practiced.

Simon Thorne's acoustics

Similarly exciting was the work that sound artist Simon Thorne made in the village of Măgura and in the hotel in the nearby city of Alexandria where the team stayed during the project.[6] Again, my prompt to Simon was to make work that evoked the village in whatever way he felt inspired to do so and using whatever materials he chose. During his time with the project, Simon recorded sounds and then remediated some of them to make acoustic work that is both of those two places, but also fully distanced from it.[7] Some of Simon's acoustic works were clear, detailed, evocations of the village that dove deeper into detail than any textual or photographic representation of the place could reach: crickets, thunder, car-tires on dirt roads, a child's unanswered question. When I listened to Simon's other sound work (made in the work rooms of the museum in Alexandria), I had little, if any, idea of what I was hearing: traces of acoustic information not normally within human hearing, captured, amplified, rearranged into never experienced representations of an institution of local cultural history. When I read the notes on the CD-liner or looked at the titles to the tracks, I started to get a sense of what I was listening to, but, if I just let my ears experience the acoustics, I was wonderfully submerged into a world without explicit reference to place or meaning or interpretation. As with Claude Heath's sighted drawings, Thorne's sound work pushed through the boundaries of what was expected (and what could easily be consumed): the results unbalanced me and other listeners. The work raised more questions than answers. More critically, it put me in a place where answers and logic and expected explanation no longer seemed relevant or necessary.

Michaël Jasmin's digging

Working at another scale and in an unavoidably physical and visual mode, French experimentalist archaeologist Michaël Jasmin inserted his work into the physical landscape of Măgura and its surroundings. Michaël's original plans for contributing to the project had been photographic, using large-format cameras to make visual work in the village. Indeed, Michaël did make that work,[8] though, his more radical work cut directly into the turf of an historical monument.

The village of Măgura sits on a low terrace above the plain of the Vedea River. Looking over the plain, one can see small hills, which, in fact, are the remains of Neolithic settlements, occupied in the late sixth and early fifth millennia. These sites are the focus of archaeological work, some of which we had carried out in collaboration with our colleagues at the Teleorman Museum. Michaël's work focused on the settlement mound (or tell) northwest of the village. This tell (Măgura-Gorgan) had been occupied for (actually, partially created by) a 500-year period by a community of Neolithic farmers, herders, hunters, and fishers. The upper strata of the tell consisted of the wood and clay houses of successive generations of people who had lived there. Long after those Neolithic inhabitants had abandoned the settlement, other people centred their lives and actions on the hill: this time in the Iron Age. Finally, and much more recently, twentieth-century rural populations (including those now living in modern Măgura) had established a small chapel and a cemetery on the top of the mound.

Michaël asked if he could make work on the tell. I asked the local authorities. They agreed. On the sloping side of the hill, using strings and wooden stakes, Michaël laid out the shapes of a set of alpha-numeric figures, each three or four metres tall and a metre wide. Seven figures in all. Then, following the outlines of the string staked into the ground, using a hand hoe and shovel, he cut through the grass and down into the earth below, and pulled the grass and topsoil away.

Each day while he worked, villagers would stop to look at what this Frenchman was doing. Talk among the villagers was that the letters and number referred to a reading from the Bible. There was, of course, a chapel on the tell. Others came up with wilder ideas about spy satellites. In the

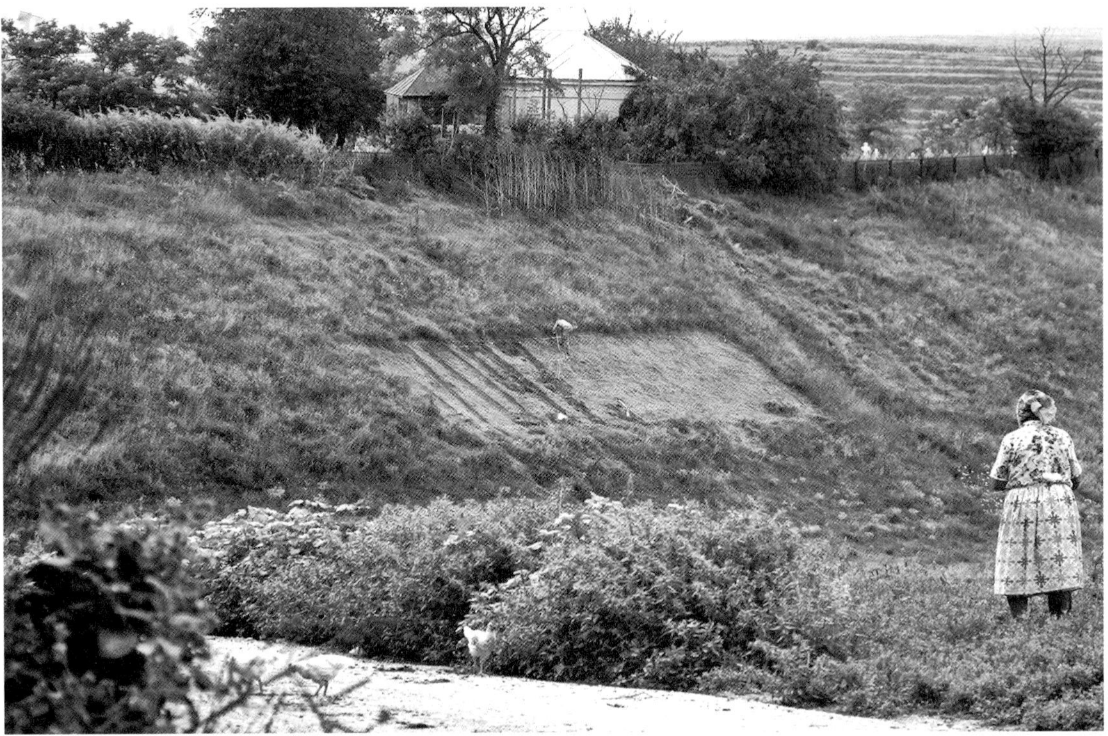

4.3 *Michaël Jasmin working at Măgura-Gorgan, Romania (2010).*

end, Michaël's cutting into the surface of the ground, into the Neolithic and Iron Age historic monument, spelt out the UTM (Universal Trans Mercator) identifier for the location of Tell Măgura-Gorgan. Michaël Jasmin's work was, perhaps, the perfect prosecution of the spirit of the original Art and Landscape Transformation project. It was work that plunged, rather dangerously in terms of the potential violation of a national historical monument, deep into the depths of the unknown. Michaël created something that was not archaeological, but something that was not artistic either. Michaël had disarticulated an archaeological site and its constituent traces of prehistoric human activities and then repurposed those newly liberated materials as if they were raw materials. In doing so he disrupted our normal understanding not only of what an archaeological site is, but also, of our understanding and our use of scientific human systems to measure the otherwise natural and unrestrained ground upon which we walk and work and live.

Dis-illusioned with archaeology

During the months when I was setting up the Măgura project, contacting potential participants from archaeological and artistic worlds, coordinating visits with colleagues and friends in Romania in the village of Măgura and the town of Alexandria, and while I was meeting with the finance people in Cardiff to make the numbers work and to help the euros flow, in none of this, did I ever see myself as a creator or a maker: certainly not an artist. When I arrived in Măgura to coordinate

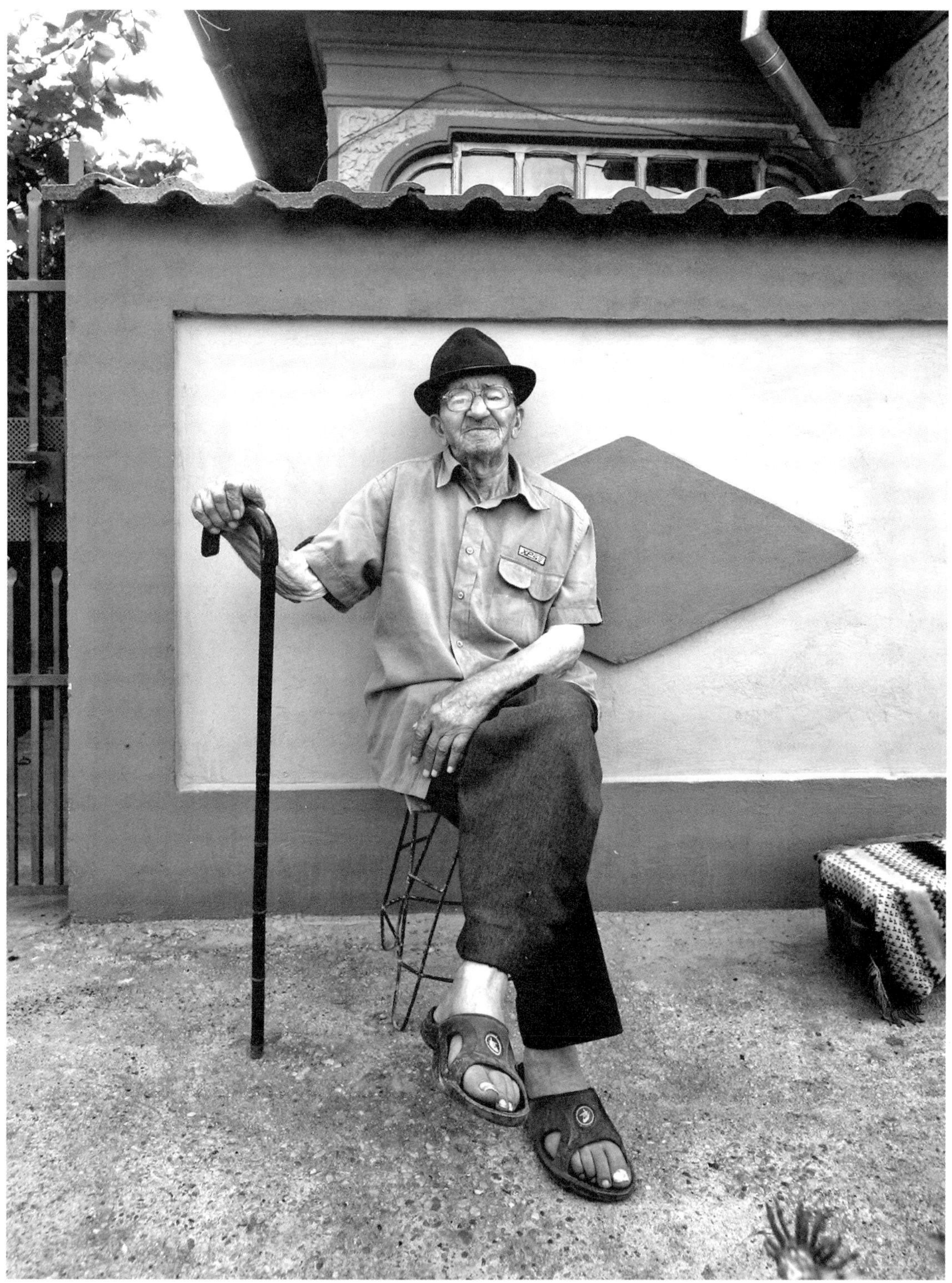

4.4 *The village of Măgura, Romania (2010).*

the project in 2010, I had no intention of making work (artistic or other). During previous periods of free time living and working in the village (1999–2003) during our archaeological excavations, however, I had made series of photographic images of life as lived around me, though I had not published any of it formally (beyond a photobook self-published with Blurb[9] and a website[10]).

When I was working watching two of the project participants (Peter Biella and Ivan Drofovka) make their work (the film *Eternity Was Born in the Village*),[11] I realized that I had the opportunity to experiment with their medium and to use their equipment and to get Peter's help recording those four, twenty-minute episodes on that side-street in the village. I was feeling it out as I went along. I could never have raised any money or secured the necessary permits to do what I ended up doing in making the film if I had set out from the start with it as my intended work. How could I have done so? I had no idea what might happen when we eventually got there.

The futility of archaeology

Another unexpected thing happened. While in the village, I felt increasingly uncomfortable about the themes of the larger EU project: landscape transformation, archaeology, and art. While I embraced the goal of making art, I was increasingly uncertain about the broader claims that

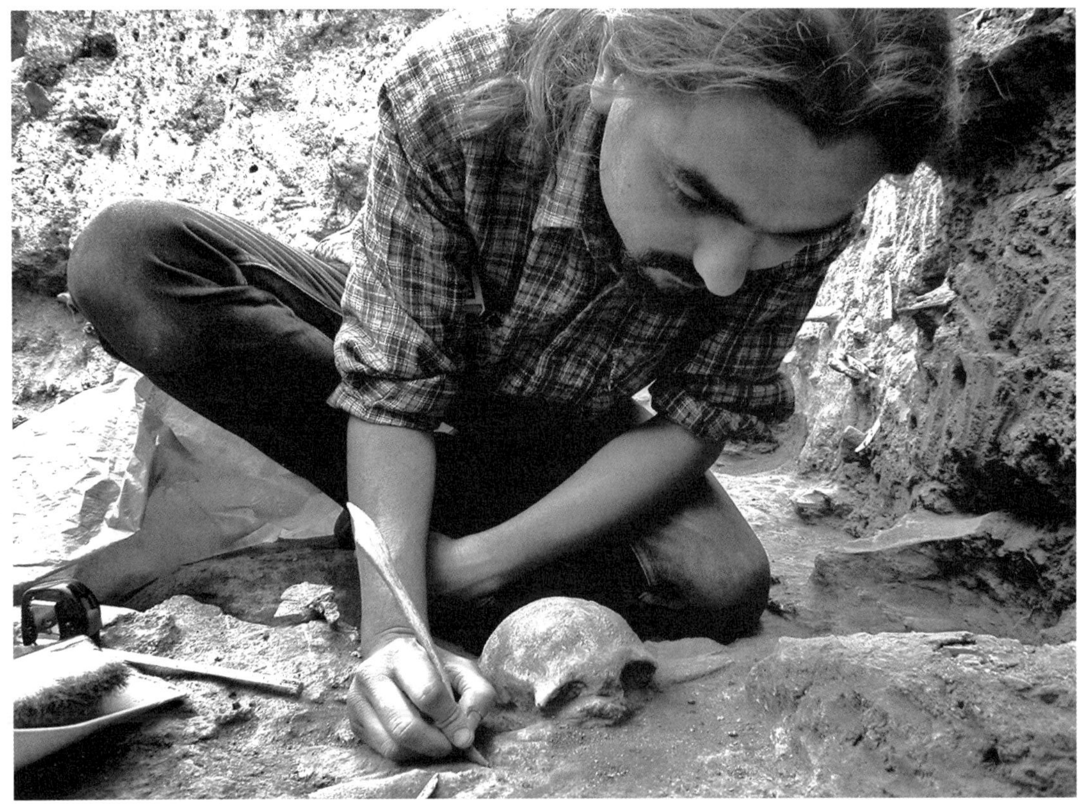

4.5 *Excavation at Măgura-Budaisca, Romania (2005).*

archaeologists make, especially based on field- and lab-research about long-term trends in the shape and character of physical and cultural landscapes. My discomfort had been during our excavations of the early and middle Neolithic site at Măgura-Budaisca. With each season's work, with each day at the site, with each grant proposal, and with each conference paper or journal publication, I felt increasingly that I was selling a story to the public, the readers, the funders, to my students and colleagues. More and more, I felt that I was making up a narrative about the past that I had no honest way of confirming was true. My arguments about how the landscape had changed around our site over 100s and 1,000s and 10,000s of years, felt less and less honourable. I realized that I was reducing an otherwise complex, long-term reality down into a dramatically simplified version of change.

Mixing my unease with the terms of the EU project resulted in a new argument that I wanted to make: to show (by doing) how facile and unrealistic are the traditional grand models of human and geographic change that archaeology produces. To me those models operated like an accordion, generating a product (acoustic or explanatory) by squeezing down into the smallest space, what was, in reality, a broad, open, and extended expanse (of musical air, of human and geomorphic actions, or of periods of time). I came to see that it would be much more honest to recognize that the reality of life (past or present) will always remain at the pace of life lived, of steps taken, of conversations had, of dogs running down a street or barking behind a fence. The reality of life is what one will see over a twenty-minute period standing at roadside in a small village in rural Romania. It will never be a set of radiocarbon dates or geomorphic sequences. This recognition of life-lived took up a place at the centre of the film that I was making, and it would stand at the base of the article that, eventually, I would write in order to turn that film into a more widely consumable academic contribution to the debate.[12]

Archaeologists create stories with image and metaphor which they set before their academic and public audiences. They do this with authority. They tell us how a landscape has changed over 10,000 years. They use studies of erosion patterns and changes in river current and river course to provide a simplified understanding of what are otherwise highly complex, dense, and numerous data points, calculations, and analyses. In reality, those 10,000 years are beyond human comprehension. You and I can understand what happens this year and the last, and we can talk coherently about other periods of our lives (when we were at school or as we grew up), but we do not have the capacity or perspective to understand the genuine pace and events that occupy 10,000 years of time. The scientist who tries to make that period comprehensible has to collapse it down like an accordion, pushing out air and moments of being.

Seen from this perspective, what many archaeologists do is a distortion. They construct a reality of time-passage which is a misrepresentation. If that is the case, and if I don't believe that this type of work is honest or positive, then what are the alternatives? One alternative is to take one day, or one part of one day (perhaps four twenty-minute sections) and promote it as a more accurate and more honest representation of change in a landscape. Change in real time is what happens (or doesn't happen) over those twenty minutes. The four-frame, gridded film was my attempt to make such a representation. Once the film had been edited, I gave it a title that would speak to its essence, but also which might attract archaeologists and researchers who held the more traditional approach to the prehistoric past. I wanted to get this work in front of the eyes of people who practised, without question, the accordionization of the past. I titled the film *Twenty Minutes Inside Out: Landscape Transformation in Neolithic southeastern Romania.*

Textualizing a film

Once I had made the film, I realized that few archaeologists were going to see it, regardless of the title, so I took advantage of another unexpected invitation to turn the film into a graphic work that could fit into a traditional academic published format. As I was finishing the film, two colleagues (Ruth Van Dyke and Reinhard Bernbeck) asked me to participate in a conference session at the annual meetings of the Society for American Archaeology. The session had the rather hefty title, 'Against objectivized subjects: alternative narratives in archaeology', and led to the production of the standard, edited anthology of rewritten and expanded versions of the papers that session participants had delivered in person at the conference.[13]

My role in the session was to be a discussant; after the other presentations had been made, I was to make detailed comments on each of the individual contributions. Instead of doing that, I ran my film *Twenty Minutes* and offered, first, a series of questions that the different conference papers had raised in my mind and which were directed at particular contributors: 'Do you have an ethical responsibility?', 'How do we facilitate multi-vocality?' Next, I made a series of suggestions, also derived from the papers, but also leaning towards my emerging thoughts on what might be possible in a more radical approach to archaeological publication. These suggestions were more general: 'Seek the incomplete', 'Focus on the mundane', 'Show don't tell', 'Avoid linearity'.

I was not sure what I could do to turn that video-plus-questions-and-suggestions into a format that would work for the academic book that Ruth and Reinhard were editing. Several years earlier,

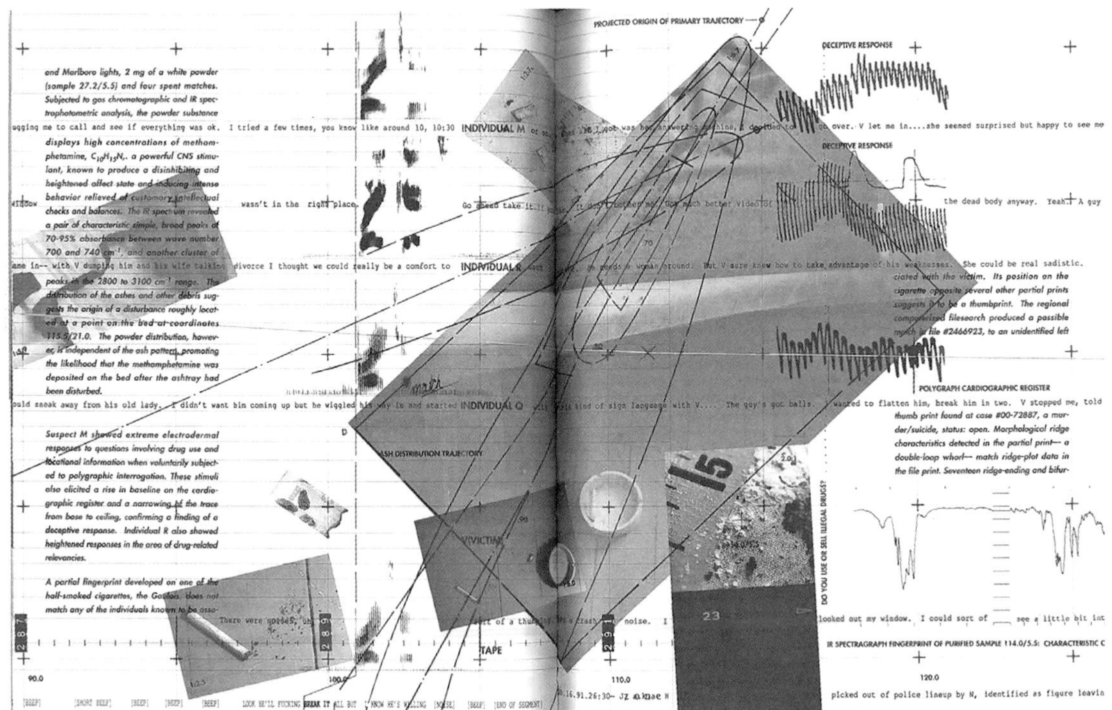

4.6 *Case no. 00-17163 by Diller and Scofidio (1992), pp. 350–1.*

I had come across Elizabeth Diller and Richard Scofidio's 1992 *Case no. 00-17163: a reworking and montage of data and images of a crime scene.*[14] The work was about the place of a murder. In a montage spread over sixteen pages, Diller and Scofidio presented questions and information in visual form. To me, *Case no. 00-17163* opened exciting possibilities for representing a place, an event, or a set of human actions (which, in truth, is what archaeologists do most of the time). I had been greatly impressed by the form, content, structure, and affect of that work. Ruth and Reinhard's invitation to contribute to their book presented me with the opportunity to explore Diller and Scofidio's experimental format.

In the work that I made for the book, I sought to present the reader/viewer with a mixture of images, texts, and data, but without any obvious or coherent argument or narrative. I wanted readers to think about key themes and to question the quotidian assumptions about archaeological data, the separation of past and present, and the unspoken leaps that we make when we attempt to present, represent, and evoke a particular place (i.e., Măgura today or the Neolithic of 6,000 years ago). I based the chapter on one of the videos that I made on the street in the village. I reproduced a series of screen grabs from the film and laid them out along the top of the twenty pages of the chapter. Above the screen grabs, I ran the time sequence for that part of the film: from five seconds to eleven minutes and forty seconds. I gave the chapter a title from these brief moments of time in the village, Eleven minutes and forty seconds in the Neolithic: underneath archaeological time.

Along the bottom of the pages, I ran a standard archaeological rendition of a time-line (6200–5900 BC) in a sequence giving the impression of time passage in its archaeological accordionized format. Thus, I created a space on the page framed at its top with the reality of time (in terms of being on that street for just over eleven minutes) and at its bottom with the scientific unreality of time (in terms of radiocarbon assessment of 3,000 years). In the space between these conflicting temporal registers, I had created a place in which to play with data, interpretation, analysis, texts, fiction, and image.

In order to bring to life the physical movements of the individuals, dogs, bicycles, and cars in the video, in this graphic place, I turned to Melanie Simpkin, a scholar of dance and dance-movement and a practitioner of Benesh notation, one of the systems that choreographers use to represent live body-movement through symbols on paper. Melanie watched the eleven minutes and forty seconds of video and she converted the movements of people, cars, and animals into Benesh symbols. I ran her notation through the chapter under the corresponding screen grabs. I engineered the chapter (as had Diller and Scofidio) as a single, long, horizontal piece, which continued across the book's gutter from one page to the next: image, text, screengrabs all running in a sequence through the chapter.

In addition to contrasting the film-time of the living with the archaeological-time of the radiocarbon sequence, I transported the reader from the position of straight, scientific archaeologist (where embodied life is disappeared by data and data analysis) to the place of sensuous humanity (where emotion and feeling dominate). To do this, I assembled a sequence of images and texts, and arranged them through the pages so that the chapter starts in full archaeological mode and ends deep in personal human emotion. The images came from our Neolithic excavations in the village: artefacts (photographs and drawings of reconstructed vessels, flint blades), palaeobotanical remains (drawings of wheat seeds), microscopic thin-sections of the analysis of micro-morphology, site-plans and stratigraphic sequences (of the site, of a pit-hut, and of an excavation baulk), graphs

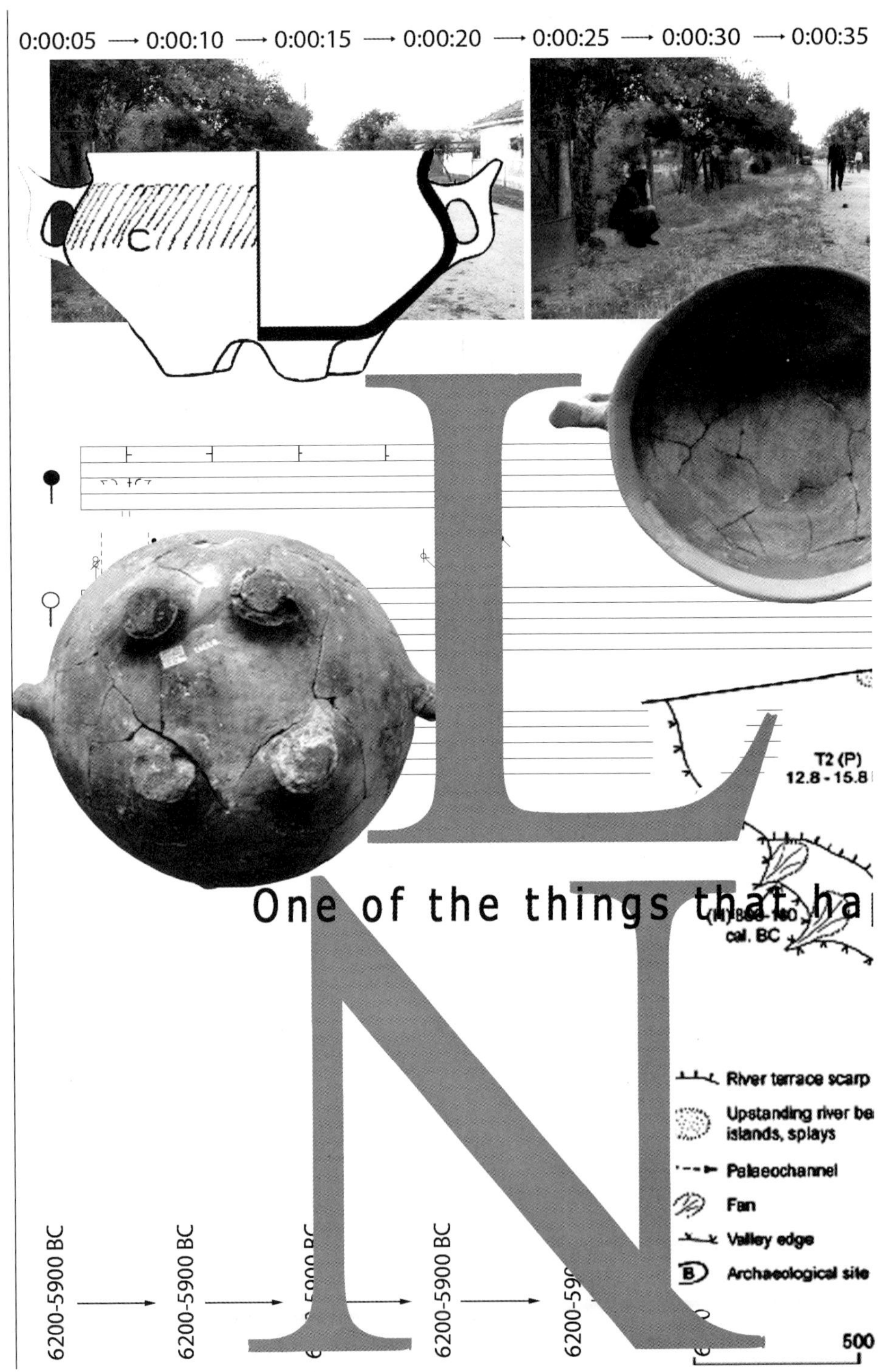

4.7 *Eleven minutes and forty seconds in the Neolithic: underneath archaeological time, p. 192 (Bailey and Simpkin 2015).*

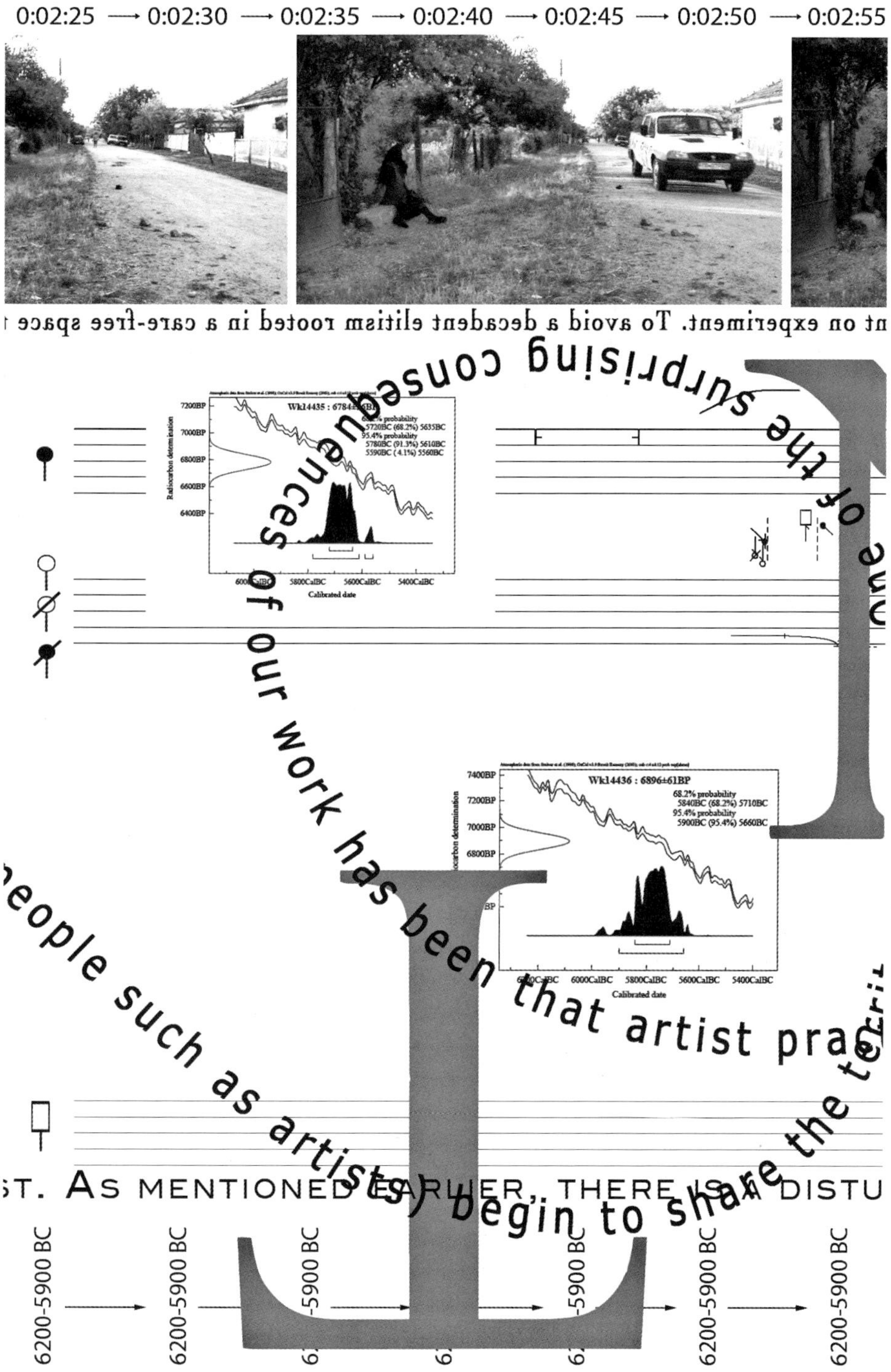

0:02:25 → 0:02:30 → 0:02:35 → 0:02:40 → 0:02:45 → 0:02:50 → 0:02:55

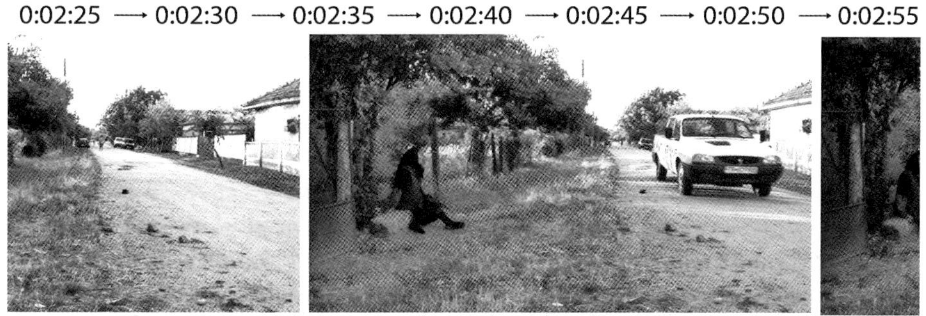

4.8 *Eleven minutes and forty seconds in the Neolithic: underneath archaeological time, p. 196 (Bailey and Simpkin 2015).*

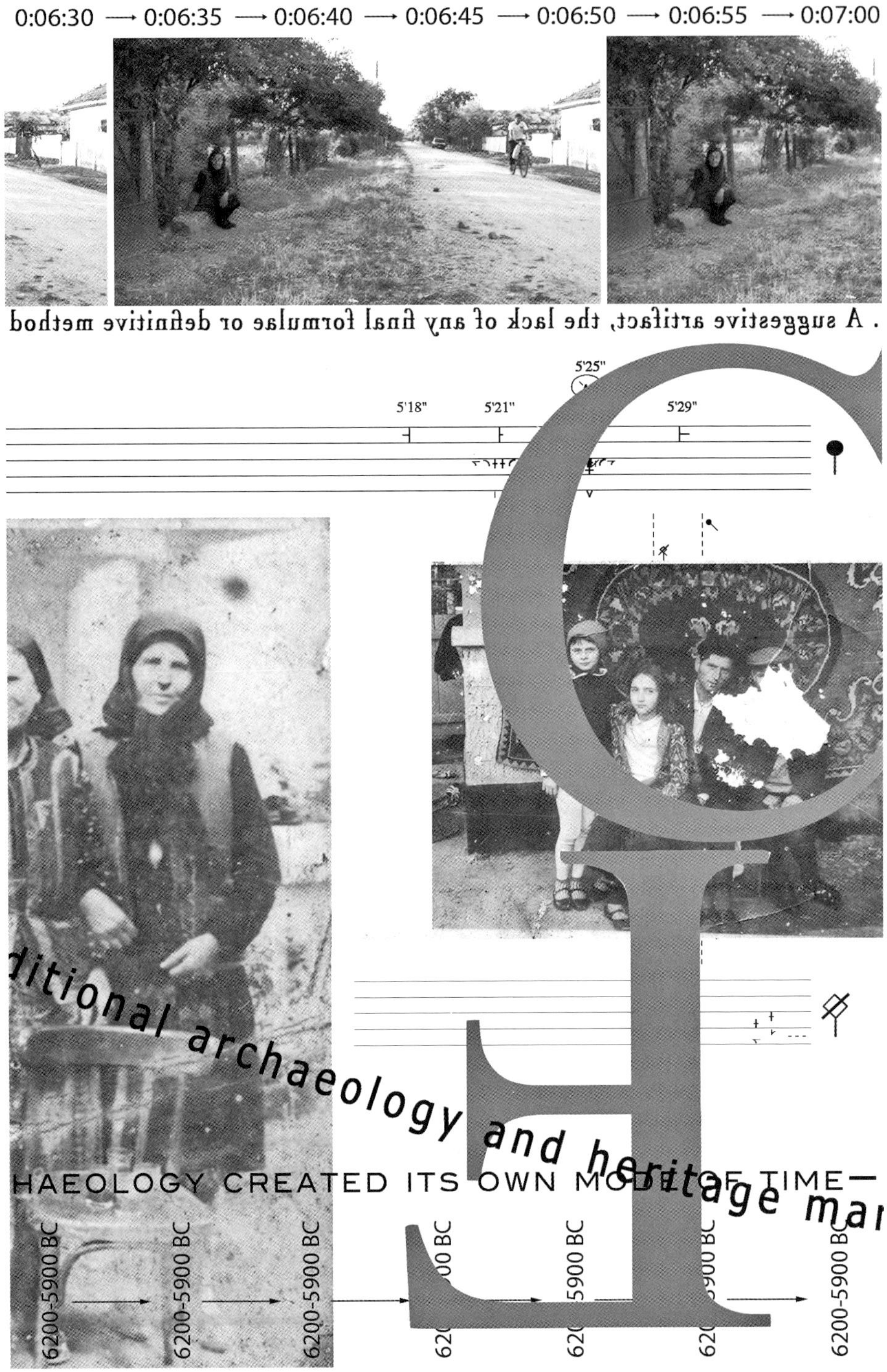

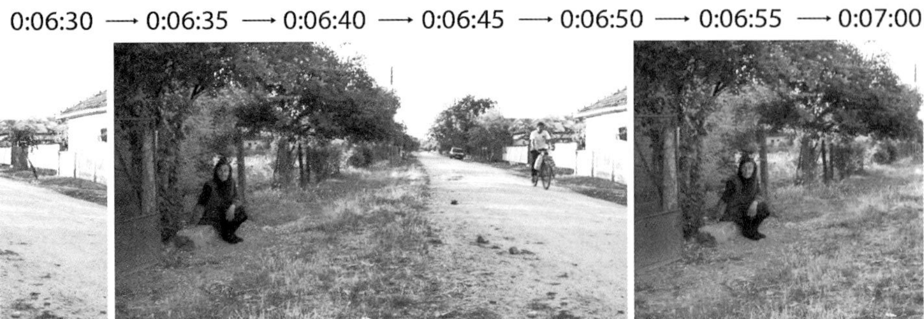

4.9 *Eleven minutes and forty seconds in the Neolithic: underneath archaeological time, p. 203 (Bailey and Simpkin 2015).*

of a radiocarbon calibration curve, and human remains (part of a mandible and a fragment of an arm bone).

The rest of the images, however, were family snapshots (given to me by Măgura residents) of current or recent villagers: four older women posing in the road; a father and three children; a wedding band leading a nuptial walk through the village; a mother in her winter coat standing with hands on her son's shoulders; a man posing on his motorcycle; a mug-shot from an identity card; three generations of a family at a wedding; a marriage party standing around the bride and groom; and the final image, the open coffin of an elderly woman at her funeral celebration. The images I chose were old and worn, some creased and others with missing corners or edges; one or two had a person's face scratched out. These photos started mid-way through the montage-chapter, slowly grading up in frequency, as the archaeological images gently became less numerous: a transition from one perspective to another. If the first pages of the chapter are fully archaeological, then the last several pages are fully humanized.

Also in this long, horizontal central space of the montage, I mixed in fragments of texts. From the start of the chapter, I shaped the texts into lines of words, one set of sentences running straight from left to right, another starting on the horizontal, but then rising and falling up and then down the surface of the page as it rambles from one page to the next, at one point performing a full loop up and over itself. On the second page, another text appears. This one is difficult to read; it is only the very end of a sentence that has been printed backwards (i.e., it starts at the end of the chapter and runs to the front). It is an academic text ending with academic citation of author's name, year, and page number. All of these found texts are quotes from scholarly articles (proper referencing is in a bibliography at the chapter's end), and they run (forward or backward) through the pages. If readers dig deeper, read each quote, and follow up in the bibliography, then they see that the texts come from key works in the archaeology of the contemporary past: that is to say, the proposition that the past doesn't exist, or if it does, then it only ever exists here in the present with us and with its remnants.

There are two other textual components to the montage. The first is easy to miss, probably because it is difficult to read. In a font so large that only one or two characters fit on any one page of the montage, I spelled out the name of the EU project that sparked the original film I had made: LANDSCAPE TRANSFORMATION. On the upper portions of the pages 'Landscape' runs horizontally from chapter start to finish; on the lower portion, 'Transformation' runs horizontally, but laid out as is spelled backwards (and upside down), starting from the end of the chapter and running to the start.

The final textual element dominates the montage's final page: a long fragment from the nineteenth-century French naturalist novelist Émile Zola: a quote from Zola's 1876 *L'Assommoir*. With rich sensations, the words evoke with the Parisian wash-house at the start of Zola's novel. With the 'pale daylight', the 'hot steam', the 'wisps of smoke', the women's 'naked arms' and 'bare necks', and the 'rhythmical beating noises and the murmurous sound of the rain', the quote (laid out on that last page, surround the funeral image of a deceased Măgura resident) brings the montage to an end and the reader to a place devoid of artefacts, radiocarbon dates, and stratigraphic sections. This, then, is the pace and lived reality of Măgura, both today and 8,000 years ago.

My argument may be best summarized by one of the photographs in the montage: the one with the band strutting down the street at the head of the wedding party, with the țambal player and the cigarette hanging out of his mouth. This image contains life in its full and richest sense.

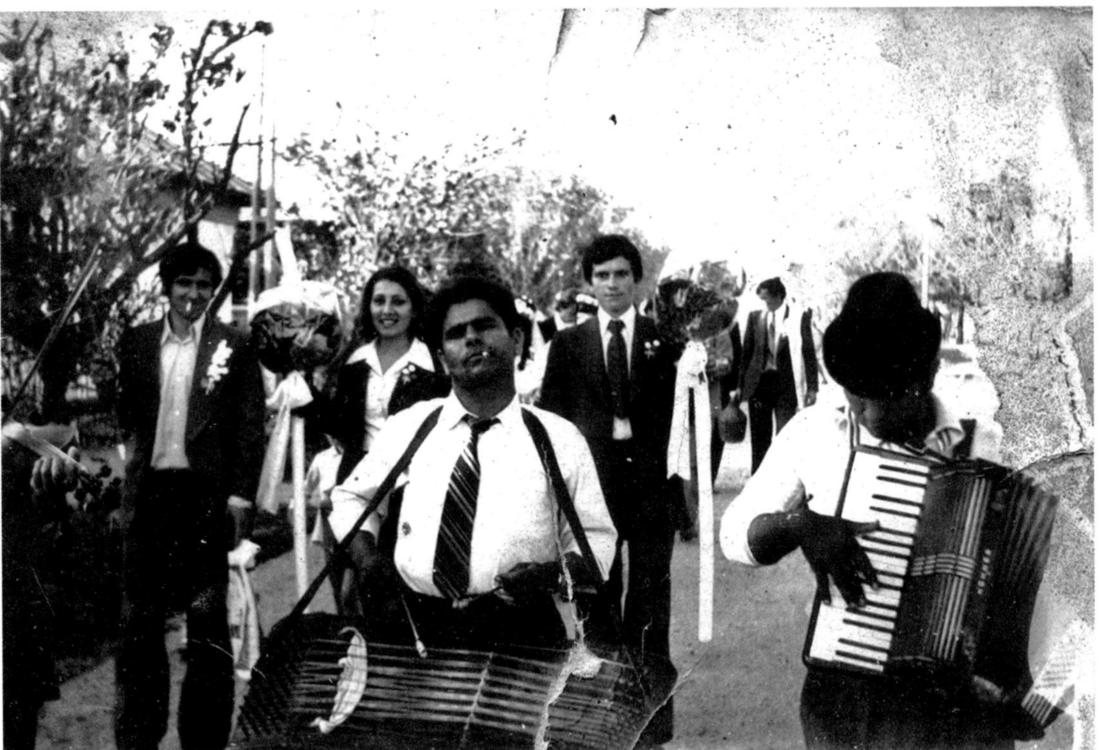

4.10 *Eleven minutes and forty seconds in the Neolithic: underneath archaeological time, p. 204 (detail) (Bailey and Simpkin 2015).*

Archaeology can't get to that level, even though, all too often, archaeologists talk about feelings and emotions and intentions in the past. Archaeology misses the intimacy of everyday life, and, as a result, archaeologists are left to speak about what happened in the past on a grander scale, in terms of long-term transformations, especially of the landscape.

When we talk about people and places in living time (today), we know that life is a chaotic complexity that combines highly specific actions and thoughts, and is wholly intimate. In the video (*Twenty Minutes Inside Out*) and in the book chapter (Eleven minutes and forty seconds in the Neolithic), life exists only at the level of the woman who is sitting on that block of stone in the lower left of one of the sequences. She sat there while the camera was running. She never said anything. That is a level of intimate-being that archaeology can never recover, even though archaeologists feel comfortable writing about persons and personhood and agency and emotion. As archaeologists, we are unable to handle that woman's emotion, and if that is the case, then what do we really know about lives lived 8,000 years ago? The answer is that we know little if anything, and if that is the case, then what is archaeology to do? The answer is that we should not pretend that we can do what we are ill-equipped to achieve. The challenge we face, therefore, is to explore in more radical ways our engagements with the past, and one potent way is through experimentation with alternative visual and textual mediations of materials, places, and lives.

5

Creating original work

Originality is highly valued in archaeology and art. In both disciplines, reputations and successful careers are built on producing original creative work. What makes an archaeological discovery, publication, or interpretation a new one? What makes an individual work of art unique or a new way of making art distinct from what has come before? When we step back and place a new work within the broader context of what has come before, we can begin to assess whether a new work has added something to existing knowledge or whether it is in fact derivative or repetitive. The examination of originality in archaeology and in art raises other questions; how do artists and archaeologists set out to create original work? Is the creative process of art-making different to archaeological process?

Setting out to create

There are myriad ways of making art and the fundamental reasons why artists' make art in the first place can differ enormously. Contemporary artists in Europe and the United States tend to make their way forward by distancing themselves from what immediately preceded them and by challenging the established conventions of the discipline. This is a strategy to narrow the field, with the aim of identifying an individual path and to set about making art of their time and from their own experience. Artists work hard to avoid producing work that might be seen as similar to other artists. This is a strategy of avoidance and distancing. Being derivative is seen as a weakness, whereas being seen to be making original work and confronting the issues of the day are the current definitions of success. Ironically, the ambition of the young artist to take on the establishment, is one of the defining characteristics of the tradition they set out to topple, whether they are aware of it or not. This is particularly clear in the contemporary art world where the emphasis on individuality and originality is given such status. The commercial art world sustains and embellishes the myth of originality and the rarity of the individual genius. Promoting an artist as unique is very good for business. These two strands of artistic ambition on the one hand, and the commercial art market on the other, are now inextricably bound together.

From an artist's point of view setting out to be original is probably a mistake and the best way of not achieving it. Surprising results emerge from throwing yourself in at the deep end and taking risks. It is in the moment of artistic desperation and with nothing to lose that you are most likely to be spontaneous and come up with something unplanned. This can be the event or the episode that can lead to opening up new ideas and new works. This opportunity exists in the moment when a work does not go to plan or when a project goes off the rails. If you remain in a comfortable position, this will not happen. Immersion in the process of making art, with a willingness to follow where it takes you, is an important creative strategy. An open-minded and free-flowing creative process has little in common with the predetermined and rigid structure of pre-planned projects and the application procedures of funding bodies.

From Simon's point of view no matter how important the issues around originality are, they are not the kind of thoughts painters should have in mind when they are in the studio preparing to work. Similar to the futility of chasing originality is an equally futile ambition to set out to make paintings that are rich and complex. These qualities are the sought after by-product of total involvement in the making process. This is a process that cannot be shortcut. The richness and complexity of a work resides in the viewer's experience of the finished painting and not with the painter at work in the studio. The painter must focus on the job of handling materials and concentrating on one of two things during this activity: making the right mark of the right physical quality; and responding to that mark with subsequent marks, actions or gestures. Step by step, the painting takes shape. Placing one touch of material next to another is what matters, and these actions accumulate and produce a third element. This is what the viewer responds to in the completed painting. Yet it is the one thing the painter must not think about when working, even for a second, or it will slip away unfixed. Unpicking the painter's process reveals evidence of how complexity is constructed. Perhaps one of the most vivid and well-known examples of this process can be found in the late works of Paul Cézanne. Revealing the process is part of the expressive ambition. Every mark vibrates in relation to the ones next to it. They are not exquisite or technically demanding in their own right; in fact most people could manage to make similar marks, but it is the sense of complexity and the richness of the experience of looking that they produce in the viewer (commonly called meaning) that is out of their reach. If a painter thought about the emotive affect of the finished painting whilst making it, then the work would be crippled early on. You do not need to live the emotional experience the work provokes when you work; you need to know how to produce it.

There may be particular places (both intellectual and physical) where there is a better chance of making new or original work. The places that exist on the periphery, on the borders, and on the boundaries, have potential and they are worth finding. When Simon works outside the studio in the landscape or in the urban environment, he gravitates to the edge of town or down to the river. He feels as if he ends up there as the only place left to act without restriction and away from unwanted attention. He cannot work in the centre, in the town-square as it were. Better to be where people are (metaphorically and literally) setting fire to things, or where they are sitting around drinking. The people in these places leave you alone and they don't care what you are up to as long as you leave them alone. It's an unwritten law. This is the perfect situation, as you are free to do what you want and you can work unselfconsciously. There is no audience and there is no monitoring and no need to explain anything. The nature of these places encourages risk taking and going the extra mile. Something from these places embeds itself in the physical material of the painting, resulting in work with a different character to a studio-based painting. Both Doug and Simon gravitate to the periphery of their disciplines and to the margins of their professional communities.

Creators and product-makers

Not all art is intended to be original or to propose new ideas. In general, artists develop by working through their influences. This is a necessary part of a process of identifying the context for their work and to either reject it or find their own place in it. Clearly, results at this stage will be derivative and intentionally so. Referencing other art, either past or present, is a positive element in most work and again helps to place it within a specific context. To some extent it is impossible to avoid leaving signs of the cultural traditions we derive from; seeking to obscure them is easy to detect. The question is how derivative we want to be and how clear we want the references to be. An aspect of the richness of an artwork can be the breadth of the references to other works. For example, a silver Elvis Presley silkscreen on canvas by Andy Warhol knowingly derives its entire aura from what is already established in the public imagination: the glamour and celebrity status of Elvis. The nerve to be so derivative and to make art in this way is part of what makes the work so exciting. It blurs the line. This is a choice, and it is a creative choice. Problems with being derivative arise when an artist does not recognize the footprint of another artist in their own work.

Repetition also has positive and negative aspects in art. The potency of a successful work drains away with every new variation made for the market. This is the point when it is possible to call an artist a product maker. In the hands of the artist with sights set on market success, the repetition of an idea, an image, or a technique, only diminishes it. There are artists who use repetition much more successfully as a creative tool. Repetition was one of the key characteristics of Minimalism, and in the hands of an artist like Don Judd it played a central role. Judd could also be called a product maker. Many of his works were fabricated by specialists in industrial workshops. The intention here was to propose an alternative to the authenticity of the handmade and the subjective focus of the Abstract Expressionists, the previous generation of American artists. The quirks and idiosyncrasies of the handmade made a return in the sculpture of Eva Hesse in combination in another form of repetition, now called seriality. The best work is creative, and it can be the most exciting and can open up new ways of thinking. The danger is when art making is reduced to a formula and is carried out without openness to the possibilities of the creative process.

Product repetition in archaeology

In the world of archaeological action, as with art, repetition without variation is also common. A team excavates a site that dates to a certain period of time, for example the early Neolithic. That excavation provides valuable new information about the Neolithic: about what people ate at the time, or how they buried their dead, or how intra-community social relations were structured, or many other sorts of past behaviours. For many archaeologists, the obvious next step is to excavate another early Neolithic site: to repeat (and confirm) the results obtained in the earlier dig. For most, this is the basis of the scientific method (discovery and confirmation, refinement, or rejection of the current state of knowledge), and if we define archaeology as a science, then all is good. In the tradition of archaeological research and fieldwork, excavation projects have value (and are most likely to be permitted, funded, and refunded) if the potential for new knowledge is high; that is, if their output is original. This could be the case also if new analytical technologies extract new types of information from long understood categories of data (recent advances in molecular archaeology are examples of this). Even in this case, however, the work is repetitive (the materials studied are the same) though the work takes place under the cover of applying a new analytical technique to that material, for example, from another early Neolithic site.

If there is no technological innovation, no novel approach, or no new research question to apply or explore, then excavating yet another early Neolithic site is the archaeological version of the product repetition that is widely practiced by non-creative artists. Understandably, the non-creative, repetitive route is an easy direction to steer a career through the archaeological workplace. Archaeologists work hard to establish their reputations in a region or a period of the past, and, as that happens, it becomes easier to obtain the permits and funding necessary to continue to excavate. Experience (gained through repetitive work), therefore, builds reputation and makes careers.

One of the obstacles to originality rests with the grant application process; the same can be said for the process of securing a contact to publish a book. Beyond developer-funded excavations, a lot of archaeological work is the result of institution-funded projects. In order to win the grant, applications must include clear descriptions of what the project will do and what the intended results will be. From the start, you have to know where you will end up. In making creative work that is original, on the other hand, it is not possible (nor even wise, perhaps), to know where you will end up. Convincing a publishing house to produce a book requires a similarly high-level of pre-creation decision making.

One way around this obstacle is to fudge it. In 2018, Doug published a book about prehistoric architecture with a major UK publisher.[1] In applying for the grant to support the research-leave needed to write the book, Doug described a non-controversial, traditional, comparative approach to the study of pit-house architecture from cultures around the world. In the end, the book that emerged didn't make any of those comparisons. As published, the book's main message is that such a comparative approach is bankrupt. The final creative output of the project was a book that made a series of unexpected and disorienting juxtapositions of art, archaeology, philosophy, linguistic anthropology, and perceptual psychology.

In addition, Doug used the published, bound book as raw material to make other original creative work, including performances of the book being made unreadable by being punctured by a high pressure drill press, and by individual creations of 'artists' copies' from which had been cut particular sections of texts from selected chapters. None of this output was predicted in the original application; nor, in fact, did Doug have any notion that this is what would happen once he started the funded project. While the original grant supported a year that was free of teaching and administrative work, the thinking and the writing (and the destructive manipulation) of the project took work in radically different, unexpected, and original direction, both as deemed worthy of support by the funders and by the publisher. It is unlikely that the UK's Arts and Humanities Research Board (as it was titled at the time) or Oxford University Press would have supported a proposal or application that listed as one of its 'objectives' the destruction of a published book.

Archaeologists as derivative product-makers

Working on excavations in Eastern Europe, Doug found that most of his archaeological colleagues there were repetitive product-makers, the products being the sites they excavated and the artefacts recovered from them. Excavation was what these archaeologists did. Archaeologists dug, and they did it in the same ways year in and year out. Sometimes excavation was necessary in the rescue or salvage sense, but most often, because it was just what they did. It was how they spent their days. It was what was expected of them. Museums were full (usually overflowing) with excavated materials. This is not to criticize these colleagues of Doug's; the same expectations and product-making in archaeology happen around the world.

In almost every way, archaeologists make derivative work. All new analytical and interpretative work in archaeology rests on objects of ancient origin, made either intentionally or as a by-product of the action of some person or some natural phenomenon. Whether it is the petrological study of a lithic flake or the mapping of patterns of ash deposition from a hearth, all the things that archaeologists focus on are objects and actions created of by other people. The archaeological creations of knowledge, publication, and exhibition, therefore, are forever securely articulated to their origins.

Archaeologists, particularly those teaching and researching in the academic world are trained to be derivative. The standard scholarly approach is to read deeply into the body of literature that already exists. That background knowledge equips the author to say something new and different. This is a fundamental measure of whether academic output is 'good' or not. Does the work bring something new into our shared understanding of the world? Does it expand or refine existing understandings, definitions, or interpretations? The gold standard of doing academic work: novel contributions to knowledge. If that knowledge is forever articulated to the past (both of objects and interpretations of the past), however, then the 'new' work can never be original. Its core will always be derivative.

A consequence of this way of making scholarly archaeological, published work is that it limits (perhaps makes impossible) creative spontaneity in what is produced. It makes it harder (perhaps equally impossible) to jump in and take the risky chances that are required for making true creative work. The tradition (read as requirement) of contextualizing academic work with a deep knowledge of the work and materials that already exist about a topic (prehistoric figurines, prehistoric architecture, and their interpretations, for example) reduces the potential for truly new, non-academic, often sensual, reactions to the cultural materials of the past and, indeed, of the past itself. The deep background familiarity and rigorous contextual knowledge that authors (and readers) are required to obtain about a topic blunts and dehumanizes any emotional reactions that authors (and readers) otherwise might have if they encountered the material in a more direct, less contaminated way.

An alternative

What if we took our engagement with the past outside of the academy? One possibility is that we might get closer to the way that artists, like Simon, react to a new artwork (and to a newly uncovered surface at a site, for that matter). We would find ourselves some distance from judging the archaeological text in terms of whether it is good or bad according to the standards of accepted academic rhetoric. We would find ourselves closer to considering what the text (and images) or the material objects and trace-remnants of the past do to us. How do they make us feel? To do so would be to focus on how the viewer reacts to an artefact or an ancient building or a prehistoric landscape. To do this would require that we place the materials (or buildings or landscapes) in front of readers (who now become as much viewers as readers) and give them the authority to react to them based on their individual experiences, personalities, desires, and prejudices. To realize these possibilities, we would have to jettison the traditional methods and media of valuing, manipulating, and presenting the past that currently control and restrict how we relate to that past and its material remains. In doing so, however, we would then be in a position to make authentically new and creative archaeological work.

The radical (paradoxical) alternative to archaeological production, therefore, is to make work that is not tied to the past, that is not derivative of artefact or trace pattern, that does not disappear archaeological action: the movement of bodies, of hands, of feet, of fingers, of eyes, of sweat glands, of muscle contraction and blister or callus formation. The same realization applies to the finds processing hut, the project laboratory (on- and off-site), the post-excavation facility, and every other place where archaeological action takes place.

Making original archaeological work: art/archaeology

What archaeological products, therefore, exist in the spaces beyond the boundaries of standard books, articles, exhibitions, and archive boxes and storage shed contents? More often than not, when archaeological work breaks with its discipline-specific traditional definitions of production, and when that work is original and innovative, critics question its status or value as being truly archaeological output.

Following a relatively traditional route, Doug established a professional reputation in the archaeological summaries and interpretations of East European prehistory and prehistoric figurines. The books that he wrote in 2000[2] and 2005[3] (and the journal articles and book chapters that he wrote before and after) built that reputation. Today, however, when someone asks him to write a book chapter or a journal article about prehistoric figurines, his response usually is to decline. His desire is to explore the alternative world on the periphery of archaeological practice, where creative originality is most likely to take place. He has been calling that creative work art/archaeology.[4] Where that project will end up, what it will create or contribute is as yet unclear. It was equally unclear where the path that Doug started down led, when he began to experiment, explore potentials, make new creative work, and felt the need to publish accompanying explanatory articles under the title art/archaeology.

What is clear, however, is that these art/archaeology projects (Chapters 4, 8, and 12 detail examples) are part of a larger attempt to break with the traditional (repetitive and derivative) work of archaeology, to expose what Doug sees as a homeostatic, and auto-limiting, tradition in which archaeologists approach the past and objects from that past: an expert studies an ancient object and where it was found, measures it, records it, determines what is made out of and how it was made, determines how old it is, how it was used in the past, and what it might have mean to its ancient makers and users. Doug's early experiments (his attempts to transform how we engage with prehistoric anthropomorphic figurines) stayed within the boundaries of traditional archaeological work: discipline-targeted publications and lectures. Is there an alternative?

One of the radical alternatives that Doug explores is to make work that is disarticulated from the past, that is not derivative of artefact or trace pattern, that does not reach backward. To do so is to make work that discards the false assumption about what archaeologists produce: the historic reconstruction, the cultural history, the heritage project. To proceed in this way requires archaeologists to let go of the belief that archaeology is a process that re-creates or recovers a past, indeed even that there is a past out there (under the ground) to be discovered, conserved, and preserved. There is nothing new in this; most critical archaeologists understand that the past is a construction of contemporary worlds. To move in this direction is to entertain exciting, but also challenging and, for some readers, threatening questions. What would this new work that engages the past in radically alternative ways look (or sound, feel, taste, or smell) like? Would that work even be archaeological, and if it is not archaeological (by conventional, conservative measure), then what is it, what potential does it have, what is its effect on us in the present?

6

Chromium Oxide Cut Pit Painting (Simon Callery, 2009)

Between 2006 and 2009 I worked on a three-year, practice-based Arts and Humanities Research Council fellowship, called the Thames Gateway Project. The aim of this research was to develop new forms for landscape-based painting in response to the changing landscape of the Thames Gateway regeneration zone. The fellowship was hosted by Wimbledon School of Art in partnership with Oxford Archaeology, the UK's largest commercial archaeology unit. One of the paintings I made in the final year of the fellowship is called *Chromium Oxide Cut Pit Painting*. The title of the painting refers to the archaeological feature that informed its shape, to its colour, and to the front face of the painting, which is cut away to expose the internal structure and space of the work.

Thames Gateway

The Thames Gateway is the name given by central government to a 40-mile stretch of land extending out of London to the east, along both the Essex and Kent shorelines of the Thames Estuary, to where it meets the North Sea. This regeneration and urbanization scheme was initiated under Labour Prime Minister Tony Blair. At its launch in 2004 the Office of the Deputy Prime Minister announced the Thames Gateway as the largest regeneration scheme in Western Europe and the most ambitious and large-scale regeneration project ever seen in the UK.

Travelling east out of London into the Thames Gateway takes you into a wide and open river valley spoilt by industrialization. Historically, the land along both sides of the river has been used as the location for oil storage facilities, petrochemical refineries, power stations, and aggregate production. A great deal of the older industry is in decline, leaving behind dereliction and contaminated land. The river is full of wharves, docks, landing jetties, terminals, and ports. The best known are the Port of London, Port of Tilbury, Purfleet Freight Terminal and now, as a key element of the regeneration, the deep-sea container port, London Gateway, at Stanford-le-Hope. The geology of the river valley is soft. There are extensive areas of marshland and wild salt marsh. The river terraces have been quarried for gravels, sands, and chalk for aggregates and fertilizers. It is not difficult to see that this estuarine landscape has been exploited extensively.

Landscape as a subject for painting occupies a central position in British art. It is easy to argue that the picturesque tradition of landscape painting has come to act as a guardian to an idea of

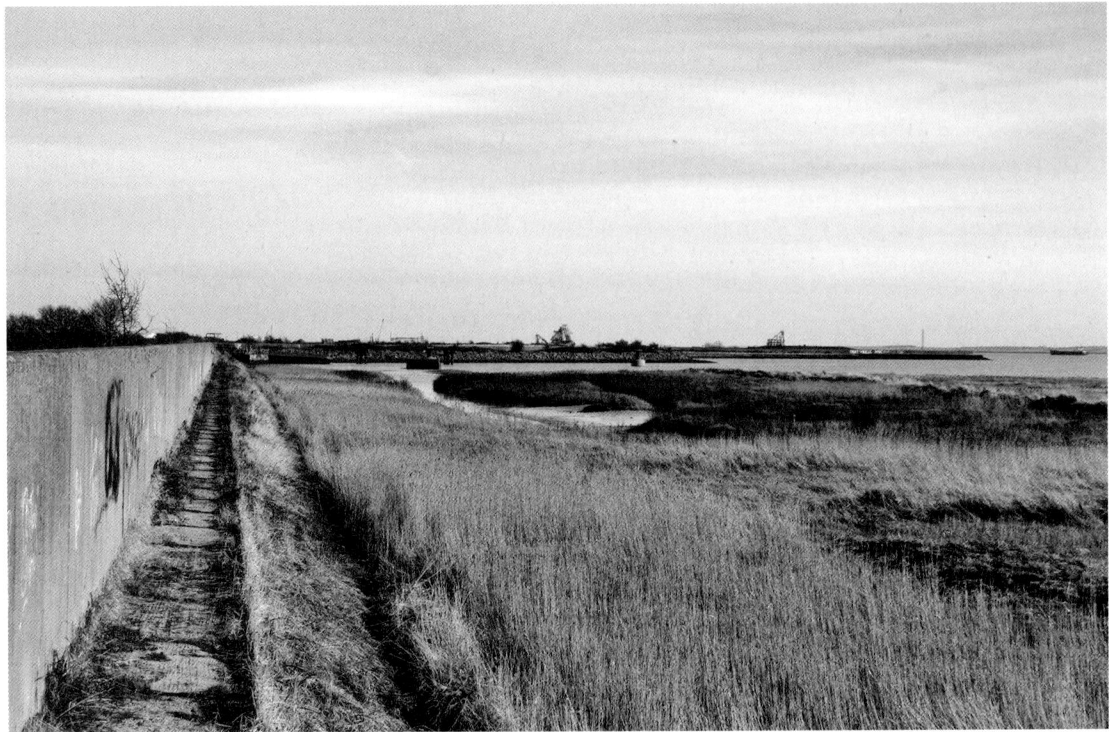

6.1 *Saltmarsh at London Gateway excavation site. Thames Estuary. Stanford-le-Hope. Essex. 2009.*

landscape as enduring and a constant in an otherwise changing and unstable world. Often the British go to the landscape for solace and much landscape-based painting also sets out to fulfil this function. In the Thames Gateway, however, I found out very quickly that reality is very different. Landscapes do not endure. We reshape and remodel the landscape to serve our ever-changing social and economic needs, and we have been doing this since prehistory.

Over the three-year fellowship I spent time on a number of the Oxford Archaeology excavation sites. They included the location of large-scale Romano-British salt production on the estuary shoreline adjacent to the deep-water container port, in the process of being built at Stanford-le-Hope. This site was returned to the water as soon as the excavation process was completed. The sea wall was breached to create marshlands for migrating birds. Another site was called Beam Washlands, Dagenham. Excavations were undertaken ahead of carrying out a flood relief scheme designed to protect local housing (and London upstream) if threatened by high water. In order to achieve this, the location was returned to wetlands. Two other sites turned out to be especially important for me. The first of these was called Woolwich Teardrop, a small triangular parcel of urban land in southeast London, close to the river and to Woolwich Arsenal, a part of the city that has been in continuous use since prehistory. The second was at Pepper Hill outside Gravesend in Kent, a long stretch of farmland excavated in advance of the rerouting of the A2, the trunk road that connects London to Dover and the south coast channel ports.

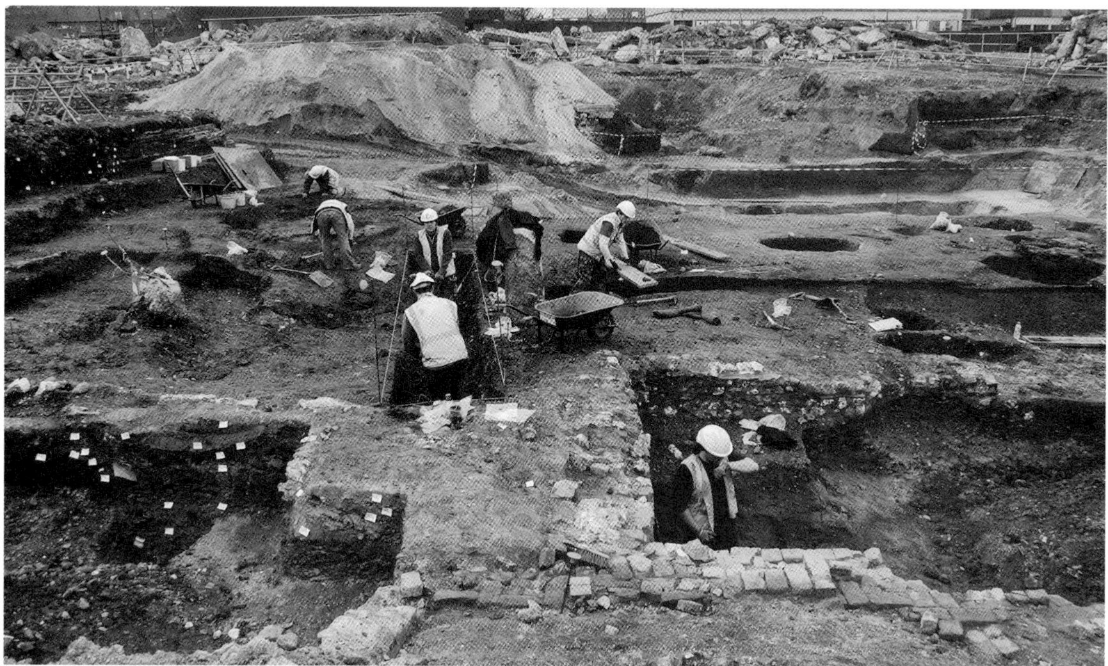

6.2 *Woolwich Teardrop excavation site. Woolwich. London. 2007.*

The archaeological pit

Pits were a recurring feature on all the sites I visited: semi-excavated, fully excavated, or sectioned pits. Ever since my time at Segsbury Camp, pits had fascinated me. I wanted to try to find a way to incorporate the circular form and spatial depth, common to many pits, in my painting, as it seemed to bring time and material together so well. My growing fascination with the archaeological pit also had a human dimension. For me, the sight of a field archaeologist in the ground excavating a pit appeared to mirror the activity of the original digger working in the distant past. Both the contemporary archaeologist and the prehistoric digger were engaged in exactly the same physical activity, in exactly the same place, and under similar conditions. Watching the archaeologists at work, I felt as if the passage of time had folded and collapsed into itself. To understand what this connection could mean for my painting I would often stay on site at the end of the working day and, once everyone else had left, I would sit quietly near the pits excavated that day and draw or use the camera. This was a special place and time and I felt I was about as close to past human activity as I could get. I knew some of those features had not seen the light of day since prehistory and would soon be backfilled.

I became attached to the pits at both Woolwich Teardrop and on the A2 site. I was often anxious that these archaeological features would be gone if I was away for too many days. The pace of work on a commercial archaeology site was totally different from a university dig. I had to learn

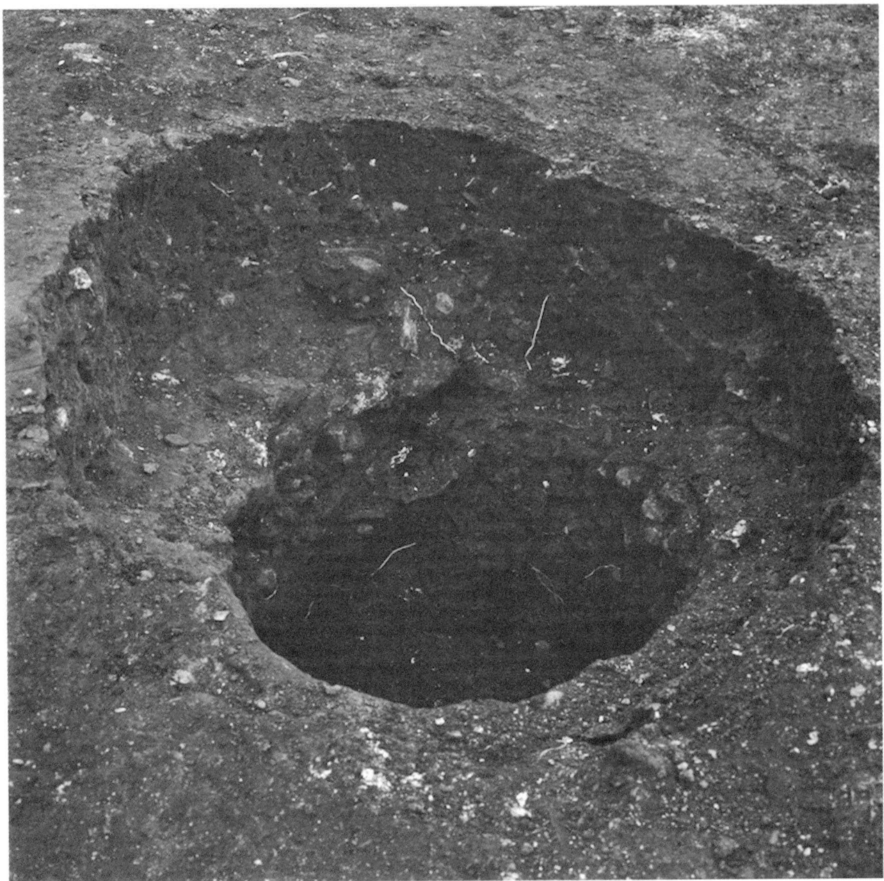

6.3 *Excavated pit Woolwich Teardrop site. Woolwich. London. 2007.*

how to be direct and to work fast. On the A2 site the contractor's earth moving machinery was ripping up the bedrock within yards of the OA diggers. Finds did not really interest me in the same way. In fact, if anyone dug an artefact, it felt as if the more important matter of moving forward with the excavation process was being held up. From my point as an artist, what was more captivating, was what was being revealed by the opening up of the landscape.

The A2 excavation site was on sloping ground and as soon as I arrived, I would immediately start looking out for the features I was following, hoping they had not been backfilled. I was aware that as you approach the pits from a distance, they slowly reveal their form. At first, they appear as dark, narrow slits or ellipses cut into the ground. As you get nearer and finally stand above them to peer down into the ground, they display their full circularity. Encountering archaeological features on site in this way suggested ideas for paintings based on circularity, of form changing as you move towards it and around it. I wanted to incorporate spatial depth, not an illusion of it, as an integral element of a painting. I also hoped that a sense of temporality, so tangible on the excavation site, would attach itself to the painting through these forms.

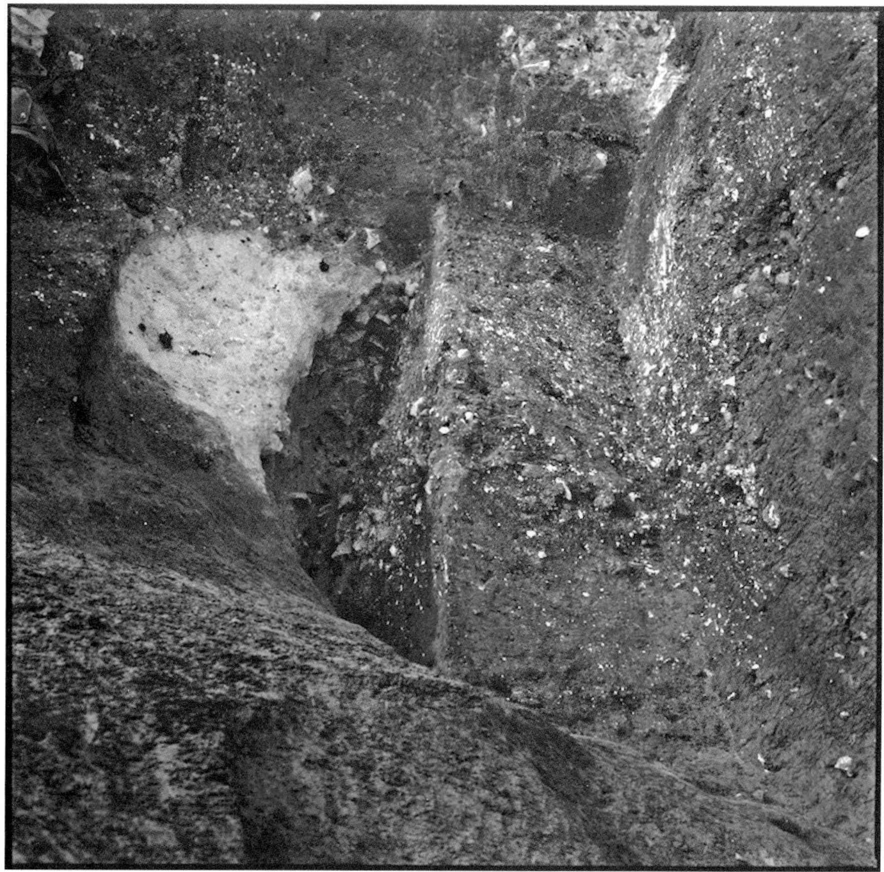

6.4 *Excavated pit A2 excavation site. Gravesend. Kent. 2008.*

Tiepolo

During the time I was working on this project I was occasionally in Italy as a tutor for a company called Art History Abroad. The circularity of the pits I was studying in the Thames Gateway was echoed in historical artworks I saw there. One work which had a real impact was Tiepolo's *Discovery of the True Cross* (1740–45) at the Galleria dell'Accademia in Venice. I remember walking through the sets of rooms that lead you through the development of painting in Venice, to the last room, to be confronted with an enormous circular Tiepolo hanging on the final wall. This 486 cm diameter painting, originally made for the ceiling of a church in Castello, was presented like a Byzantine icon, hanging at an angle above the heads of the visitors. I could see the back of the work from underneath it, and I could see how it was attached to the wall and how it was held in place. For me all of these physical elements were as much a part of the painting as the image, and I could not edit them out of the experience. The painting depicted the moment Helena (mother of Emperor Constantine) unearthed the True Cross. We see her triumphant, above our heads, from the point of view in the bottom of the excavation. Researching the painting at a later date, I read that St Helena is the patron saint of archaeology. The clues I needed for my work were coming in from a number of directions.

I tend to avoid making drawings in anticipation of a painting. I am careful about when I start the work. I do not start preparing it in advance, because the excitement of the discovery of making the work can be lost; it can slip out of your hands. When I first go on site, I normally take a camera and tripod for general documentation. This kind of photography is quite mechanical and it helps me orientate myself, to assimilate, and to give me time to think. I talk to the diggers as much as possible during the breaks and try to absorb as much as I can about the archaeology. Paintings generally give birth to the next painting. Ideas accumulate and get passed on and are modified from one work to the next. However, I recognized the idea of making paintings informed by archaeological pits represented a break from previous works. As a consequence, it led me to re-examine and question the roles and the functions of the materials of painting. I began by questioning colour.

Colour as a material

For many years I had very intentionally restricted colour in order to concentrate on the white paintings. Restricting colour in a painting allowed me to prioritize one aspect and suppress others. It is quite a common strategy used by painters. My understanding of whiteness and tonality has been informed by the subtleties and the qualities of the chalk surfaces of the downlands at

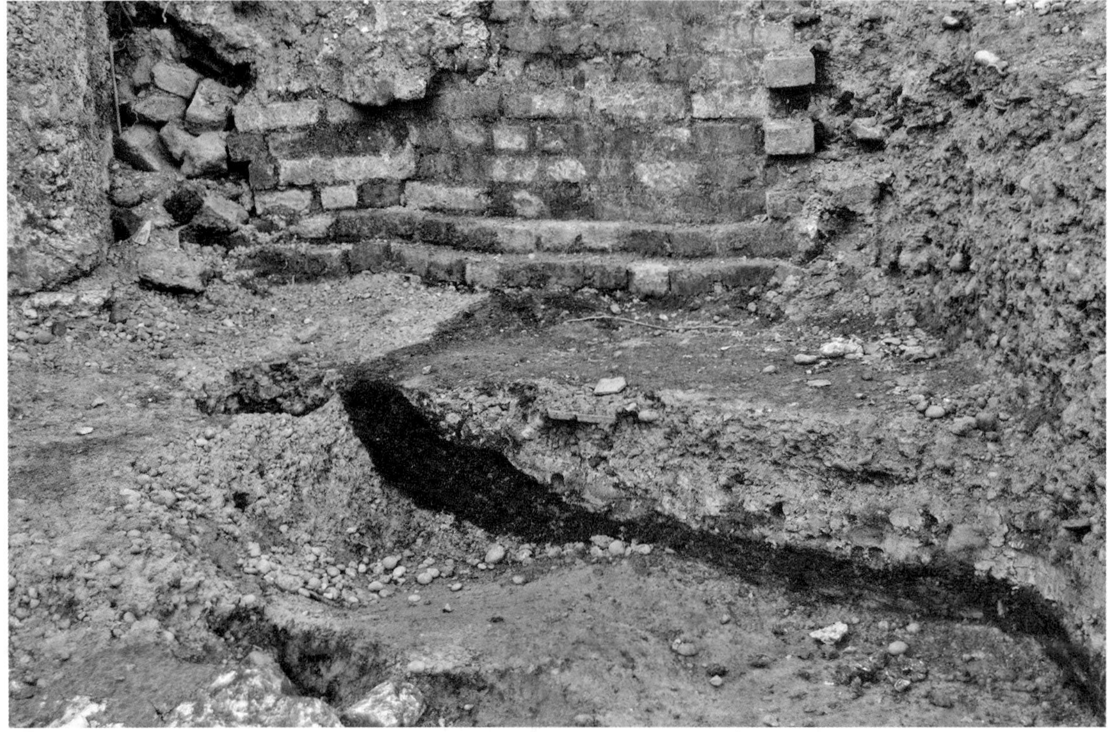

6.5 *Burnt material in section. Woolwich Teardrop site. Woolwich. London. 2007.*

Segsbury Camp and Alfred's Castle. Chalk, in both wet and dry states could be slightly yellow, with green markings, off-white or grey and, on site, a specific colour when topsoil is ground into the chalk by the diggers' boots. The Thames Gateway Project sites were completely different from the chalk downlands. On the site of the A2 motorway rerouting in Kent, for example, the earth movers had chopped right through the side of a hill and revealed thick layers of blue clay. At Woolwich Teardrop, the spectrum of colour of the deposits of the numerous phases was so rich and varied that I had no choice but to face what these places were urging me to do. If I was going to work in response to them, I had to work with fully saturated colour.

Initially, I experimented by simply changing the colour of my oil paint and I continued to make paintings in the same way as I had before. So, instead of making a white painting with lead white oil, I made one with a cadmium red. It did not work. The red paint could not be applied and worked with the methods I had developed for the white paintings. While a red painting is fundamentally different from a white painting, interestingly, the clue to understanding the difference was not just related to its colour. I began to realize that to stand in front of a cadmium red painting is an experience of cadmium the material, even if that thought was not a conscious one. It became clear that a cadmium red painting is very different from a lead white painting because of the physical properties as much as their chromatic differences. I needed to have better reasons for choosing the colour that I wanted to work with and then develop the appropriate methods to use it.

Distemper

I began to experiment with distemper instead of oil paint. Distemper is a traditional paint made with rabbit skin glue as the medium, mixed with dry powder pigment. It dries to a matt and non-reflective film as opposed to the reflective and glossy surface of oil paint. I made some distemper and painted it onto a strip of unprimed canvas cut straight off the roll as an initial test. It dried and then it flaked off. I took advice and was told that I must wash the canvas first to remove the starch. Starch is put into the cotton canvas threads to make them stiff to aid the weaving process. I cut a 3-metre length of canvas off a roll and soaked it in a builder's tub full of hot water. The starch dissolved and leaked out of the canvas. It was dark yellow and looked like urine. I rinsed the canvas and let it dry. Once the canvas was fully dry, it was soft to touch and the individual fibres were open. I threw the canvas down onto the studio floor and sponged on hot distemper. The medium soaked deep into the fabric and the grains of the pigment were caught in the cotton fibres. It was important to work fast because as the distemper cools it turns into an unworkable jelly quite quickly. My experiments with different colours taught me that some dry pigments have fine grains and others are larger. All the iron-based pigments (caput mortuum, mars yellow or mars red, for example) have large coarse grains and they tend not to be absorbed so deeply. The cadmium-based pigments have fine grain and are drawn deeper into the fabric. One fine grained pigment that I found especially convincing was the green chromium oxide. When dry, the matt distemper surface absorbs light, which emphasizes its tactile qualities and its materiality and is quite different from the reflective surfaces of the earlier lead white paintings.

Getting to know the material properties of my pigments meant I could choose to make paintings with different physical qualities. A painting could be soft, if I worked with earth pigments like raw umber, red oxide or lamp black. Or it could be hard, if I used a cadmium red or a cadmium yellow. I wanted the colour of the new paintings to be compelling in the same way that the colour was compelling in the ground at Woolwich or in the cut open hillside in Kent. Colour in the material landscape does not depict anything; it is itself, and that is enough. The breakthrough I needed was to think of colour as a material.

The questioning of colour led to more questions about the functions of other aspects of painting. Traditionally, the conventional stretched canvas has a single purpose; to act as a support for an image. Since I was not working with images, then the functions of the structure and the roles of the materials could be challenged. The stretcher need not be a rectangle. It need not be hung on the wall at the standard viewing height of 145 cm to centre. In fact, it need not be flat on the wall at all. It could tip out and be above your head or even on the floor or in a corner and still be a painting. It could have an exposed interior space as well as a front face and it could have open sides. The means by which it hangs on the wall could be visible rather than hidden. Recasting the roles of the materials of painting, in response to the materiality of the excavation sites, meant the works could communicate on a physical register rather than solely a visual one. My works are paintings, made entirely within the context of painting but no longer defined by the enduring conventions established in the Italian Renaissance.

Woodwork and stretchers

Making a pit painting involves quite a lot of woodwork. I approach it in an expedient way and make the work by hand as much as possible. I want these elements of the painting to do what I have in mind for them and to go no further. I try not to elaborate, and I make decisions based on everyday practicality. For example, through the open sides of the completed *Chromium Oxide Cut Pit Painting*, you can see a number of chocks of timber screwed together to hold the stretchers apart. Although these chocks serve a practical purpose to wedge the parts open and to separate one from another, they also clearly reveal the construction process of the work. I want the way a painting has been made to be traceable and evident as a part of the finished painting. Revealing how a painting has been made is an important part of the original intention of the painting. If a viewer connects with the evidence of the making process, then there is a chance their experience of the work will slow down a little. I prefer a strategy of revealing the physical process, no matter how rough or rudimentary, over the traditional convention of arriving at a flawless and impenetrable final surface.

The timber elements that I used while making *Chromium Oxide Cut Pit Painting* came out of the studio wood pile. On a normal working day, the studio is full of all kinds of things. There are paintings and drawings there, some finished and others in various states of semi-completion. Some works are on the wall, many on the floor and often drying canvasses hanging from suspended lengths of wood. In amongst it all are my raw materials: piles of wood, bags of pigments, rolls of coloured canvasses, woodworking tools, sewing equipment, and more conventional painting tools such as brushes, sponges, and cloths. My current studio is next to the Royal Opera House production workshop in Purfleet, Essex, and we share a yard. The opera house has a skip where they throw all the off-cuts at the end of each day. I scavenge from the skip, and I accumulate a stock of irregular pieces of wood. When I need wood for a painting, I reach out and I take what I need from the pile. There is a degree of chance involved in using what I come across first. Often it can be better than using pre-prepared material. For example, I might find that a marked block of wood, that had a previous life, is the ideal shape and size for holding open the inside of a painting.

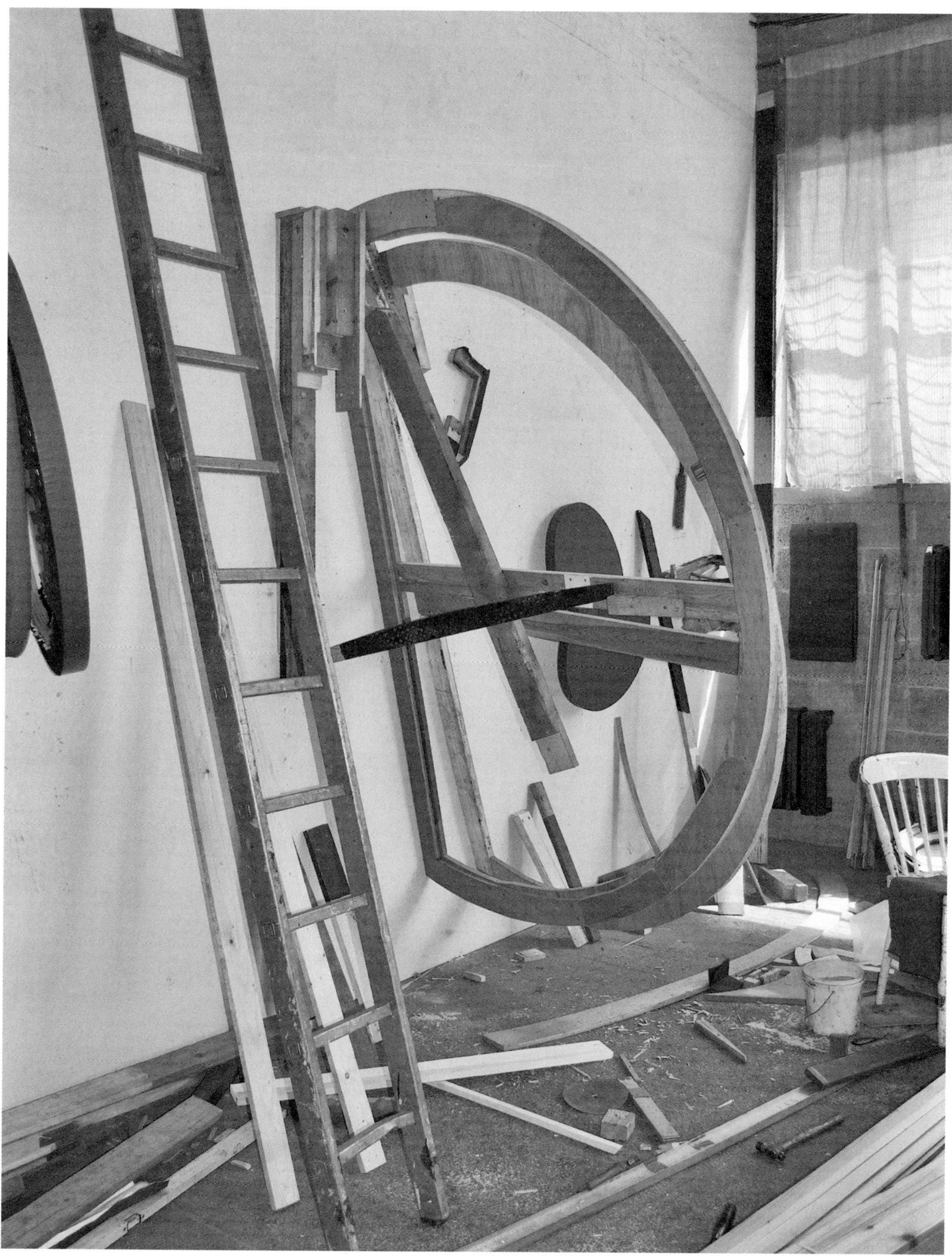

6.6 *Constructing stretchers for a pit painting. London. 2009.*

The majority of the physical process of making *Chromium Oxide Cut Pit Painting* took place on the floor of my studio. The painting was lifted, to be worked on the wall vertically, only when it was close to completion. Of particular importance to the character of the painting is the function of the wood stretchers. The stretcher, or strainer, is the structural element that is normally a hidden part of a conventional painting's substructure. The left-hand side of *Chromium Oxide Cut Pit Painting* is a perfect half circle. The exposed wood stretchers that are visible on the right hand side are elliptical. The painting consists of three separate wooden stretchers and a wood support. Each stretcher plays a different and specific role. The cut circle functions in a conventional way as the stretcher for the canvas front face. The other two stretchers have less conventional functions. They articulate the overall form of the work and they stack to bring the painting off the wall. As a result of being stacked they form the internal space of the painting.

The first of these two circular stretchers is fixed to a vertical wood post. This post has a number of customized wooden parts attached to it with grooves and slots for the stretchers to sit into or onto. The post is screwed to the wall firmly, and it carries the full weight of the painting. The post is a practical element of the work, but, rather than being hidden, it is a visible and an integral part. A crossbar runs horizontally through the centre of the stretcher, and it is screwed to the post where they cross. All three of the stretchers are handmade versions of what you might expect to find as a support for a traditional oil painting except I have elevated the job of the stretcher from a supporting role to a leading role.

To make the stretchers, I laid out on the floor two standard 18 mm, 122 x 244 cm sheets of plywood next to each other, to form a 244 x 244 cm square. I banged a nail in the centre of these sheets and, with a string, scribed out a precise half circle on one side of the plywood. I put in a screw at the top and at the bottom of this half circle and tied a long iron rod to them. By pushing this rod hard against the screws, I was able to flex it into an ellipse. With a pencil, I traced the profile of that ellipse onto the other side of the board. This line connected with the drawn half-circle forming a single continuous flowing line, circular on one side and elliptical on the other. I cut along this line with a jigsaw to form the external edge of the largest stretcher. The two other stretchers are also cut circles using this initial cut form as a template. As I made each stretcher, I customized the slots and grooves on the vertical post so that they sit correctly in relation to each other and so that they would enclose an internal space. I think of this internal space, or void, as the body of the painting.

I use a fifteen-ounce cotton duck canvas that I buy in fifty-metre rolls from a textile supplier in Stockport near Manchester. It is a good quality and a heavy weight. After it is washed it is pliable and flexible enough to pull around the side of the first stretcher so it lies flat along the visible edge. It must be stapled to the stretcher and it must be taut, so there are often a series of adjustments that need to be made to get the tension even across the surface. Again, this takes place on the floor. Once this is done, I make up a bucket of distemper and sponge it into the stretched canvas when it is hot. The hot liquid tightens the canvas even more, like a drum. I try to be mechanical and apply the distemper in a uniform way. The priority is to get the pigment deep into the fabric so the canvas and the pigment are unified. When I painted *Chromium Oxide Pit Painting* there were a number of marks and irregularities in the painted surface when it dried. These were finger marks and sponge marks which I used to consider flaws and I worried about them. Gradually, I came to accept these marks as an inevitable sign of the handmade. The colour connects the painting to ideas of landscape, but it is not being used to represent it. The intention was to colour the canvas

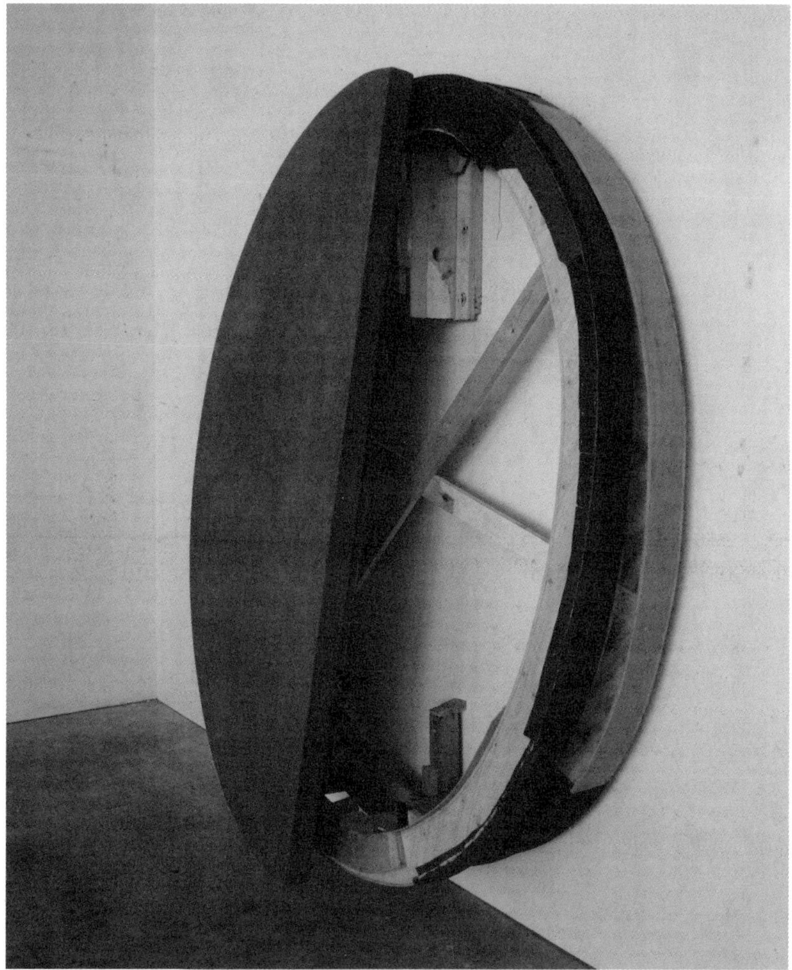

6.7 Woolwich Teardrop. *2008–09. Canvas, distemper, oil, aluminium, wood. 206 x 183 x 64.5 cm.*

in a practical way so the viewer would recognize that its role was a material one and not a depictive one. When I carry out this part of the painting process, I try not to make any judgments about it until the following day. I paint the distemper surface at the end of the day in the most expedient way I can, then I turn the lights off and go home. Walking into the studio in the morning, there is a brief moment of objectively, when I can see what I have done the previous day. In this moment I can feel, instinctively, if it is right or wrong.

The finished painting

Standing in front of the finished painting, you can see straight through it to the wall on the right hand side. On the left hand side, the canvas obscures any view of the interior. The stretchers are

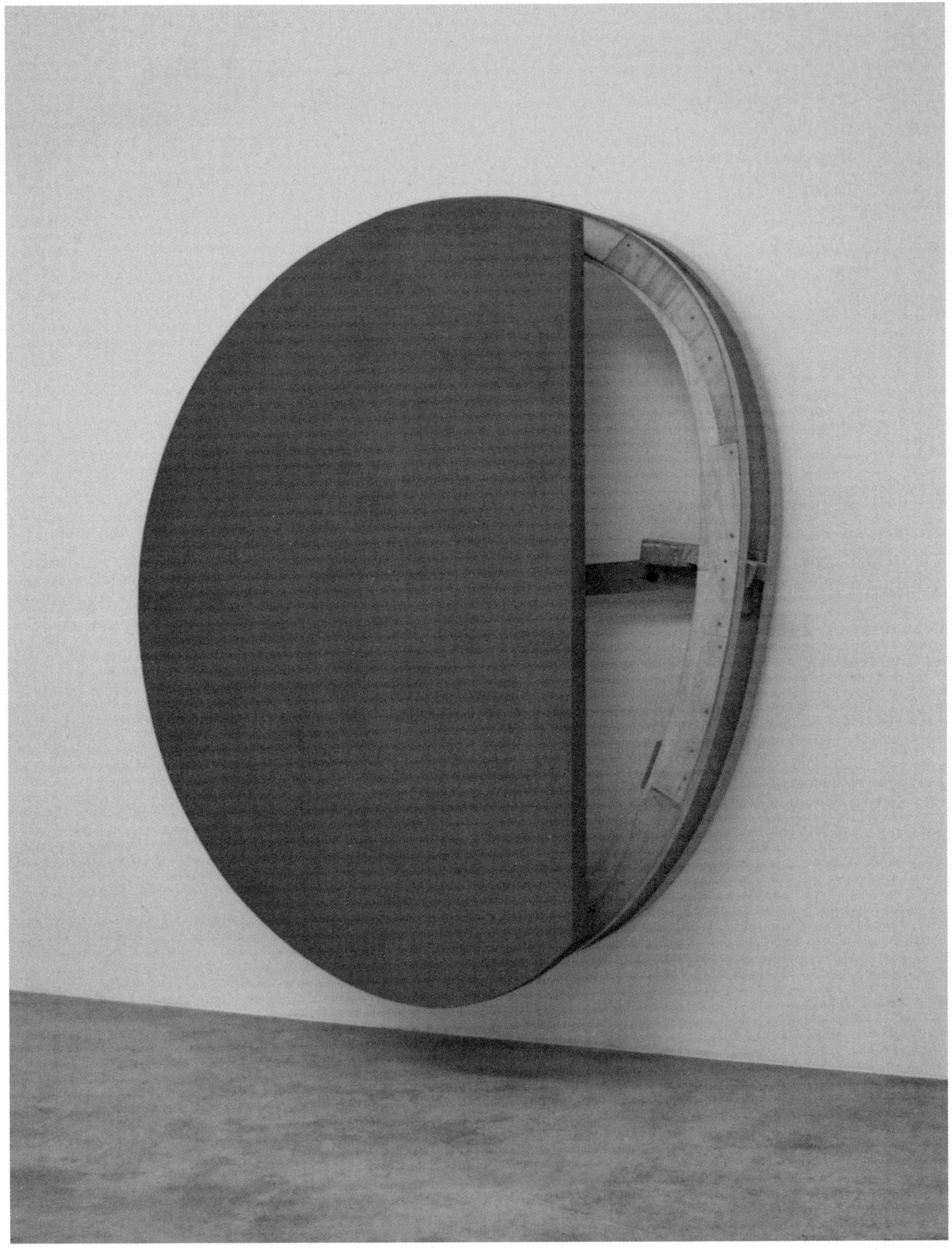

6.8 *Simon Callery. Chromium Oxide Cut Pit Painting. 2009. Distemper, canvas, wood, rope, aluminium. 230 x 218 x 60 cm.*

held apart on the right hand side to a greater degree than they are on the left side; this difference causes the front plane of the painting to tilt away from the flat plane of the supporting wall. The aperture on the left side between the painted surface and the rear stretcher is tighter and the interior space of the painting is less accessible. The painting is 230 cm high. When you add the space between the floor and the bottom of the work, the top is close to 300 cm above the floor. This is well above the height of the average person. At 218 cm wide, it is certainly broader. Scale is an important consideration. I use large-scale to encourage viewers to move around a painting, moving from one side to the other in order to peer inside the open body of the work. The incentive to do this came from my growing awareness of how we experience landscape with all of our senses when we are in motion. I wanted to move away from a static encounter of painting, something that I associate with the image-based tradition in European painting, which prioritizes the visual sense over all others.

This is a difficult work. I call it a pit painting but it is not a painting of a pit or an attempt to represent a pit. It is evidence of the impact of the physicality of the archaeological excavation site on painting. It does not hang discretely on the wall. It is fragile and it is heavy at the same time. The shape of the flowing line unifies the individual elements from one point of view, which then breaks down from another. The painting is an obstacle. It is not a seamless object that you can just slip past. The emphasis is on materiality, on the physical and spatial elements and on the circularly impressed on me by the numerous pits I had seen on the Thames Gateway excavation sites.

Quite early on in the fellowship I knew working in the changing landscape of the regeneration zone would not lead me to making paintings about 'change'. The commercial excavation site, always the first sign of approaching change in the landscape or the urban environment, was the place to recognize change as a dynamic and to apply it to my work. This led me, as the fellowship progressed, to recognize the need for change in my thinking about what a landscape-based painting could look like, about how it could be made and what it might do. In terms of making any judgement about whether *Chromium Oxide Cut Pit Painting* is a successful painting or not, I have to watch a viewer in front of the work. If they are active and they are in motion, exploring the painting from one side to the other and pausing to look inside, I can see it is doing its job and I need not say a word.

7

Different times: Perspectives from art and archaeology

What time is it?

Reflections on how people think about time as a concept (for example: Is time universal?; Does it exist at all if it isn't created by human thought?) are vibrant parts of debates in contemporary archaeology and have been part of longer trends in archaeological and ethnographic discussions. When Doug and Simon talk about how they each think of time they are struck by the differences.

Time in archaeology

In his montage publications, Doug has been approaching time in a way that is distinct from how most other archaeologists approach the subject. His work illustrates how time is dependent on the living being who experiences it: that time is not universal. To expand the potential realities of variability in conceptions of time possible in different populations, Doug found inspiration in the work of an early twentieth-century biologist (Jakob Von Uexküll, 1864–1944) and then created a montage to illustrate the different rates with which animals (including humans), fish, birds, bugs, and other creatures experience the speed of time. As Von Uexküll originally argued, different animals experience the passage of time at different rates.[1] For some, the world moves more slowly than it does for others. For others still it moves more quickly. Think how difficult it is to move your hand fast enough to catch a fly, or how easily it is to lean over and pick up a tortoise. Different animals perceive time at different speeds. In Doug's montage-chapter,[2] he juxtaposed standard archaeological ways of marking, measuring, and counting time with images of different beings (human and other) that perceived time in a variety of rates, from turtles through to squirrels.

If this is the case for different members of the living world today, it is also likely that similar variabilities exist if we compare humans living today and humans living in the past, or for that matter, if we think about how people may come to understand (or even ignore) the variable of time thousands of years into the future. Can archaeologists honestly know how the people who made coloured figurative and abstract markings on the walls of caves in the Upper Palaeolithic 35,000 years ago perceived time? The honest answer is that we don't have a clear idea. In fact, Doug would suggest that we don't have any idea, clear or otherwise. However, we can ask questions about how those people might have thought about time (indeed, if they thought about time at all);

to do so though we need to start with the basic assumption that they didn't understand time in the same way that we do today.

Contemporary interests in the past (both archaeological and public) are phenomena of relatively recent origin. There is little (if any) proof that a common and unchanging sense of the past has been in human minds for the last 300,000 or so years since humans on this planet have shared our cognitive abilities. For their part, anthropologists, ethnographers, and linguists have shown that perceptions of the past (and of time, more generally) differ among the different living communities of today's world and of the recent, historic past. For their part, archaeologists have focused on how communities other than ours (in the past, but also, critically, in the present) perceive the world. One thing is clear: the more we learn, the less certain we can be that peoples of the past saw the world as we see it today. This applies to how we conceptualize time, but also to many other perceptions of the worlds we inhabit.

It is helpful to look at the work of linguistic anthropologists and their investigations of how different living communities use varieties of words and grammar to talk about the objects, places, people, animals (everything, actually) of their worlds. This includes time. Most contemporary Western popular (and academic) conversations share a conception that something called time exists, that there was a past, that there is a future, and that we live in the present. However, the more effort that archaeologists direct at reading ethnographies and linguistic studies of non-Western communities, the clearer it becomes to them that the way in which we see the world today is neither constant nor invariable. Not across the world today and, we would argue, not through times past.

Time, therefore, is one of many variables about which we now have to question the assumption that today's understandings of it are the same as were past understandings. Because of this, most archaeologists no longer feel comfortable implanting their modern understanding of time into people who lived, for example, 3,500 years ago in the Bronze Age.

As with many people who are not trained as archaeologists, Simon's thoughts about time do not come from an archaeological education. Visiting an excavation provides an experience different from visiting a museum that might exhibit archaeological artefacts. In the museum display, they see the end product of a longer, multi-component process: excavation, analysis, conservation, restoration, and display. When they visit an excavation in action, they see something very different: action, movement, events, behaviour, but, for the most part, they do not see artefacts. They see the real-time physical endeavour of excavation in its place, in the trench or the test pit.

This difference is important. The conserved ceramic vessel in the museum vitrine is of a particular time, perhaps the Iron Age. The excavation trench from which that vessel was recovered, however, is of a different time: today, or more precisely the time of the excavation event. The pot was made in the past; the trench was made in the present. One entity, the pot, will be valorized (and analysed, conserved, and displayed); the other, the trench, will be abandoned (and backfilled and, thus, made to disappear). The pot was made by other people, long silent, in some other time, long ago. The trench was made today by people who the site-visitor watches, hearing them talking amongst themselves as their digging creates newly exposed surfaces of soil. The archaeologically-trained vision of an excavation focuses on a past long gone (it is what is sought, uncovered, and recorded); the excavators work to recover fragments and traces of human actions from that past. As an artist, Simon's vision focuses on what the excavators make, today, in their trowelling, clearing, and removal of soils, samples, and cultural materials.

Simon's questions about time are in the present, but they also reach out in connections to past peoples and their actions. In contrast to how an archaeologist might think, Simon found it difficult to measure time when he encountered an excavation or an artefact. He wonders, what does it mean to say that something happened 3,000 or 2,000 years ago? How should he (or other non-archaeologists) understand that idea of time? Even when he holds a Bronze Age axe-head in his hand, and someone tells him that it is 3,500 years old, that measure of time is nothing more than a concept. For Simon, this idea of archaeological time remained only an intellectual way of thinking about something that he senses as physical and present. As Simon's relationship with archaeology deepened, increasingly he thought about time as something tangible, as something material, and, in the works that he makes, as his response to that material manifestation of an otherwise abstract concept.

In this way, Simon was drawn to the connection (through time) of the two temporally separate processes of digging which are manifest on an excavation, to take one example, of an Iron Age grain storage pit. For Simon, the pit is a material and temporal link between two much-separated digging actions: the original removal of soil (in the Iron Age) required to create a hole in the ground as needed to keep grain from one planting season to the next; and the removal of the soil (in the recent excavation season), from that same pit by a team of excavators. Though the tools used may be different, the two actions were/are the same, and it is in that likeness that Simon finds his interest in the concept of time on an archaeological excavation.

For Simon, everything is partially about site and partially about art, particularly the relationships between time and the material he uses to engage it: to catch a moment. Time is central to European painting, and the material is how you go about engaging with time, the material, and the relationship between them. This relationship is at the core of how Simon feels when he is on site. For the first time in his life, time was more than just a concept or an idea. It was a tangible experience. When diggers section an Iron Age pit, they realize that the last time that newly opened surface saw daylight was when some earlier person (in the Iron Age) dug into the ground. For Simon, this was an emotive realization. It was incredible. Other people working on excavations may have their own emotive reasons for doing so and reactions from participating. For Simon, the emotive response rests in the way in which the excavation brings time and material together.

Time in painting

Time has always been an important subject for the painter. In European art history we find numerous paintings, religious or otherwise, where the brevity and fragility of human life is the focus of the work. There are countless images of this subject. Time, defined in human terms, takes its place as a central theme in painting. In contemporary painting, however, time is more likely to constitute an element of the experience of looking at painting rather than being an idea represented by an image. Despite the differences in approaches and concepts of time that separate past painting from contemporary, there is a common and unifying quality in all painting. This is an experience of time made manifest by the pace of a painting. The pace of a painting is the speed at which the viewer's eye is drawn across the surface to gather and connect the details of a work, which lead in a structured manner to a grasp of the work as a whole. It is clear that an artist has to make a decision, consciously or not, about how this time-based procedure in a painting will work.

In this frame, time is not a concept, it is a lived experience. Considerations about the pace of a painting have a fundamental impact on how a painting is made, on the choice of visual language and on how the physical materials are handled by the painter.

Simon recalls an exhibition at the National Gallery in London in 1987, curated by the painter Lucian Freud, in which time and painting revealed their connections. The exhibition was one in a series called the Artist's Eye, in which contemporary artists were invited to curate a show and present their paintings alongside historic works they chose from the collection. On one wall Freud placed two Rembrandt paintings close to each other. Both were portraits of women. One sitter was an old woman (Margareta de Geer, painted in 1661) and the other a younger woman (Hendrickje Stoffels, the artist's partner, painted during the last years of his life, 1654–56). To the left of the two portraits, Freud had hung a large-scale Turner seascape (Sun Rising through Vapour: Fishermen Cleaning and Selling Fish, 1807), which cast a brown light. The placement set up a straight-forward reflection on time and ageing which was emotive and affecting. What made the experience very special, beyond the quality of these works, was the way the viewer was drawn into a net constructed by the dialogue between one work and another and by the knowledge that these works are hundreds of years old. The age of the paintings, the subjects of the paintings, and our moment in front of them spun a temporal web connecting all three. This created a sense of time and an awareness of our place in it, which was extraordinary and moving.

There is a strong link between the visual language of contemporary painting and the visual language of popular mass culture and advertising. Pop Art, for example, is the child of this relationship. Much contemporary art is caught in the persuasive influence of the language of Pop, some of it intentionally and some of it unintentionally. The ability to communicate to a target audience as directly as possible is as important to the artist as it is to an advertising agency. In this context, an artist's interest in time is more likely to be fixed on the speed at which they can grab the attention of the audience. The symbiosis that exists between contemporary art and the world of commerce favours the art that uses a common visual language. This artwork can be promoted in exactly the same way as any other product on the market; seamlessly and quickly, through the established advertising networks.

Slowness

There is another way to think about time in painting, and it is connected to slowness. Before Simon began to work with archaeology, he was already searching for ways to slow down the experience of looking at painting, to make it more contemplative and to shift the attention away from the artist and towards the viewer. For Simon, the ambition was to make paintings with qualities that set them apart from the speed and attention-grabbing characteristics of Pop-influenced art and the strategies of his YBA peers. It was almost an obligation for Simon to resist joining this mainstream, no matter how successful and popular it was. A function of his work was to act as a counterbalance. There were risks involved in following an alternative path. Most people are visually sophisticated. Many of us are born into image-based cultures and when it comes to looking at images, we are able to grasp the purpose and consume the message very quickly. This enables us to move on to the next one almost straight away, whether it is an artwork in a museum or an advertisement on social media. Slowing down the process of looking and engaging an audience for longer is a challenge. We are not used to slowness and do not always understand its value.

When Simon first went on site at Segsbury Camp it was clear that there was much shared by painter and field archaeologist. A site might attract a visitor for certain reasons on the first day but there are other motives that emerge to hold the visitors' attention and to bring them back over a longer period. In this process, there is a moment when you stop being a visitor and you start to become a part of the place. One of the most compelling reasons for this is that you recognize your position in that place's continuity of use, connecting you with past human activity on the site. An excavation is not the end of a story, it is not a summation. It is another episode in a history to which the individuals present on that site (the digger working on a section in a pit, an artist drawing, or someone visiting for the day) all contribute. By recognizing this Simon was able to begin to find his place in the landscape and to start to ask questions of painting that he started to phrase in archaeological terms. This implied that the questions that drove the archaeological inquiry could equally be applied to questioning how and why to make art. The excavation process implied that an emphasis on materiality, rather than image, was necessary to slow down the experience of looking at painting and a strategy to engage a viewer for longer, was to involve more than just the eye.

Time as material

Stepping into an archaeological trench you are aware that you have crossed a threshold. Time does not remain a concept. It ceases to be an idea; instead, it finds tangible form in the materiality of the site. This is the place where time and material come together most convincingly. The excavation site acted as a model for the artist. It provoked a turn to materiality and a letting go of image in the painting. The excavation process educated Simon as an artist and offered clues of how to connect material and time in painting. Importantly, it suggested that involving all our senses, mirroring the artist's experience on site, was a way to achieve this. A path has to be structured, similar to setting up the pace of a painting, but one that begins with the eye and leads incrementally to the body. The artist must consider the viewer as fully sentient at all times and must aim to engage that individual completely. A painting is not a message, it is an experience.

Standing in front of a painting

When Simon starts making a work he thinks about the viewer and what it will be like for that viewer to stand in front of the work. This way of thinking gives form to the work. Will it be taller than the viewer? Will they need to look upwards? How high will it hang from the floor? Will it relate to the legs of the viewer, to the knees, or lower even to the ankle? Archaeologists seldom (if ever) think about this: how a member of the public will receive their work, where work is understood as the actions of excavation, and related field-based investigations. Most of the time, archaeologists think about how other archaeologists (distinct from members of the general public) will react when they read their published texts or hear their lectures at conferences or in departmental seminars. This academic and intellectual tradition sits securely in the broader goal of what archaeologists see themselves doing: creating knowledge. Most archaeologists (especially those working in academic or research spaces) just don't think that much about the public. A different case, of course, applies for people who work in the heritage industry or in museums; their focus is often directly on the public. For the rest, however, the public seldom enters the equation.

Fast archaeology

In many ways, archaeology does the opposite of what Simon calls for in his attention to slowness. Archaeology rushes people through time at, literally, super-human speed. Archaeologists are comfortable, for example, talking with authority about the European Bronze Age (a period that covered 2,500 years). Can we truthfully understand what a period of 2,500 years means? How do we conceptualize that span of time? We can understand what happened today, and we can understand what happened last night or three weeks ago. Doug may have some sort of a grasp on what it means that his ninety-eight-year-old mother was born in 1926, but in order to do so, he needs assistance. He wasn't there when she was born, nor is there anyone alive today who Doug knows who was there at that time in that place.

In response to this type of unfilled gaps in time passage, we create and rely on mechanisms of remembering longer periods of our personal pasts: photographs, diaries, older relatives, personal memories, grandpa's stories. Beyond that, however, we are not well-suited as a species to hold the rest of time-passed in our minds in a coherent way. We need the help of the intellectual phenomena and practical technologies that have been constructed by the industries and perspectives of modern disciplinary projects like the study of archaeology or history. In this sense then, archaeology collapses time to a scale that is conceivable: centuries, millennia, epochs, eras.

If this is the case, then we have to accept that archaeologists manipulate and fake the passage of time. They cram all kinds of people, events, storms and floods, droughts, and long winters into something that might be called, for example, the Bronze Age, and then they talk about a 2,500-year period in terms of settlement patterns or warfare or technological innovation or environmental pattern. Archaeologists are so skilled at this that they can collapse thousands of years into a 60,000-word book, or a 5,000-word book chapter, or even a paragraph. Because we cannot otherwise conceive of such a long period of time, we find assistance and relief in temporal categorizations and chronological creations; archaeology provides the intellectual and scientific tools to make this happen.

For Simon, the pit, and his observation of it are the raw material for his painting. To understand why connections like this exist and how they operate is to understand what stimulates the artist to make paintings. To be clear, Simon doesn't connect with the Iron Age pit. It works the other way round; the pit has a deep connection with him. The power of this connection comes from Simon's response to that association, particularly to its materiality: to it as a physically manifest connection. While this connection makes Simon reflect on the relationship that time has with material, he recognizes that his response is not universal; it is only his personal take on it.

Simon's experience with archaeology is an experience of being on site during excavation. A particular feature on a site (for example, the Iron Age pit in the trench) activates Simon to think and respond. Other people (both public and professional) undoubtedly engage archaeology in other ways and through other connections. This may include a visit to an excavation-in-process (as for

Simon), but it may also take place on a broader, perhaps, less connected, scale: in the news media, in the classroom, in the museum.

These other engagements with archaeology most often have objects as their points of connection: artefacts, mosaics, sculptures, coins, pots, axe-heads, for example, but also human and animal bones or preserved textiles. In most (perhaps all) of these other engagements with the past, people don't conceptualize the pit, or the trench, as if it were an object. Most never see the excavated feature from which the axe-head or cattle skull was removed. For many people (archaeologists and non-archaeologists alike), once the pit has been excavated, it no longer has historical, cultural, or aesthetic value. The pit becomes an object to be thrown away and discarded. It is backfilled. It disappears, and once again, is submerged from sight.

The importance that Simon finds in a newly excavated pit rests firmly in his knowledge that, though he may be sitting next to it one afternoon, he knows that the next day the pit will unceremoniously be filled with dirt. Again, time is in play. The excavated surface is transitory: only present for half a day or so, before it is erased. In this, Simon sees a temporal overlap. The surface of the pit, once it is cleared by an excavator, sees light again after 2,500 years. Two widely separated moments of time overlap, the connection is made, even though the temporal connection may last no more than half a day, an evening and a night, before backfilling intervenes.

Up to a point, Simon's pit and contact paintings (see Chapters 6 and 10) are registrations of this moment of temporal overlap, when the newly connected surface of the pit is temporarily present. His moment of contact and connection with that particular surface on that particular afternoon and evening is brief, lasting until the wind blows loose soils and leaves onto the surface, or when the team backfills the trench and moves on to work on another part of the site. Before that disappears, of course, archaeologists record the surface with accuracy and detail in site-plan and photography. Archaeological recording, however, is not the same thing or process as Simon's registration.

Part of Simon's emotive reaction to features (such as pits) on site comes from his recognition of the amount of work performed by the excavators and the site recorders and photographers. He respects the sheer amount of work required and the people who do it, both in the excavation today, but also in the original digging, 2,500 years ago. Effort and labour form yet more connections between Simon with the people of that past. On site all day, watching the excavation, Simon understands the effort made, during the excavation and during the Iron Age; he is witness to it.

There is no better way to understand someone else than to do exactly what they do, to know the effort it takes. Through the actions and process of making his contact paintings and pit paintings, Simon works in that newly excavated trench. Crawling over the canvas that he has laid onto the cleared surface of the pit, he starts to make his work and, in doing so, he expands and deepens his temporal connection to the past. Common action in a common place: Iron Age pit digger – archaeological excavator – modern painter. There can be no closer connections for these three people.

It is in these action zones where Simon finds the greatest commonalities. His connection is in his contact with the site. With his contact paintings and pit paintings, the connection is physical: literally grounded, as he lays out his canvas on the newly excavated surface and then crawls across it marking and cutting the cloth. Then, he takes the canvases back to his studio where he works and reworks (and reworks again) them and their component parts into a finished painting for exhibition. The excavation team had crawled across that surface (or knelt on protective planks or plastic), trowelling and brushing, before lifting the cultural or environmental materials, taking them to laboratories for analysis and treatment and study. While Simon doesn't try to get inside the head of the pit-digging Iron Age person (as many interpretative and explanatory archaeologists would do), he shares an intimacy with the man, woman, or child who scraped out the soils and stone and chalk in the Iron Age. Shared experience crosses time and creates Simon's emotional response to temporality.

To be sure, other visitors to the same excavation, or to a museum, or to a project's open days and public outreach efforts, also get a thrill, and part of that thrill is feeling a temporal connection to the people of the past. Most often, however, their connection comes when they hold in their hands an object that once was held by a person who lived in the distant past: a Neolithic flint blade, a Roman glass vase. Simon's interest and work is within the process of excavation, without regard for objects uncovered. His focus is not archaeological nor about landscape context or environmental conditions of a distant past. Simon's focus is on excavation, though he admits that occasionally some particular object emerges that may amaze him: an Iron Age pottery vessel, the rim of which holds the thumb and index finger impressions of the person who made the pot. In a moment of fundamental human sensation, those fingerprints collapse temporality into another connection.

8

Which Ruins do we Valorize (Doug Bailey, 2014)

In 2012, Bjornar Olsen and Þóra Pétursdóttir invited me to contribute to a book that they were assembling and which they published in 2014 with Routledge titled *Ruin Memories: Materiality, Aesthetics, and the Archaeology of the Recent Past*.[1] In most ways, it is a traditional academic book, published by a mainstream commercial publisher of archaeology (and other humanities and social sciences): a collection of academic essays written in narrative prose with supporting illustrations as well as a few photo essays.

At the time that Bjornar and Þóra asked me to write something for them, I was enthused about montage and collage, particularly the works of Hannah Höch and Erwin Blumenfeld. I was especially attracted to the graphic medium of montage as a way of getting a message across to the viewer/reader without providing direct descriptive texts or obvious rational argument grounded in words, sentences, and logical writing. I was also excited about the potential for making work for an archaeological audience that would provoke readers and viewers to respond in their own way to what they were seeing and reading, without the standard signposts and messaging required in traditional academic production. I was (and remain) taken with the strategy of provocation. I like the idea of making something that will shock, disturb, or disrupt. I am particularly taken by the potential that comes with a process that makes its argument through the use of found images without explanatory or justification texts.

In response to Bjornar and Þóra's invitation, I made a twelve-page visual and textual work. At first sight, the book chapter that I sent them (titled *Which ruins do we valorize? A new calibration curve for the Balkan past)*[2] both confuses and intrigues. Images, found-text, quotations, artefacts, and photographs jumble on each page and even tumble over the edges of the printed pages. Glimpses of rational structure do appear here and there, but they slip away in increasing acceleration as the readers/viewers navigate through the work. Along that journey, things are not as they seem: images start on one page and seem to bend around the paper's edge and continue onto the next; streams of words do the same. In other places, the chapter ignores the power of the bound book's gutter, breaking the reader's linear progress through the work. In all, it is a chaos of information, textual and graphic, lacking any adherence to the rules of what an academic argument within an edited book should be or look like.

I was drawn to collage and montage and to taking images or objects and putting them together in different ways, particularly in ways unexpected and confounding. My interests in montage and collage may have come from reading about, looking at, and listening to Dada and Surrealism.

Conceptually, I found that much of what was happening with these movements was an archaeological process: find objects (or texts or sounds or images), put them together, make a story through juxtaposing combinations, sometimes with clear intent, and other times in a more open way, but always allowing spectators to take from the work whatever they may.

I was drawn once again to the format and openness of Diller and Scofidio's 1992 montage *Case no. 00-17163* (discussed above, p. 43). Thinking back on this, I wonder if I came to the Diller and Scofidio work via a work by Cliff McLucas, the late British performance artist: his *Ten feet and three quarters of an inch of theatre: a documentation of a site-specific theatre work*.[3] *Ten feet...* used a similar conceit to present material in printed form in an academic book. Both of these works were multi-page creations, published within traditional, edited books, and both works deployed visual images in provocative ways. I saw strong similarities between the materials that both works presented and the materials that archaeologists work with and publish: evidence, facts, records, traces, representations and reconstructions of place, time, and past events.

Particularly, I was taken by the way that each work had been built through sequences of pages within the larger edited books. There were no breaks of the imagery in the gutters, between the pages of the bound books. Each work presented a full bleed (up to and over the edges of the paper), and the whole work flowed from one page to the next: something that never happened in standard academic publishing. In some ways it was chaotic, but in other ways, it made complete sense. Both works broke the rules that normally regulate the production of information in book form.

When I 'read' the Diller and Scofidio and the McLucas work, I sensed the openness of experimental potential more than the promise of an answer or a clear understanding of data or argument. The works operated through evocation rather than by telling. I was attracted to this alternative way of producing work that appeared in a book (the majority medium of my academic archaeology) and of representing facts and traces of past actions (the goal of archaeology). So, when Bjornar and Þóra asked me to write something for their *Ruin Memories* book, I responded that I wouldn't write an article for them, but that I would make a montage.

Political context: Romania's past and present

At the time of Bjornar and Þóra's invitation, I had just finished two decades of running archaeological projects and publishing books, journal articles, and excavation reports about prehistoric Bulgaria and Romania. I had a lot of experience with Romanian prehistoric archaeology, but also with twentieth-century history and politics in the totalitarian regimes in Eastern Europe. I had a lot of things running around in my head. On the one hand, I had been studying the Neolithic period of southeastern Europe, a span of time that ran from 6,500 to 3,500 BC. Indeed, I had written a book about this which, at the time, became the standard (or the only) clear introduction to the period.[4]

Then and now, many people see the Neolithic in this region of Europe as the origin of what popular culture understands by the term civilization. The period was one of important developments in the human story writ large: the origins of agriculture; the origins of settled habitations into houses and villages; significant changes in representative art forms (pottery-making and its decoration, as well as the creation of human figurines); early metalworking; and the first substantial cemeteries with prestige grave-goods, made of gold, copper, and marine shell.

Not surprisingly, archaeologists and historians write about the Neolithic as a remarkable period of the past, as an explosion of cultural achievement and human advancement. They valorize it. And, in the countries where these long past events had taken place, authorities, academics, and politicians (especially politicians) use the polished brilliance of the Neolithic in modern celebrations of national heritage and the peoples' history.

Just as significant, a second result of my archaeological collaborations and academic integration with these regions was that I had learned a lot about (and was intrigued by) a different period of time: the second half of the twentieth century. People look at this period of time (especially the decades following the end of the Second World War) in a light very different from the one under which they see the Neolithic and its record of technological and social innovation and advance. People stigmatized this post-war period as a time of totalitarian hardship and uncivil society. In Romania, where I had been working the most recently, the period had been dominated by Nicolae Ceauşescu (and his wife, Elena), and before that by Gheorghe Gheorghiu-Dej. Before the coup (in which Ceauşescu and his wife were executed) and subsequent changes of 1989, the country had been a police state of great poverty, corruption, and human misery.

Thinking about these two vastly separate periods, a question emerged: why do we value one period of time (the Neolithic) as worthy of praise and useful in displays of nationalist pride, at the same time that we scorn another period of time as one of darkness and despair? Put another way, how do we come to value certain patterns of human behaviour or periods of our past in a positive light (and valorize them publicly), yet do the opposite for other periods?

I realized that there was no simple answer to this question. Further, I was certain that I did not want to assume an academic position of authority on the question (or to propose some absolute answer). I wanted to find a way to provoke readers to ask themselves the question of the differential valorization of periods of the past. The more I thought about it, the more I felt that a traditional, purely textual, presentation of my thoughts and of the two, separate, historic situations would limit discussion and debate. Increasingly, I sensed that images offered more options and possibilities for provoking thought and reaction in the viewer. I came to realize that I didn't want to write 5,000 words about differential valorizations of the past. In the end, I made a chapter for Bjornar and Þóra's book that was purely visual, a montage that juxtaposed images of the Neolithic with found images and texts from the second half of the twentieth century. I wanted to make a point, but I wanted to make it indirectly. I wanted to ask the viewers to sift through the images and my arrangement of them, and then to make up their own minds, though of course, I was pushing them in a particular direction.

Making the work

I started to look for visual material: both about the Neolithic and about life in Romania in the more recent past. I treated images that I found as if each was an artefact, excavated from a 1960s or 1970s Romanian newspaper, tourist brochure, party platform circular, or an archaeological report about a Neolithic excavation.

I arranged the images over a fifteen-page sequence. I followed a structure one would normally find in a standard write-up of an archaeological excavation: each page of the montage analogous to the title page of a chapter in an excavation report. Archaeological publications and excavation reports usually include a chapter each for the key categories of material or research themes: architecture and the built environment, social structure, technology, art, agriculture, mortuary ritual and so on. In the montage, I made each page as if it was the title page for such chapters. Those title pages became the armature for the montage and it was around, on, though, and past that armature that I arranged and juxtaposed the found images.

My hope was that the readers would see the mixtures of imagery and ask themselves what was going on: why are images of archaeological elements jumbled up with images of life in twentieth-century Romania? I wanted to unbalance viewers, especially as those viewers (or readers) would have come across the montage-chapter in the middle of what was otherwise a standard collection of academic essays. My hope was that they would be drawn into the challenge of figuring out what was going on: to unpick the puzzle that I was setting for them.

The montages

The rest of the work that created *Which ruins…* involved finding, choosing, juxtaposing, resizing, and arranging images for each of the chapter title pages. For example, the first page (or 'chapter') of the montage is about agriculture. On that page I arranged images of standard archaeological artefacts and analyses from Neolithic sites in Romania: flint and bone sickles, diagrams from the analysis of pollen, a digging-stick made from a cattle bone, and chaff left from threshing Neolithic wheat. And that was it. Except that I tucked in one image from the mid-twentieth century: an image of a farm tractor which I found in a 1960s pamphlet about collectivized agriculture in Romania. The image of the tractor is almost completely hidden, down in the lower right hand corner of the page. Having started with a relatively straight-forward page of images, the pattern and pace of juxtapositioning accelerated with each succeeding page as I moved forward making the rest of the work.

The second montage-page was titled 'Built Environment'. Like agriculture, the built environment (or architecture) is a mainstream topic for archaeologists. As with the preceding page about agriculture, I juxtaposed and arranged images (most prominently for the page's background) of archaeological materials with found images from mid- to late-twentieth-century newspapers, pamphlets, and political guides: an aerial photo of the common apartment block that was the standard living accommodation created in Eastern Europe since the Second World War. Also, running on the left side of the page from page bottom to page top, I inserted a found text of 1964 propaganda about the Romanian contemporary architecture (i.e., the Soviet-style apartment block) presenting that architectural achievement as evidence for a better life for its occupants, as well as peace, progress, and good will. In front of that background (and thus, perhaps, attempting to cover it over), I arranged archaeological visual material from Neolithic sites in the region: a plan-drawing of a small hut; an excavation drawing recording postholes marking shapes of circular shelters; a reconstruction of the wattle-and-daub core of huts and houses of those prehistoric buildings; a larger cut-away drawing of the interior of one of these village houses with a clay oven in one room's corner. Two other images of Neolithic material culture appeared, both truncated: on the lower left edge of the page, the end section of the flint-and-antler sickle, the photograph of which had started on the previous page (i.e., in Chapter 1 Agriculture); and running vertically near the top of the page, part of a finely knapped long flint blade, the remainder of which would be found on the following page (Chapter 2 Mortuary Record).

The third 'chapter' of *Which ruins …* was about death, and was titled 'Mortuary Record'. In archaeological reports we read about inhumations or cremations, grave-goods, age and sex demographics of the population, and learn of egalitarian or ranked social status in a community. This montage started with standard archaeological material: a photograph of an excavated skeleton from a late Neolithic cemetery; a plan from an excavation of a contemporary burial; Neolithic grave-goods (an elegant, long, flint blade; an arm-ring made from the marine mollusk spondylus). Also, onto this page about death, I continued two images that had appeared in part on the preceding page: the remaining part of the long flint blade, and the rest of the cut-away reconstruction of the Neolithic house. I wrapped both images around the edge of the page, ignoring the page break that the book-format normally would have inserted in my sequencing of images.

Among the archaeological images of death and its study, I inserted images from the twentieth century. From a classic patriotic poster from the 1970s, I found an image of the face of the dictator Nicolae Ceaușescu and ran it over and through the layout gutter that separated this page from the next (about production). I added a short text written by Constantin Giurescu (1901–77), a Romanian historian. Giurescu had been a professor at the University of București, editor of the *Romanian Historical Review* (1931), Director of the National Institute for History (1933), and a member of the Chamber of Deputies of Romania (1932–33). He had also served as secretary of the National Renaissance Front government (1939–40), the last of several attempts to counter the popularity of the fascist and antisemitic Iron Guard. Giurescu's story is noteworthy. While I was looking for image material for this montage, I found a short booklet that Giurescu had written. In it he describes his arrest and the time he spent in jail under the totalitarian regime. Here were the words and experiences of a professor of history (someone whose job it is to make the past) who was arrested because of his views and because of the inherent power he held as a producer of the past, as a historian. In his booklet, Giurescu reconstructed conversations he had had with his jailers, and he published his own hand-drawn plans of the prison at Sighet and of his cell (no. 21). From his book, I selected a short section of text. The quote begins 'They started to die on their way to the prison …' and I continued the quote as it described who had died (General Chihoski, General Popovici-Epure, Costel Tătăreanu) and how they died (heart failure, liver disease, suicide). Giurescu's account contains a close and intimate specificity that enlivens the otherwise static archaeological materials. The juxtapositions that result create a dark glimpse into death and dying at a level that is seldom reached in our treatments of the prehistoric pasts.

The next chapter-montage focused on another standard archaeological topic: production. Archaeologists write a lot about production whether that is of pottery, or metal, or textiles, or flint tools, or about how people produced the food that they ate. On the archaeological side of this juxtaposition, again, running over the gutter of the page break, I continued one of the images (the long flint grave-good) from the death page, and I added images of Neolithic artefacts (a flint core that would have been used to make blades that would have been used as cutting tools; multiples of a copper shaft-hole axe; multiples of a deep ceramic bowl), and a graph from an analysis of prehistoric tool production. For the twentieth century, I continued the large image of a young (and patriotic) Ceaușescu from the previous page and added an image of the government/party medal awarded to exemplary workers (the Order of Labour). Running horizontally to the right (and off of the page,) I laid out the beginning of a line of found text that starts 'The astonishing and little-known artistic and…' and which continues on the following page to conclude about the 'peoples' achievements'.

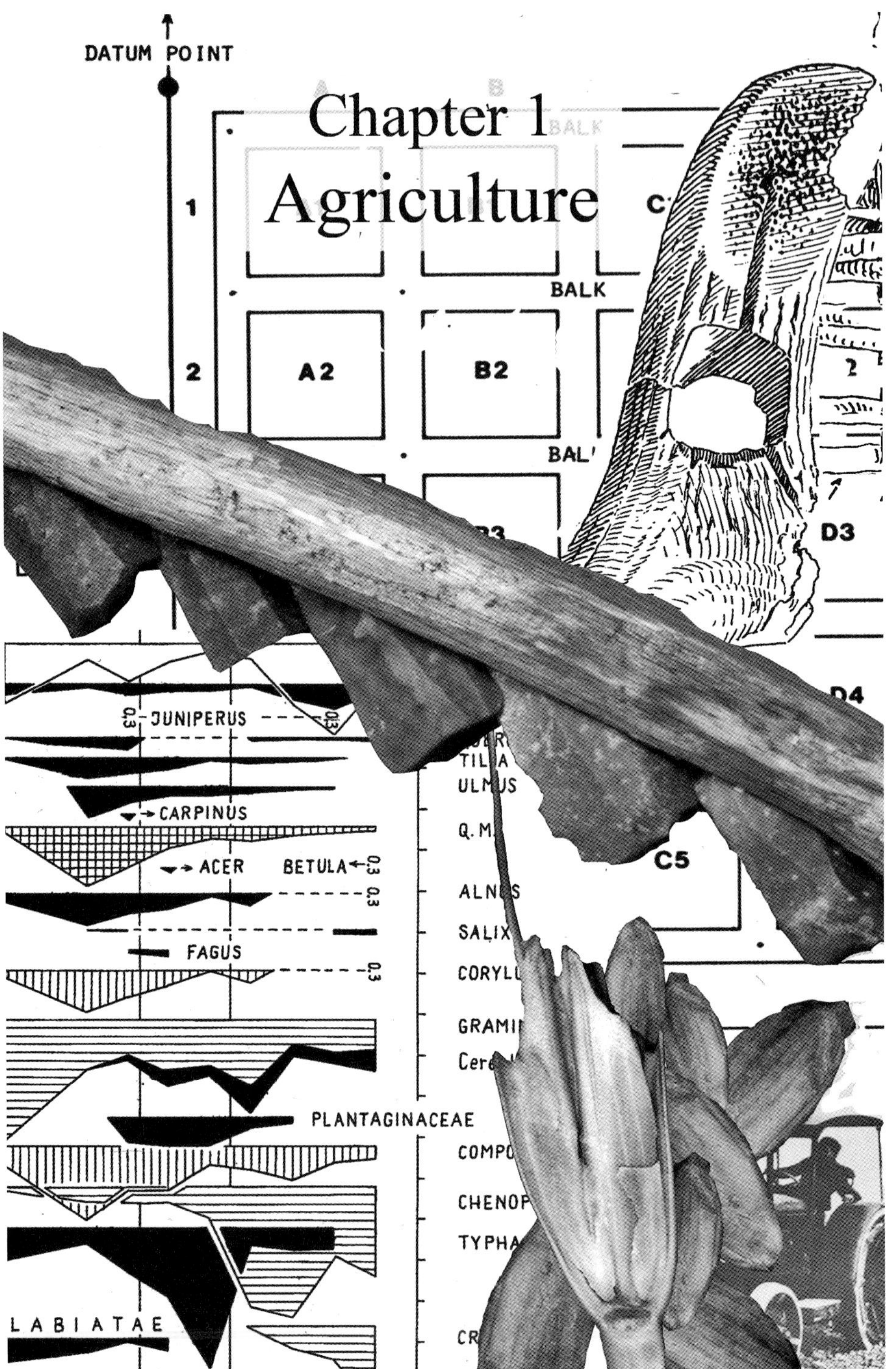

8.1 *Which ruins do we valorize? A new calibration curve for the Balkan past, p. 216 (Bailey 2014b).*

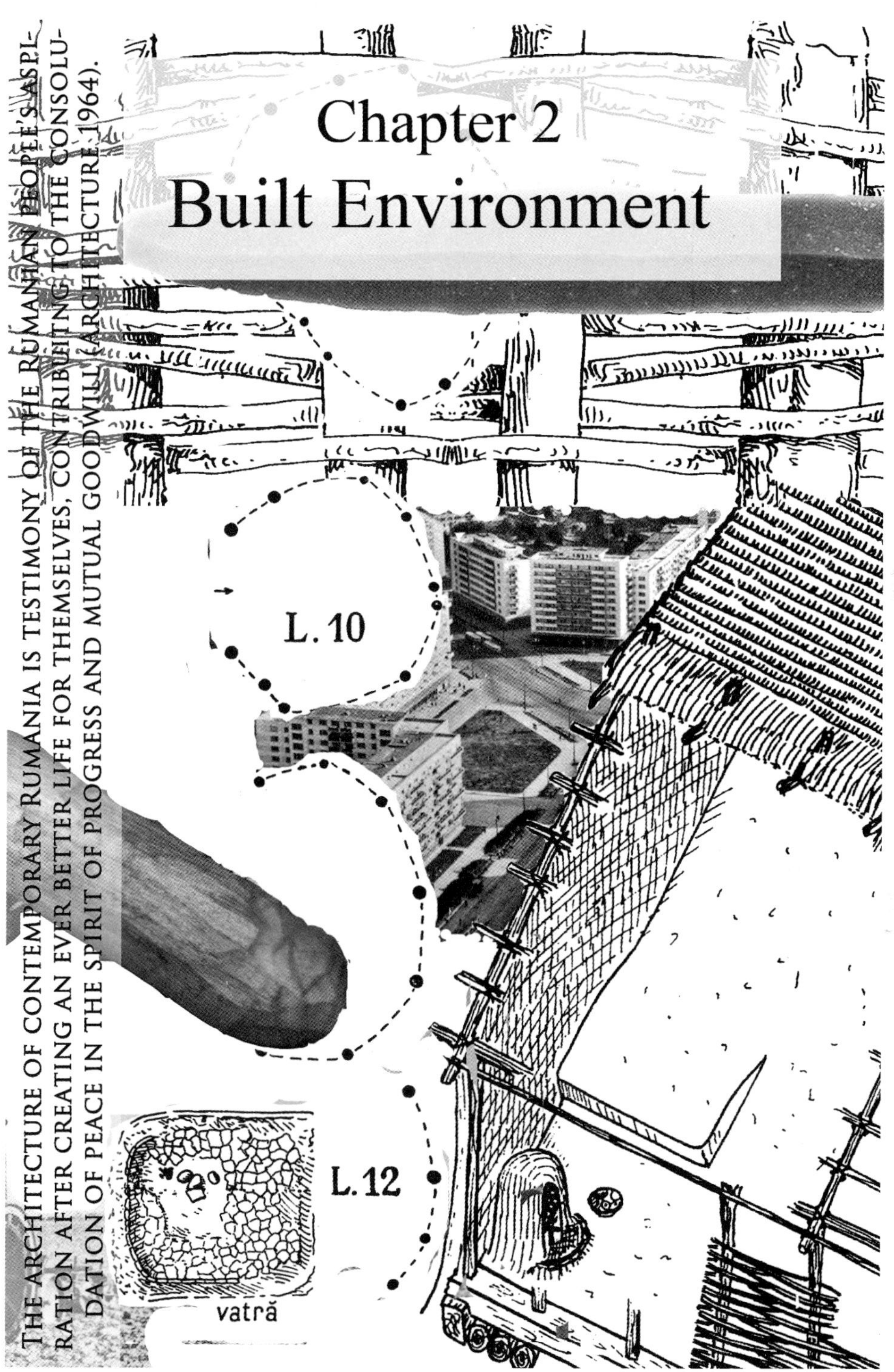

8.2 *Which ruins do we valorize? A new calibration curve for the Balkan past, p. 217 (Bailey 2014b).*

Chapter 3
Mortuary Record

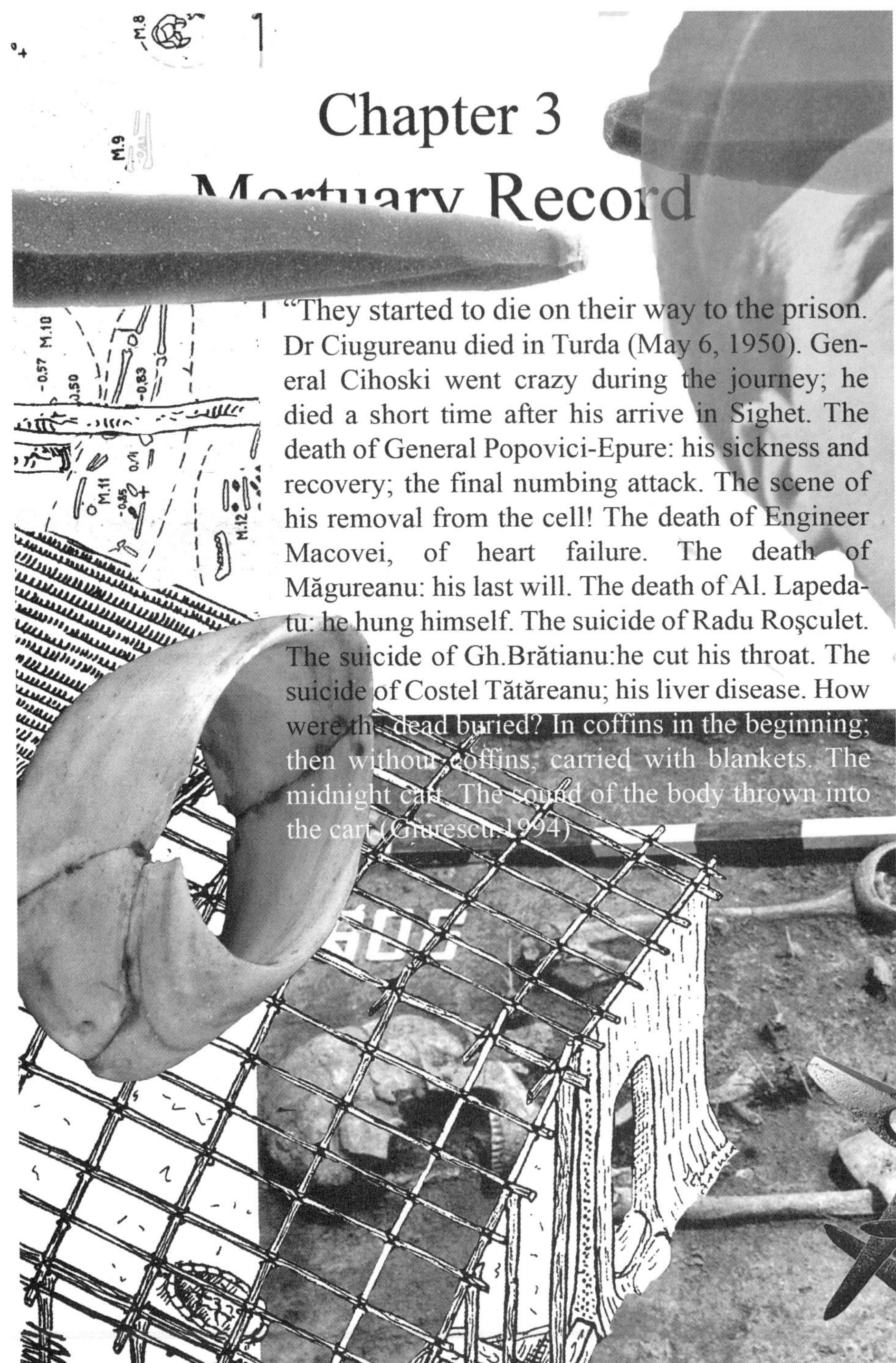

"They started to die on their way to the prison. Dr Ciugureanu died in Turda (May 6, 1950). General Cihoski went crazy during the journey; he died a short time after his arrive in Sighet. The death of General Popovici-Epure: his sickness and recovery; the final numbing attack. The scene of his removal from the cell! The death of Engineer Macovei, of heart failure. The death of Măgureanu: his last will. The death of Al. Lapedatu: he hung himself. The suicide of Radu Roşculet. The suicide of Gh.Brătianu:he cut his throat. The suicide of Costel Tătăreanu; his liver disease. How were the dead buried? In coffins in the beginning; then without coffins, carried with blankets. The midnight cart. The sound of the body thrown into the cart (Giurescu 1994)

8.3 *Which ruins do we valorize? A new calibration curve for the Balkan past, p. 218 (Bailey 2014b).*

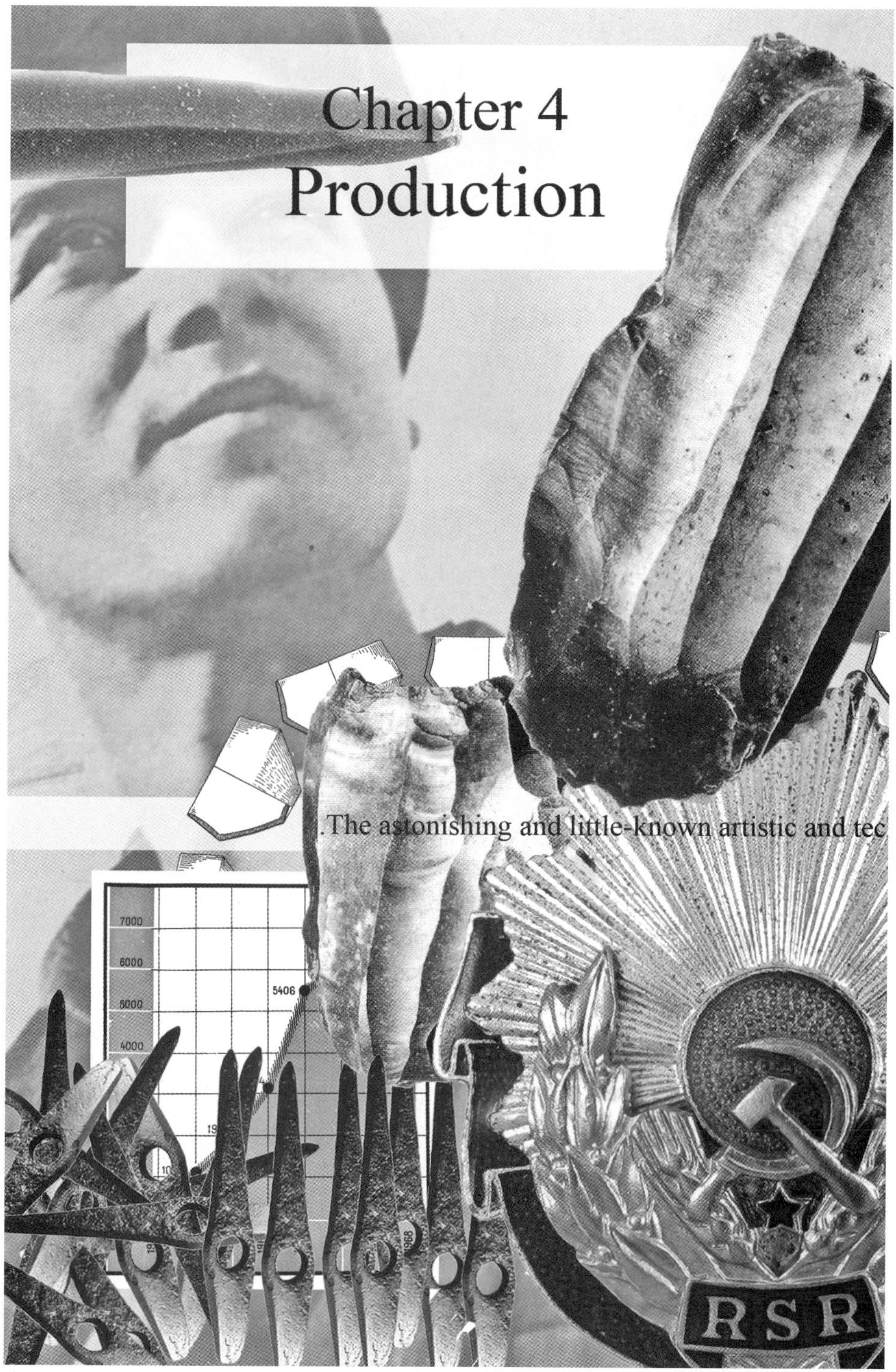

8.4 *Which ruins do we valorize? A new calibration curve for the Balkan past*, p. 219 (Bailey 2014b).

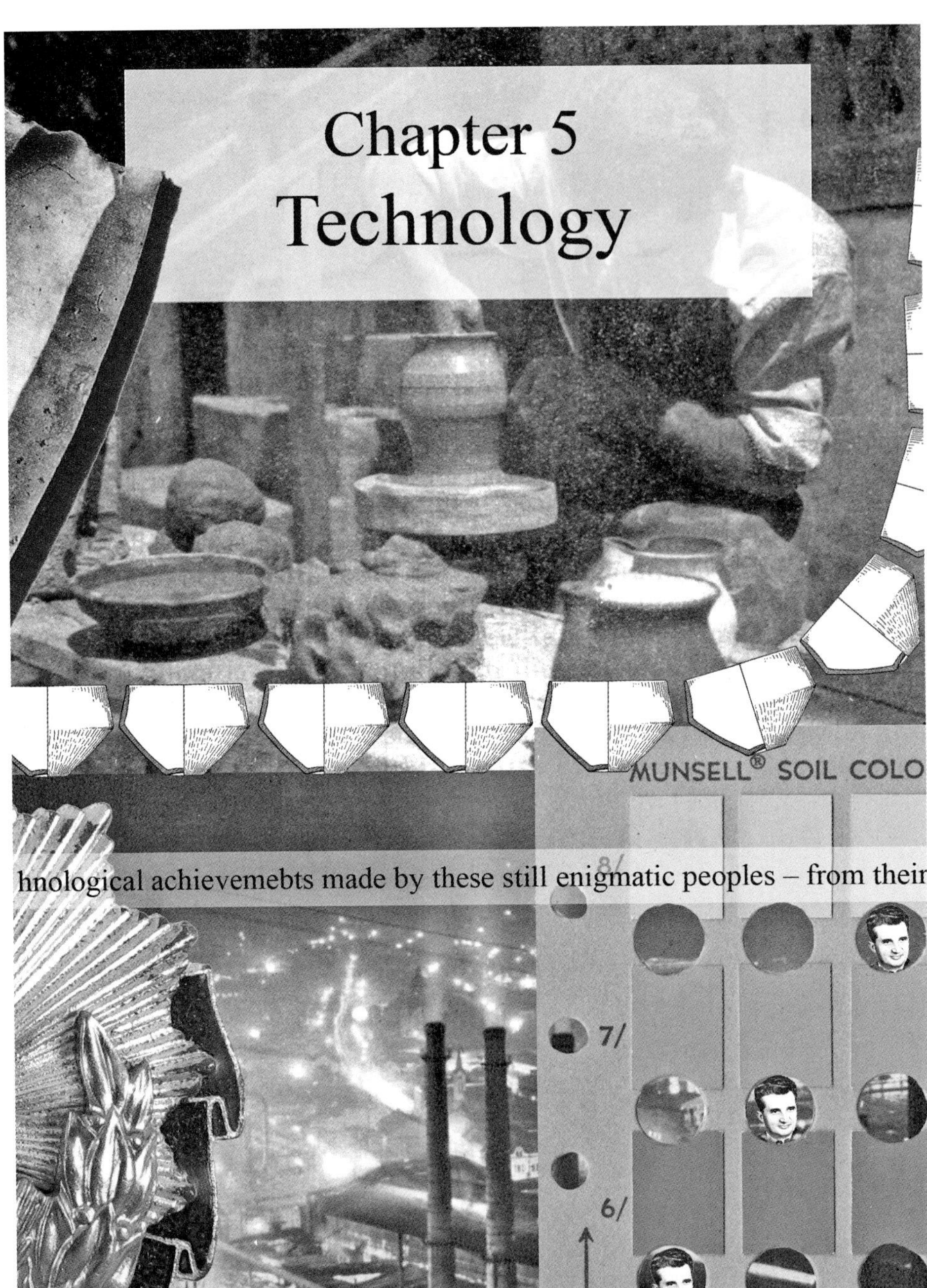

8.5 *Which ruins do we valorize? A new calibration curve for the Balkan past, p. 220 (Bailey 2014b).*

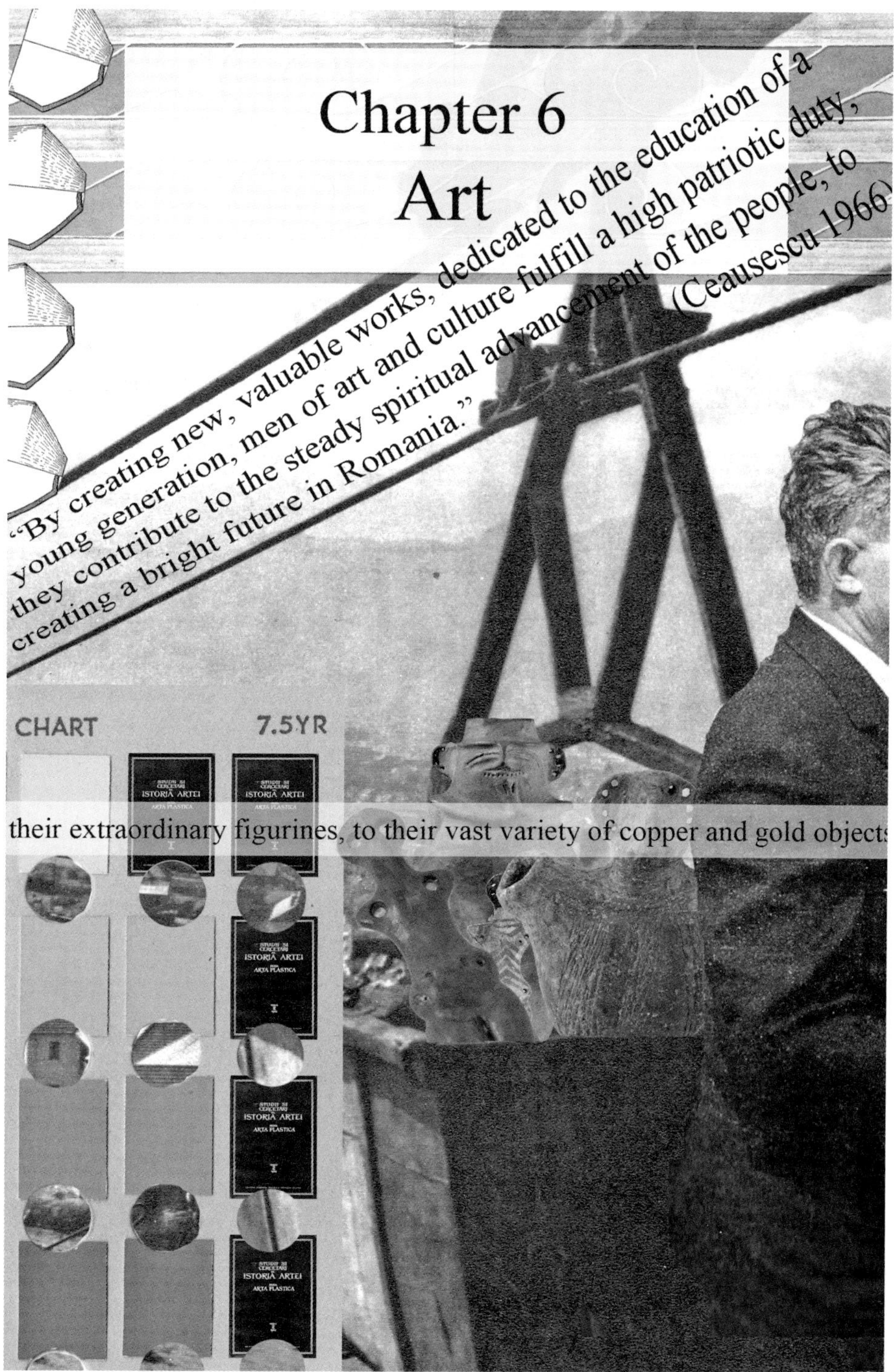

8.6 *Which ruins do we valorize? A new calibration curve for the Balkan past, p. 221 (Bailey 2014b).*

Also, part of the image of the Order of Labor medal wraps around the right edge of the page and continues on, into the next montage which is titled 'Chapter 5: Technology': another archetypic archaeological theme. That found text about 'astonishing' that started on the previous page, continues '… technological achievements made by these still enigmatic peoples …'). I found and inserted images from mid-twentieth-century Romanian pottery producers, as well as an image (taken at night) of a hellish industrial landscape of Romanian factories and foundries, ablaze with light and industry and pumping out columns of smoke. I cut out and cropped a portrait photo of Ceauşescu, made multiples of it, and then dropped several of them into cut out windows of a standard tool of archaeological field work (a Munsell soil colour chart).

The found horizontal text bleeds off of the technology page, continues across the gutter and onto the next montage page: 'Chapter 6: Art'. Bleeding images off of one page, across the gutter, and on to the next page worked to connect the pages in ways not acceptable in academic publishing (with texts and images neatly contained and controlled within the boundaries of each page, or perhaps of a single double-page spread). Two consequences come from the cross-gutter and round-page-edge bleeds. First, I wanted to suggest (by showing) that the boundaries that define and isolate the major themes of archaeological thinking (e.g., built environment, technology) are unhelpful at best, and at worst give the false sense that one can divide up life (past or present) into easily defined, distinct categories of actions and object: that there is something called 'art' and something called 'resources' and that these two portions of life do not overlap or intermingle. The second consequence was to suggest that the physical conditions of disseminating archaeological knowledge in printed book form have restricted what archaeologists can say and how they can say it: if we ignore the limitations of the edges of the page and the boundary normally identified as the book's gutter, then we will find unexpected and provocative ways to think about the past.

For these reasons, the Munsell colour chart that started on the Technology page continues over the gutter and onto the Art page, as do the multiples of the deep pottery vessels, and as does the running horizontal text ('…their extraordinary figurines, to their vast variety of copper and gold objects…?'). For this new page about art ('Chapter 6'), the other archaeological elements are limited to images of anthropomorphic figurines, which are presented in an unorderly, chaotic, and non-archaeological jumble and heaped into a huge, metal, industrial bucket suspended from the overhead cabling at a factory and mining complex. The two parallel cables suspending the bucket became the framing lines for a 1966 Ceauşescu quote about the patriotic duty that 'men of art and culture' make to the 'spiritual advancement of the people'. Ceauşescu himself appears (or the left half of his head and upper body appears) on the right edge of the page (perhaps even being carried away in the bucket), bleeding off to the next page, which focuses on the archaeological topic of 'resources'.

Archaeologists devote tremendous effort and thought to recovering patterns of resource availability, exploitation, and control in the past. The next montage page ('Chapter 7: Resources') attacks this topic. The archaeological elements for this page relate to animal and mineral resources. Running along the bottom of the page are multiples of animal bone, and a jaw from a sheep or goat sits in the page's upper right hand corner: both links to Neolithic food sources and textile raw materials (wool). For the background of the page, I reproduced a fragment of a table presenting the proportions of trace metal elements that laboratory analysis found in a study of Late Neolithic copper axes. Bleeding onto the page from the left (from the technology page) is the other half of Ceauşescu's head and torso. He smiles and his hand is aloft in adulation of a group of applauding school children: another common patriotic image from his propaganda campaigns of the 1960s and 1970s. The most powerful image on the resources page, though, is of a Romanian miner, face darkened with soot and dirt, a percussion drill held heavy in his hands; on the page, I have positioned the miner at work so that the drill plunges into Ceaușescu's chest.

Next comes another standard archaeological chapter: 'Chapter 8: Textiles'. Here images include more jaws and skulls of Neolithic sheep or goats (the producers of the wool spun and woven since prehistory), Neolithic clay spindle whorls to produce the yarn, and Neolithic clay loom weights once part of weaving looms. From the twentieth century, the main image is of a woman working an industrial loom (leaning into the machine, adjusting the weft or the weave). Added to this is a series of images of embroidery patterns used by rural modern weavers, and a 1950 caption for the image of the woman at work: 'Cinča Maria, Textile worker of the "Cotton Industry B", awarded the Order of Labor, operates 34 looms simultaneously'.

The images jostle and have no explanatory commentary or caption. It is for the reader/viewer to provide the dialogue or to make the connections, if they see any, or if there are any. Some may make an unsettling connection between what is commonly seen as one a development of human technological innovations (Neolithic breeding and shearing of sheep for wool, the invention of a technology to turn that wool into textiles for clothing, decoration, or commodity) with what is equally seen as one of humanity's sources of labour exploitation (sweat-shop labour in modern communities where women and children are trapped in factories with low-paying jobs working in life-threatening conditions).

The next montage in the chapter ('Chapter 9: Social Structure') picks up the life, interrogation, and imprisonment of Constantin Giurescu, the history professor the viewer last saw in the montage about death and mortuary archaeology. Here, I inserted an image of Giurescu that I placed on top of the sketch-map that he made of his prison wing at the Sighet Prison and his cell there. With its details, its bird's eye view, and its layout, my thoughts drift to the types of sketch maps made on archaeological excavations, though there is no reason to assume that the viewer will make the same connection. At the bottom of the page, I have inserted the first (left) half of a quote from Giurescu's notes (the right half bleeds over to the montage on the next page, about cultural identity): the quote relates Giurescu's encounter with a guard at the prison (and as the reader will see on the following page) shows the way that the totalitarian regimes of the mid-twentieth century weighed (and controlled) the dangerous powers deployed by historians.

Archaeological elements inserted into the 'Social Structure' page include more Neolithic animal skulls (though also a human skull from a burial of the same period), Neolithic grave-goods (copper axes), and a Neolithic pottery vessel made in the shape of the human body. I cropped, rearranged, and positioned more grave-goods (two *spondylus* bracelets and a copper axe) as if they were the erect male genitalia of the anthropomorphic pot. Where the head of the pot should have been, I have placed the head of Gheorghe Gheorghiu-Dej (1901–65), Ceaușescu's predecessor, who was the Communist leader of Romania from 1947 to 1965), the time when Constantin Giurescu was in the Sighet Prison. In the bottom left section of the page, I placed two tapestry figures of women (the embroidery made in the middle of the twentieth century in a Romanian village): the sewn figures seem to dance, or at least wave or perhaps salute: one hand on hip, hair blowing to the right, eyes covered with a partial mask.

As with the previous chapter, the text of the page's title ('Chapter 9: Social Structure') is partially obscured by the images and their arrangement on the page. Throughout the work, as the chapters

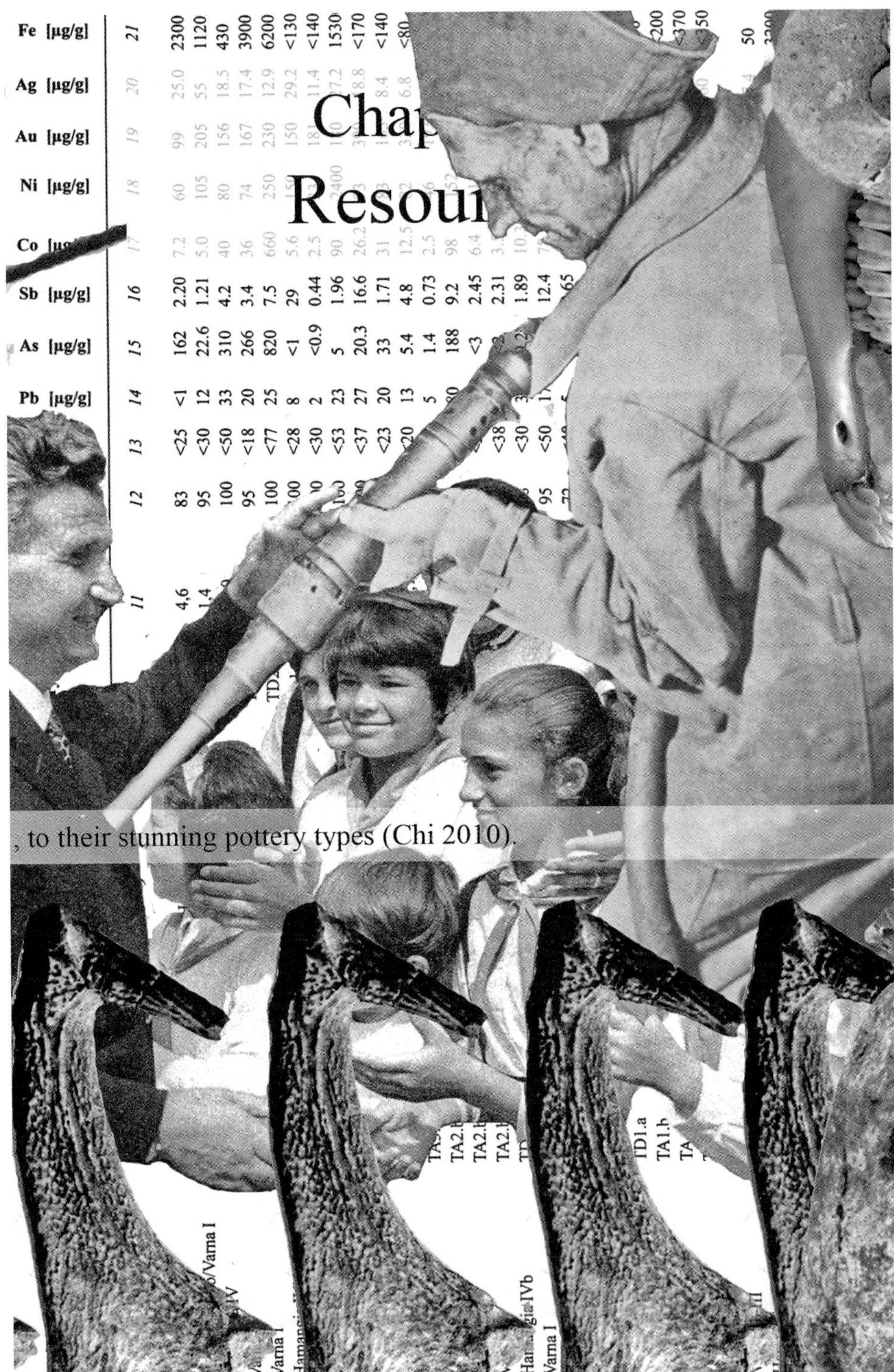

8.7 *Which ruins do we valorize? A new calibration curve for the Balkan past, p. 222 (Bailey 2014b).*

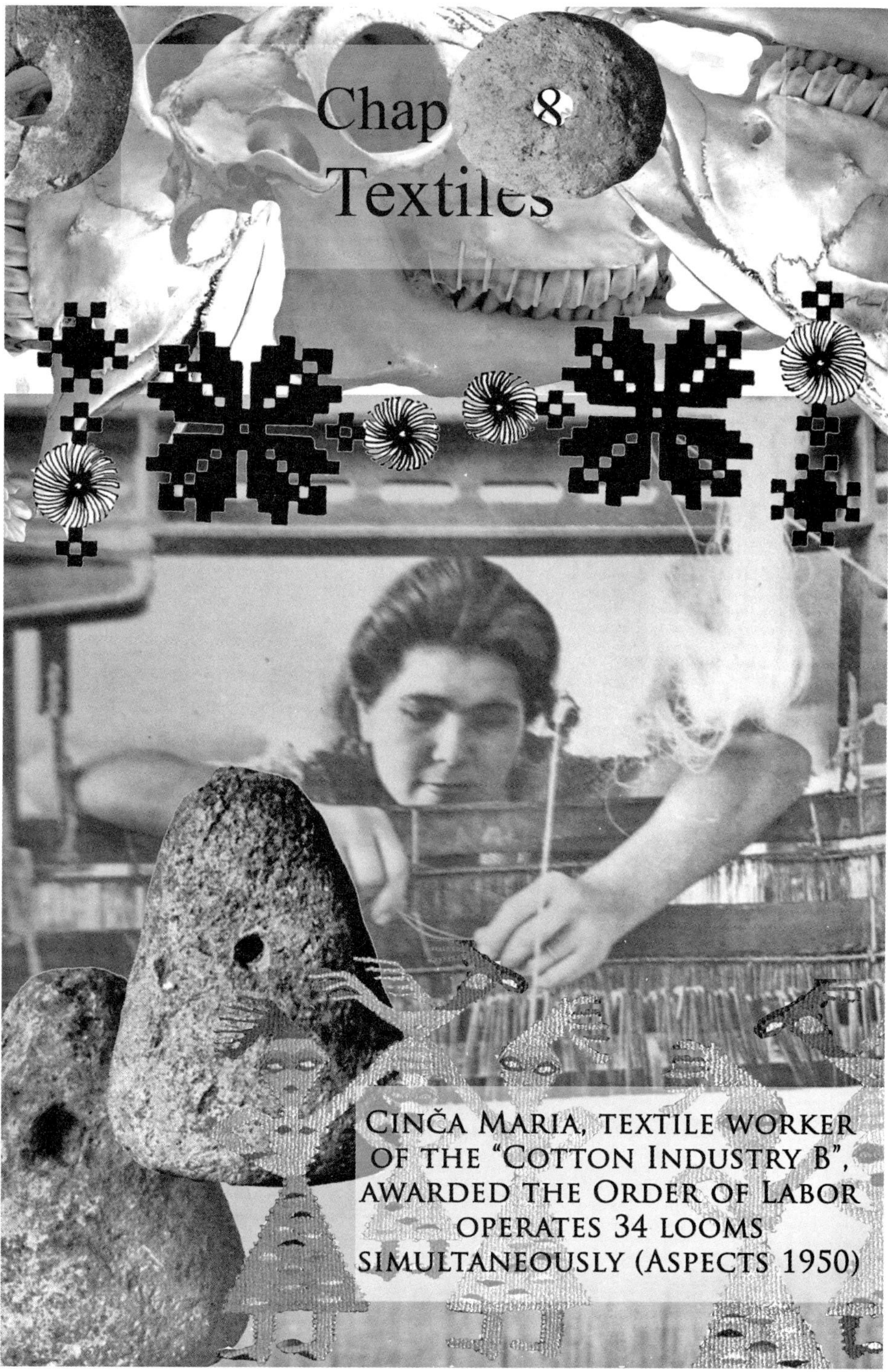

8.8 *Which ruins do we valorize? A new calibration curve for the Balkan past*, p. 223 (Bailey 2014b).

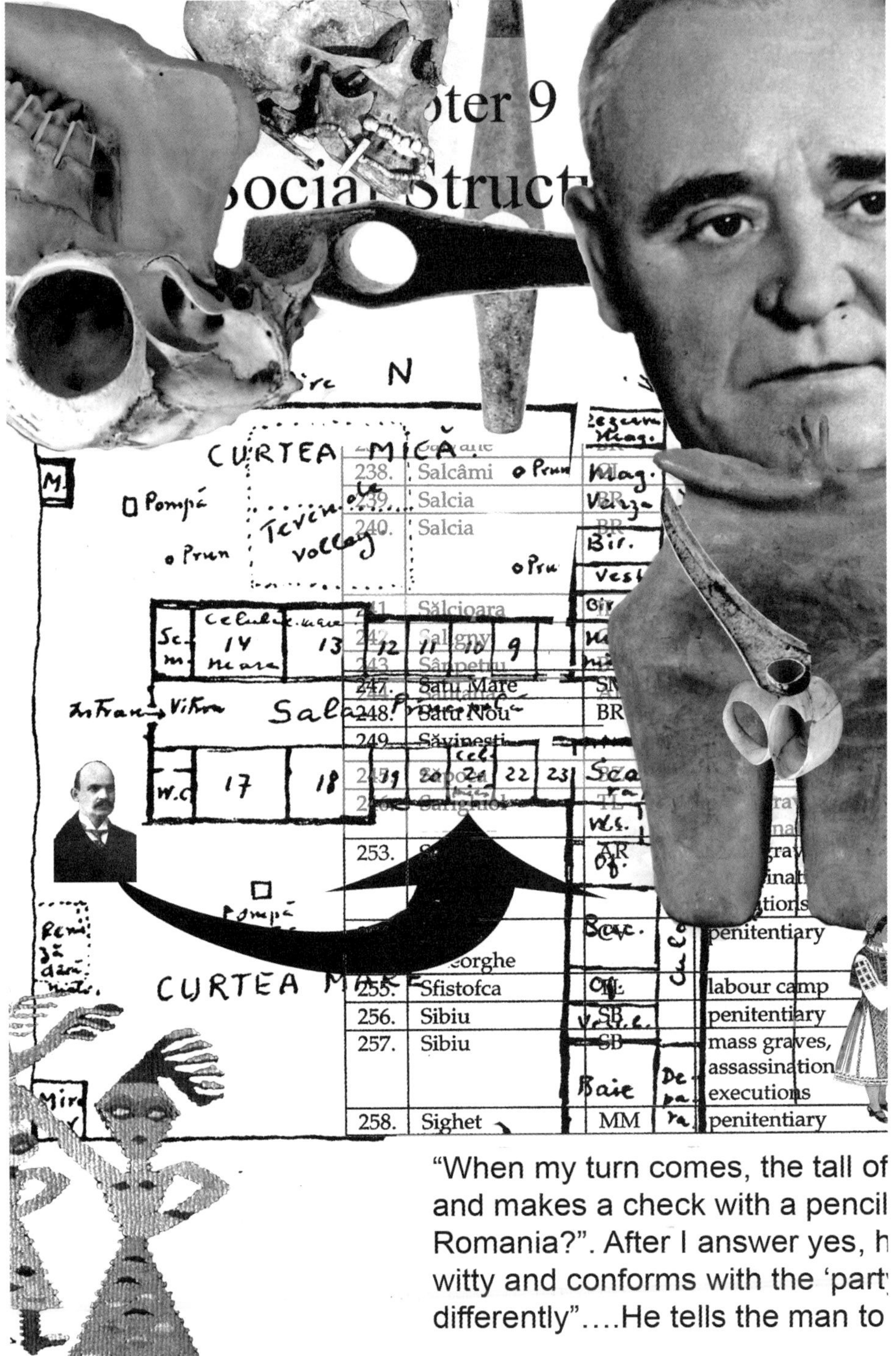

8.9 *Which ruins do we valorize? A new calibration curve for the Balkan past, p. 224 (Bailey 2014b).*

Chapter 10
Cultural Identity

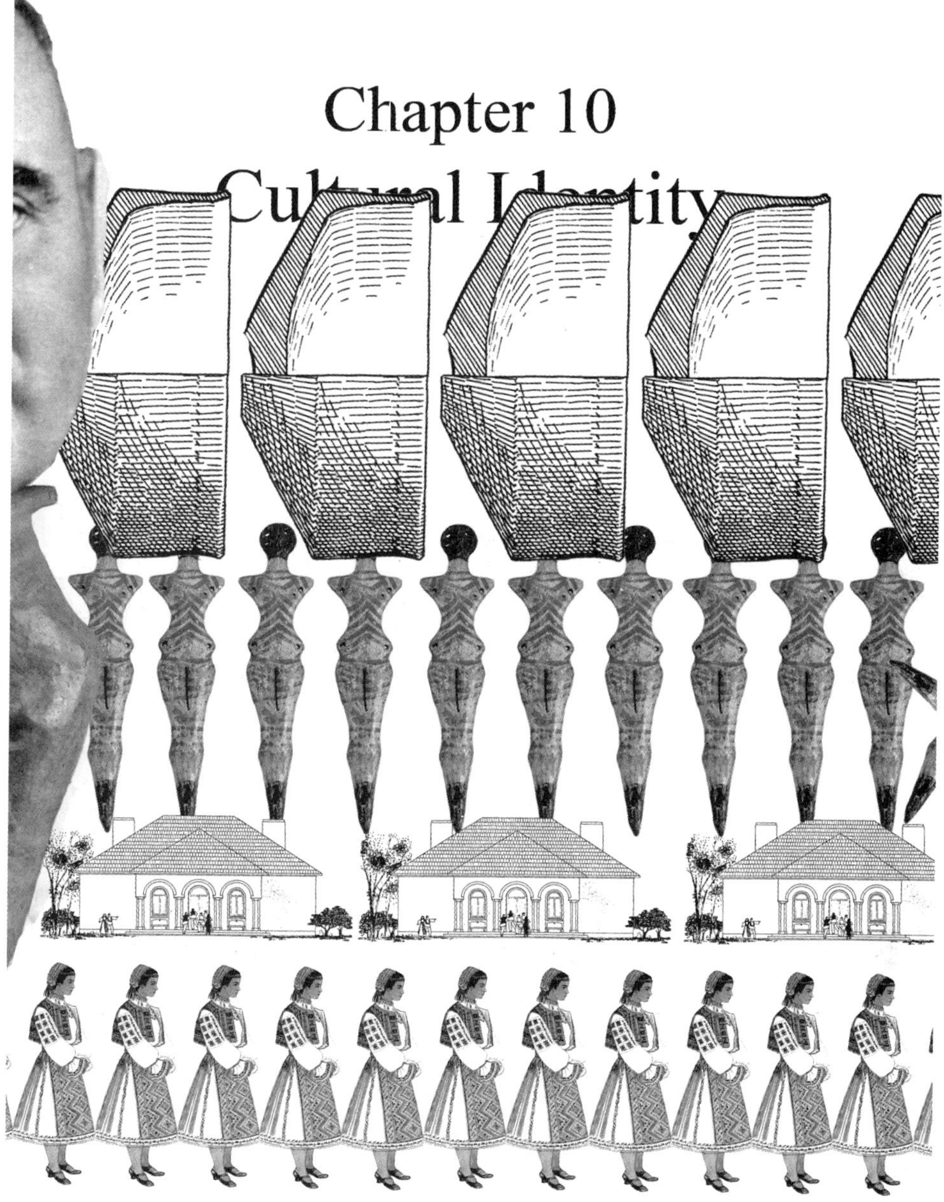

ficer asks me what my name is. I tell him; he looks on the list
, then he asks again: "Are you the author of the History of
e considers it appropriate to make a remark that he thinks is
y line': "Nowadays the history of Romania is written
take me to Cell 21 on the first floor." (C. Giurescu 1994)

8.10 *Which ruins do we valorize? A new calibration curve for the Balkan past, p. 225*
(Bailey 2014b).

proceed, the images increasingly dominate the printed space and the standard archaeological classificatory topics; the text loses its position and capacity to communicate. Images (and their arrangement) are the medium; increasingly, text emerges as less capable of doing the work that I want to complete: to provoke and stimulate the audience. If used at all (as on the Social Structure page), words appear as found text, as if they were an artefact that I found, selected, cropped, and deployed in a larger, looser production.

Along the left margin of the next page, 'Chapter 10: Cultural Identity' (another standard theme in archaeological research) appears the rest of the Gheorghiu-Dej-anthropomorphic-pot-erect-genitalia image. Along the bottom of the page continues the found text from Constantin Giurescu and his encounter with the Sighet Prison guard. The remainder of this page consists of four horizontal lines of multiples, arranged one line above another: first, a line of multiples of Neolithic open-shaped bowls (pottery-shape similarity is a common way for many archaeologists – particularly Romanian ones – to identify the ethnic character of prehistoric peoples); next, a line of Neolithic, fired, painted clay anthropomorphic figures (another standard marker proposed by archaeologists for prehistory identities); then, facades of state-sanctioned, twentieth-century buildings designed for the rebuilding of Romania as a modern state in the post-war period; and finally a found image of a woman in twentieth-century regional folk costume (styles of which are often used to promote and identify ethnic or regional identities). In total, the page contrasts the regimented identification of standards in object form, body shape, building plans, and dress (i.e., the horizontal multiples) with the reality of one man's identity (a history professor) as that identity is turned from a member of civilian society to that of outcast and criminal (i.e., the Giurescu text).

The penultimate page ('Chapter 11: Conclusion') continues the juxtaposition of Neolithic and twentieth century: another horizontal line of bowl multiples running across the page; several Neolithic figures (the same ones which lined up so regularly on the previous montage-page) now tumble and spin, as if out of control. A huge industrial crane dominates the rest of the page. From its hook hangs a heavy chain holding up a map of modern Romania and a portrait of Nicolae Ceauşescu: both map and totalitarian leader are constructions, projects of industrial scale. Angling up and to the right from the bottom of the page is a piece of 1964 found text from Gheorghiu-Dej about the role that architects and construction workers play in Romania's 'aspiration for peace'. Above that text I placed a photograph of Bucureşti during the period when Ceauşescu's rebuilding of the city when he razed large parts of the historic centre to make way for his vision of a modern urban world. The montage contrasts the reality of the building of a modern Romania, especially by Ceauşescu, which was founded on the destruction of its old core, with the chaotic tumbling Neolithic figures; in both worlds, the past and the present are managed, manipulated, used, and repositioned.

At the centre of the final montage-page, I placed an image of the first page of the 1976 law that underwrote Ceauşescu's grand plan: the *sistematizarea* or systemization of the nation that called for a huge increase in the number of urban centres, the relocation of the populace from the countryside to the cities, the destruction of villages, and the construction of apartment blocks and the centralization of services. Behind the found text of the law, there continues the horizontal march of the Neolithic pot multiples (though now almost completely obscured by the twentieth-century plans). To the left of the law-text are floor-plans of buildings: one a Late Neolithic village; the other, one storey in a twentieth-century tower block. Also below the image of the law there continue the multiples of women in regional folk dress, marching in exact similarity to each other,

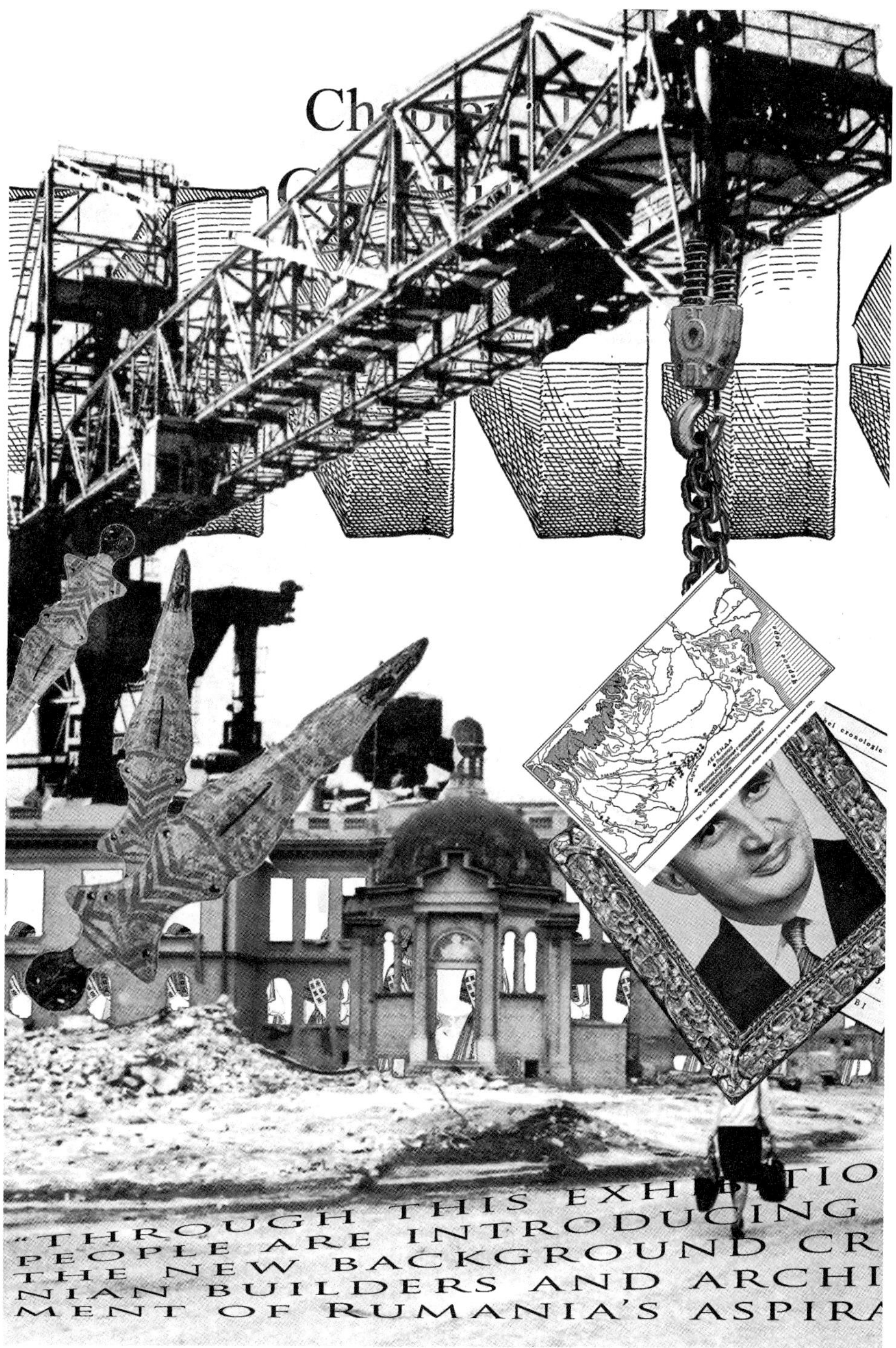

8.11 *Which ruins do we valorize? A new calibration curve for the Balkan past, p. 226 (Bailey 2014b).*

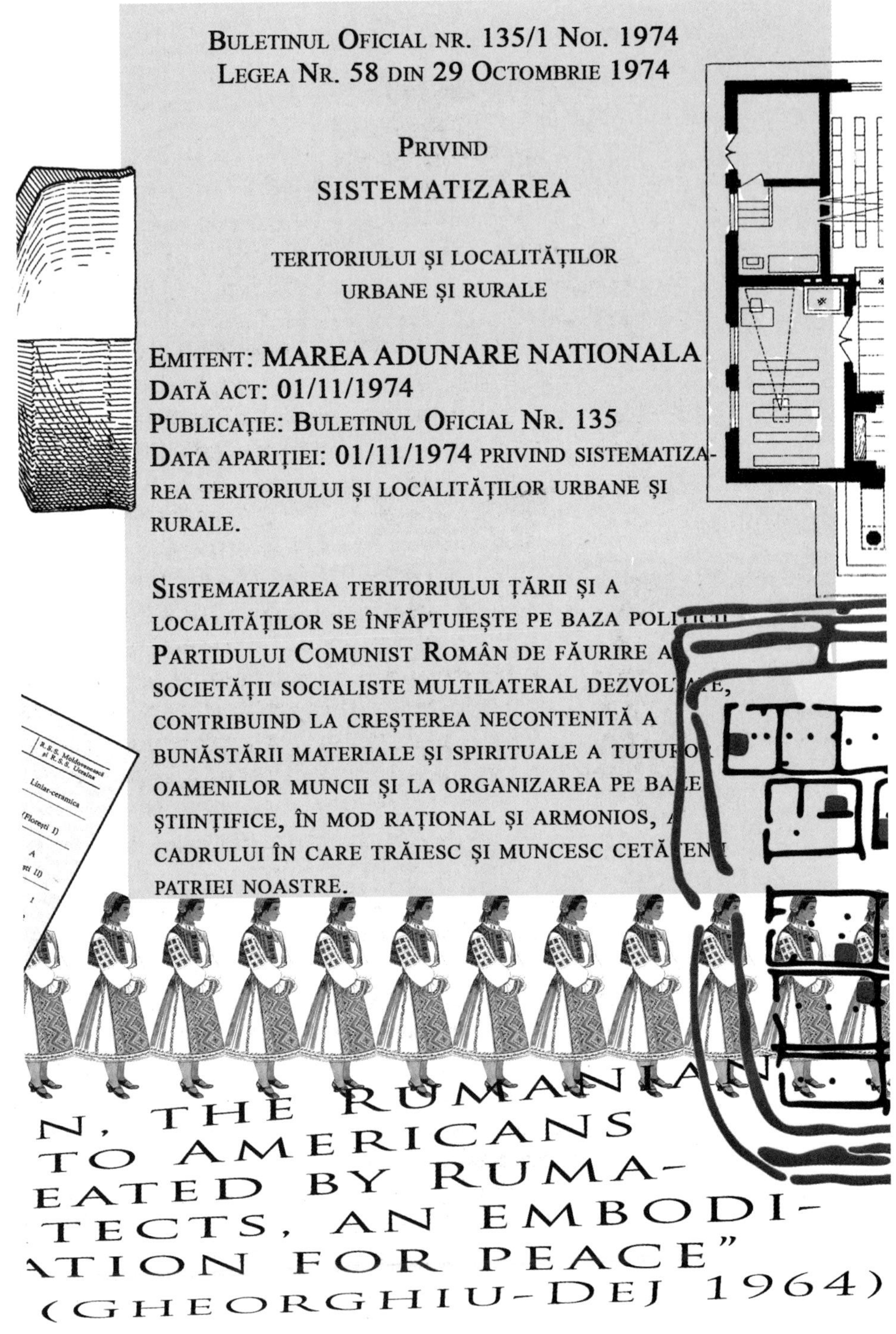

8.12 *Which ruins do we valorize? A new calibration curve for the Balkan past, p. 227 (Bailey 2014b).*

moving onward to the right. At the bottom of the page is the final portion of the Gheorghiu-Dej 1964 text about the role that architects and construction workers play in the aspirations of modern Romania.

Intent

Though many subtle contractions and juxtapositions lurk in each of the individual montage-pages of *Which ruins…*, my intention was to create a continuously running scene that brought together important elements from two vastly separate periods: the Neolithic (6,500–3,500 BC) and the middle and third quarter of the twentieth century. In making the work, the scenes unfolded and took form as I found images and texts both in my own library but also in the library of the Hoover Institute at Stanford University. I started with my personal thoughts about these two periods, about each of which I already had some knowledge, but then I dug deeper into both eras. Through all of it, I was faced with a slowly forming question: why do we hold up the Neolithic period of this region as such a major step forward in human cultural, economic, and technological achievement, but we castigate the late twentieth century as a failed step backwards through totalitarian crises?

In all of this, there was (and remains) no overt political statement about the Ceaușescu regime or judgment about its repressive and dictatorial practices; nor is there an explicit glorification about the wonders of the Neolithic. I wanted to make the reader/viewer think about how we address these two periods in different ways and make different judgements about them. I wanted to ask the viewers (and to provoke them to ask themselves) about the processes and practices that shape our perceptions of different historic periods, whether that is the Neolithic, the second half of the twentieth century, or beyond. Hence the full title of the montage-chapter: 'Which ruins do we valorize? A new calibration curve for the Balkan past'. Calibration is a potent archaeological word and concept, used in relation to correcting naturally occurring errors in estimations of radiocarbon dates; with the term calibration comes a recognition that the past (both Neolithic and twentieth century) is not as straightforward or objective as it may appear.

The other theme that provided direction for the work was an acceptance (now common among reflective and critical archaeologists) that we (historians and archaeologists) construct the past, and that we construct it in the context of modern, contemporary debates, and under political pressures, and within certain economic and social conditions. I aimed to present this sense most clearly in the chapter's title image. Here, I started with a Romanian postage stamp (stamps as common, nation-based, mass-produced images of constructed cultural identities); the one that I used was a portrait of Gheorghe Gheorghiu-Dej. I added the title of the chapter to the stamp. After that, the main work was replacing most of Gheorghiu-Dej's face with a mixture of archaeological objects from the Neolithic (all of which featured in the montage-pages): flint blades, animal skulls, *spondylus* arm-rings, anthropomorphic pottery vessels, copper axes, bone digging-sticks.

9

Avoiding meaning: Non-figurative painting and non-interpretive archaeologies

Archaeology and the construction of interpretation

The goal of archaeological action is to understand what happened in the past, when and where, and especially why it happened: what were the causes for the effects seen in the traces of behaviour uncovered and recorded during excavation. Archaeologists see themselves (and the public sees them) as certified expert authorities trained to deploy sets of skills honed through experience in field, laboratory, and library. This goal is part of a larger project to inform others (often assumed to be the public, though more accurately other archaeological professionals and students) about past intent and action. Determining the when, where, how, and why of past behaviours and events is the contribution to human knowledge by which readers, reviewers, and academic examiners judge archaeological output; does the work that is produced add to the knowledge that exists about a particular people in a particular place at a particular time?

The best work in the last forty years of archaeological output has shown that there exists no single, prioritized way to know or see the past. Few now question the understanding that the past itself is a construction made by archaeologists. In this sense, archaeology is the creation and use of the past in the present. Such usage can be political, as seen in the ways that it creates versions of history and prehistory that benefit one constituency and disenfranchise others. In this way, archaeology serves to support (or deny) territorial (and thus social, political, and economic) claims about which particular group of people occupied which particular region earliest, and thus who holds the rights of occupation or resource exploitation. Examples are widespread, from confrontations that set indigenous communities against colonizers, to unresolvable arguments about the rights to settle in purported religious homelands.

Recognizing that archaeologists create the past in the present requires a reassessment of the value that interpretation holds as the central product of archaeological action. This reassessment forces a re-examination of the ways that archaeologists go about their work, and of the consequences of what many assume are the objective, non-interpretive output of field and laboratory work. There is nothing new in the recognition that the act of interpretation happens before an excavation or survey begins, though many continue to assume that interpretation is something that happens after the fact, after the analyses are completed, during some disparate and culminating 'writing up' process. On the contrary, each decision about recovery method, sample size, site location, recording strategies, size and demographic make-up of excavation team, and every other element of a field project fixes important conditions about how much (and what type of) material (and information) will be recovered, and how much time and money will be required to do so. In line with archaeology's standards of best practice, explicitly identifying these variables at the start of a project is the way to successfully meet that project's aims and objectives. The consequence, however, is that making these decisions at the start of work (and almost always before work begins) defines and sets borders that constrain and shape the types of knowledge that a project will produce.

The problem with measurement

Measurement is one of the definitive characteristics of archaeological action, whether as it applies to the precise location of an artefact within a site grid, the location of one artefact to another within a feature, the location of one site within a landscape and with respect to other sites, or whether measurement is taken along other scales: chronologic, ecologic, evolutionary, or socio-economic. Measurement is at the core of archaeological work: it brings order out of chaos, and allows both archaeologist and the public to understand and to see what happened when and where in the past and to recognize how it relates both to other moments of the past and to our moment in the contemporary present. Precise measurement (of object, of landscape, of constituent material elements, and perhaps most centrally, of time) is at the core of methodologies in the field and laboratory. So much archaeological action is measurement-based that many would argue that field and laboratory archaeologies are at their bases quantitative processes. Though measurement is essential to archaeology, it is equally a problem that conditions and limits what archaeological action produces.

At a metaphysical level, the primacy of constructing the past through the measurement of its ephemeral traces and physical remains spiritually determines the shape and character of what archaeology creates. Contrary to common assumption, and regardless of the level of precision employed (e.g., millimetres, nano-particles, molecules), quantitative measurement is not an objective process. As employed at each level of archaeological action, decisions that are made about the scale of measurement and of analysis determine the types of data recovered and, thus, the types of reconstructions of past behaviour that can emerge. Further, decisions about scales of measurement determine the types of interpretations that one can offer to explain how and why, how, when, and where past events happened.

At this ontological level, and in a dangerous way, the actions of measurement reduce and confine the complexities of realities that archaeologists record. At the simplest level, maps, photographs, and site plans reduce the three-dimensional things to two-dimensional ones; even digital data that create three-dimensional or virtual reality reconstructions are, at their core, the transformation of otherwise random relations of materials in space recorded along a limited number of spatial dimensions: most often only three (x-, y-, and z-axes), with the potential addition of a fourth dimension (time).

Measurement as wave collapse

In all of this, archaeological measurement assumes (and at the same time creates and imposes) an inertia on a past that it presumes is unaffected or unaltered by the very actions of making record and image. Approaching measurement from the perspective of quantum theory raises objections to this standard way of archaeological thinking: measurement reduces complexity and prevents the recognition of alternative states of being that exist beyond those three (or four) dimensions. In line with the work started almost one hundred years ago by Werner Heisenberg,[1] quantum theorists would redefine the archaeological actions of measurement in terms of what they call the collapse of the wave function: measurement interferes with the natural state of what is being measured.

A quantum approach sees all matter as co-existing in at least two states (primarily as wave and as particle). When an observer measures any phenomenon, that phenomenon collapses to one of the different states of being: specifically, the state of the observer. All other potential dimensions and states of existence are eliminated. When archaeological action measures matter (for example artefact, landscape, carbon isotope), it prevents that two-state-status from existing; one state is preferred at the cost of the other. To accept the existence and significance of wave function collapse, then, is to destabilize a central foundation of archaeological action: measurement. From a quantum position, one can see that other fundamental parts of archaeology similarly collapse multiple possibilities of reality: reconstruction reduces material complexity to comprehendible simplicity; interpretation reduces incidental, random, or contingent patterns to single (or multi-) cause sources.

What would happen, then, if we released the objects of the past from the imprisonment of archaeological measurement? What would happen to the chronologies, site-grids, stratigraphies, typologies, and interpretations if they were no longer locked into the restricted set of dimensions that archaeology mandates for its practice? What would happen if we abandoned the soothing comfort of the ordered and the precise, and, instead, embraced the chaos of the free-flowing and dynamic, and of an openness to possibilities and dimensions of reality that may exist beyond those recognized by (or, as argued above, actually created by) precise scientific measurement? Much has been written in archaeological literature about the agency of the artefact and about the application of a biological/biographic metaphor to material culture, yet so little has been gained from the potential for these attempts to breathe life into objects of the past. One might suggest it is not a great leap from the promotion of an agency-approach-to-artefacts to a quantum approach to the same. If archaeologists truly believe in the agency of material culture, then why does archaeology still trap those (supposedly wilful) objects, buildings, images, landscapes, and sites inside of the confines of measurement, interpretation, and archival captivity?

Much of what we see in the value of an art/archaeology is exploring the potential that comes with an abandonment of measurement (and the consequent limiting consequence of wave collapse), and with an embrace of a practice of archaeological action that releases the past from its conscription to objectivity and that lets the materials of the past follow their potentials to affect the viewer, reader, or exhibition visitor. Though not founded on quantum theory, art/archaeology aims to prevent the collapse that comes with measurement in archaeology. As an important consequence, art/archaeology is a call to dispense with interpretation, at least when that interpretation is delivered by the archaeologist-as-authority to the reader/museum-visitor-as-passive-consumer. If acts of interpretation are present in art/archaeology at all, then they occur as, when, and to the extent to which the viewer of the art/archaeological work so desires.

The goal of science is to make simple what is otherwise complex. To make something simple so that someone else (the public, the student, even other archaeologists) can understand it, however, requires a smoothing off of rough edges, and an elimination of the extraneous, peripheral, and epiphenomenal information, observations, and data. The standard goal is to provide the reader, public, and classroom audience with a coherent version of reality that they can easily consume. In that tradition, the interpretive process selects and promotes particular elements, patterns, and observations, and excludes others.

To get away from this type of interpretative mandate requires a recognition that there may not exist any stable interpretations at all; life is chaotic, whether that life is in the past or in the present. We argue that for the vast majority of time when modern humans have lived on this planet, they have accepted the world as chaotic. Our becoming modern (in biological and cognitive senses) has included learning how to find efficient shortcuts to knowing what is otherwise difficult to understand. We call those shortcuts understanding, explanation, and interpretation. The majority of people in the contemporary West desires the opposite of complexity and chaos. They desire something that they can consume quickly, so that they can move on to the next thing. The consequence, however, is that the complexities of detail and the immeasurability of the chaotic non-patterns of life are disassembled, ignored, and superficially paraphrased to suit the needs of the majority.

The role of the viewer/audience

One way to dispense with interpretation is to elevate the role of viewers and readers. Give them the opportunity to make their own ideas, to form their own opinions, to have their own reactions. Unfortunately, the chances of this shift in authority are slim; the majority of archaeologists see themselves as authorities on a particular topic, period, or region; theirs is the role of interpreter. From the perspective of an academic tradition, one sees the logic to their authority claims. Each archaeologist possesses a set of specific skills and deep knowledges. Each was the person at the excavation. Each has acquired and assimilated the radiocarbon dates, analysed the soil samples, and completed the pollen analysis. Each knows what animals lived in that place at that time, what the vegetation was, and how the climate was different from how they are today. Each knows how the river valley landscape formed, and what affect the deeper geology had on the soils that formed and the crops that could grow and the animals that could survive.

Without question in the past decade or two, a growing number of archaeologists have started to grant the viewer/reader control of this information, but only (and this is the vital threshold guarded by the gatekeepers of knowledge production) after the archaeologist has already sorted, assessed, assimilated, and packaged that data for them. In addition, and following the discussion above, the delivery of knowledge to the reader and viewer occurs long after the moment when the most powerful event of interpretation occurred: when the original project was planned, when scientific objectives were set, when methods were selected to meet those objectives, and when estimates were made of the type and form of the results that would be obtained by applying those methods.

What are the alternatives to interpretation in archaeology? One way to reframe archaeological action is to explore practices of disinterpretation. Disinterpretation is distinct, not only from interpretation, but more precisely from misinterpretation or non-interpretation or anti-interpretation. The prefix 'dis' inserts a sense beyond mere opposition to interpretation. It is more than just ignoring interpretation; it works in a space where interpretation never has existed. Disinterpretation is more than a passive stance that welcomes alternatives; it is an active project to undermine and disappear interpretation and the pursuit of meaning before they can attack and deflate the robust actions and objects of the past.

In the art world, a corresponding call for a disconnection of work from interpretation is louder and has been heard for longer than it has in archaeology, particularly over a century from the mouths of American artists and their drive to make non-figurative work: whether that is the abstract expressionism of Jackson Pollock or Barnett Newman, the ephemeral land art of Robert Smithson or Maya Lin, or the minimal art of Agnes Martin or Don Judd. A better equivalent of disinterpretation for an artist would be to recognize that a show is merely one step in an ongoing process and not an end or a summing up of work.

Examples of disinterpretation

In most of Doug's recent publications, exhibitions, and visual work, a central aim has been to intentionally avoid telling people what to think. One of the central intentions of his 2005 book about prehistoric figurines was to move the reader away from a desire for a single easily consumable answer to that topic's most common question: 'what does a prehistoric figurine mean?' In a series of subsequent publications, Doug has repeated and expanded that strategy. Many readers found this disinterpretive approach both provocative and exciting; others reacted less enthusiastically. The latter readership felt cheated of the expected (and desired) authoritative interpretation or explanation about how the figurines had been used or what they had meant to the people who made, handled, and discarded them 6,000 or so years ago.

Where Doug did suggest answers, he went little farther than the suggestions that each prehistoric figurine meant many different things to many different people in the past, but (and this was critical) also to many different people in the present, for example, people who go to a museum or who read the late Marija Gimbutas' influential books, or even to Marija Gimbutas herself. People want answers from archaeologists; they want to know solid, stable facts and explanations and function and meaning. When you suggest that the readers (and not the authors) are the authorities, that they should do the interpretive work themselves, that they need to take the time to reflect and respond and react to the material, then usually the result is that the readers are dissatisfied (at best) and angry (at worst). Regardless, they move off quickly to find some other text by someone more comfortable in their own ego (or professional need) to claim authority and to provide an easily consumed explanation; the reader then can gulp down whatever interpretation they can most easily find that suits their taste. In the case of prehistoric figurines, some prefer a goddess interpretation, others that the figurines were toys, or portraits, or guides to sexual education.

The Unearthed *exhibition*

In a more extended and specific challenge to interpretation in our engagement with prehistoric material, Doug attempted to disrupt what is normally expected as form and content of archaeological museum exhibition. In 2010, he curated a show at the UK's Sainsbury Centre for the Visual Arts in

Norwich (SCVA) and designed and created the show's accompanying catalogue. The original grant (won in collaboration with Simon Kaner at the University of East Anglia) was a large award for a project that compared prehistoric figurines from two chronological and geographically disparate cultures: the Neolithic communities of the Southeast European Neolithic and the Jōmon of Japan.

Doug's plans for the exhibition included abnormal and sometimes disturbing mixes of prehistoric artefacts and modern material culture (e.g., erotic images, 1950s Bild-Lilli dolls, bonsai trees). In the end, however, in the galleries and vitrines at SCVA, the exhibition failed to take advantage of the radical alternative proposed; the curators at the museum refused to allow a mix of the ancient and the modern. The objects from two different eras were kept in separate rooms. The museum was unadventurous, but also afraid. They couldn't (or wouldn't) leave the safety of the status quo of what was supposed to happen in an archaeological exhibit. Doug found this short-sighted and antithetical to making intellectually provocative work, particularly at the SCVA: a museum on a university campus and an institution that was more art-driven than archaeology-based.

The book that accompanied the exhibition, however, was more successful. It was produced without input from the curators at the SCVA, who only saw a final mock-up of the published volume when it was too late in the production stages to make any changes to it. To create the book's layout, Doug worked with a graphic designer (Jean Zambelli) who understood immediately what Doug wanted to do. Together they created a non-narrative, 200-page exhibition catalogue (though perhaps it is best understood as an 'anti-catalogue') that mixed images, texts, interviews, and objects in disruptive yet provocative and aesthetically engaging ways. Unusually, the book had no table of contents or scene-setting foreword, preface, or introduction, and no index. It contained no narrative trail for the reader to follow.

As readers turned each page, they were met with a new object or quotation or image, but with no clear connection with the contents of the preceding or following page. On their own, the readers had to pause and take the time to make whatever connection or sense they could make out of what was on the page, if indeed any connection was possible or intended. The goal was to face the reader with the same degree of disconnected chaos that faces the archaeologist at work: a disorganized, chaotic scramble of traces and objects. If there was a meaning or an interpretation or an explanation to be found about the two categories of prehistoric objects (the Jōmon dogū and the Balkan figurines), then that would come from the reader and not from Doug as the creator of the book.

The book did contain a glossary, though even here the intention was to foil expectations and avoid clarity. An otherwise normal concept such as 'the Neolithic' was defined in an unhelpful and subversive way: where a more traditional entry would have provided specific chronological and geographic terms, this glossary offered, 'An overgeneralization by arrogant academics from the industrialized western world'. The book bore the most traditional of titles (Unearthed: A Comparative Study of Jōmon Dogū and Neolithic Figurines) specifically aimed at attracting readers and researchers who were interested in the standard comparative approach. The goal was to invite them in and then let them react to the disinterpretive presentation of the material. As they turned the pages of the book, readers felt as if they were on a non-directional ride through unexpected territories that included the following disparate elements: 1970s US television shows, pornographic dioramas, Chinese scholars' rocks, and general or theoretical comments on portraiture as an art form. Also included were (carefully) rewritten emails from local University of East Anglia faculty experts; these email texts represented (in legally acceptable paraphrasing) the institution's reactions to the exhibition's original, disruptive proposal, and their arguments that Doug's plans *were unworkable and not appropriate for the museum. These redrafted internal documents showed (but didn't judge) the unresolved arguments and disagreement that went on behind the scenes during the exhibition planning phases.*

In the end, particularly in the action of the book, the project left the visitor and reader without a single or even multiple explanations for either the Japanese dogū or the southeast European figurines. Perhaps the book's cover best summed up the approach. At its centre is the body from a southeastern European figurine; where its head should be we positioned the decapitated head of a Barbie doll suspended from the end of a construction crane. Surrounding the figurine's body, were placed carpenters' and plumbers' tools and materials: wrenches and pliers; nuts, bolts, and screws. Speech bubbles come from Barbie's mouth: 'I am an ancestor', 'I am a mother', 'I am a portrait', 'I am a goddess', and 'I am a toy'. The intended message was that figurines and our understanding of them are constructions (i.e., they have no ultimate, original or definitive function or meaning), and that each of the main scholarly suggestions for interpretation is of equal potential value.

The problem with meaning in contemporary painting

How does interpretation operate in contemporary painting? In the archaeological sense a work could be interpreted, and that would be the job of an art historian once time has passed. In the everyday sense of the word meaning, the desire to interpret a painting takes the form of looking for its meaning. There is a widely held assumption that paintings have a meaning which can be revealed by the viewer through careful looking and an understanding of art history. This is certainly true of early European painting; religious images rely on iconography and a viewer's knowledge of it in order to construct the painting's narrative meaning. However, the great adventure in painting from the early twentieth century onwards has been abstraction. The decision to move away from depiction and verisimilitude led inevitably to the loss of meaning communicated in the traditional sense. Non-image-based painters are often asked of their work 'What does it mean?' or even 'What is it supposed to be?' Perhaps it is not such an unreasonable question, but any answer, rather than supplying the sought for meaning, tends to reveal the chasm separating the artist's intentions from the viewer's expectations.

The language of painting is primarily visual; to resort to spoken language to explain an artwork represents a failure of the visual language to communicate in the first place. This confusing situation is often the result of a misunderstanding of the intention and a misplaced expectation of what a contemporary painting is supposed to be and what it is supposed to do. An artist can talk about their work but they cannot really describe what it does. An attempt to describe this experience is notoriously difficult and is perhaps the sign that painting communicates in a unique way with its own vocabulary of mark, line, and colour. What it can do is bound entirely within its language. Any development of this language should hypothetically extend what a painting can do. The problem for anybody not fully up to date with current art theory is further confused by institutions' and museums' labelling of works, which offer explanations enabling a visitor to feel they know enough to move on to the next work. In fact, more often than not, these brief descriptions short-circuit the intention of the artist. What these labels can never do is to describe the sensory nature of an encounter with painting, which more than anything, is now the site of meaning.

Subjective measurement

Partly as a result of working on excavation sites, Simon's painting gradually shifted from a visual language rooted in the pictorial landscape tradition to one based in materiality. Measurement played an important role in this transition. The function of measurement in the making of a painting was not intended to provide objective data but to be subjective. Its role was a part of a strategy to connect a viewer with an artwork. Initially the artist worked with measurements and proportional relationships taken from his own body: the width of a hand, the length from fingertip to elbow and elbow to shoulder (the body, broken down, to provide numbers as a source for the dimensions of paintings).

Suggestions for the overall sizes, internal depths as well as the shapes of paintings came from dimensions of trenches and from fully excavated or sectioned pits and postholes. During the process of making a painting any initial set of dimensions could and often was modified to conform to the needs of the individual painting, much like the extension of a trench, to extend the exploration. Well-thought out measurements and proportions can relate the body of a viewer to the artwork, and thus establish an immediate and direct connection with the physicality of a work. The proportions of a painting are one of the fundamental elements we respond to and yet they are often taken for granted until the form of a painting deviates from the standard rectangle. Deviating from the accepted standard form is a way to establish new form.

Simon wanted to work on an excavation site in the landscape but wanted to resist depicting it in any conventional way. This created a dilemma in how to record the place. How could you make a painting if you were unable to record it visually? Over several seasons on the excavation sites of Segsbury Camp and Alfred's Castle, Simon was educated to understand landscape as material: an understanding close to that of the diggers in the trenches and away from the traditional pictorial conception of landscape as image. Sensitized to the realm of materiality, the artworks could be based on information gathered from the wide range of colour of excavated soils, from the textures of the pitted and stepped surfaces of a trench under excavation, or from its spatial depth.

All of this information came from another form of measuring. A significant turning point for the artist resulted from an internalization of the measuring process and an awareness that we (as painter or viewer) can be the measuring device with our senses collecting and storing data. We can use ourselves as a measuring tool of the physical world and how we relate to it. On site, the artist was fully engaged with all senses active and alert. This was precisely the condition that Simon wanted to encourage in a viewer of a finished work hanging on the wall. The ambition was for this viewer to be active and mobile in an encounter with a painting. At this point, the function of the painting is to involve the viewer, to engage their senses and to encourage an awareness of themselves in relation to the work. The objective function of measuring was given a subjective role with the aim of converting a passive position for the viewer to an active one.

The value of misinterpretation

Perhaps this way of thinking about measuring is an example of a misinterpretation of the purpose of its use in field archaeology. As an artist, Simon is aware that he is the only individual on an excavation site permitted to misinterpret. For an artist, misinterpretation is a valuable tool. The dialogue carried out on site by archaeologists, involving the diggers or not, is to look at and discuss a problem from all sides and to weigh up all possibilities. The artist, on the other hand, must grasp whatever emerges from a dig or from a conversation as a clue whether it is a correct or an incorrect understanding. Sometimes the clues can be highly marginal to the growing, central narrative of the site; nevertheless, they must be explored. In art-making, often the only way forward is to break the rules, to critique what has come before and propose an alternative view.

10

Country Register (Simon Callery, 2018)

For two weeks every summer from 2013 to 2018, I travelled up to North Wales for the excavations at Moel-y-Gaer, Bodfari, an Iron Age hill fort situated in the Clwydian Range in Denbighshire. The excavation was directed by Gary Lock and John Pouncett, from the School of Archaeology, University of Oxford. The diggers were a combination of a core team that had dug with Gary for a number of years and local volunteers who would come in each day.

Moel-y-Gaer, Bodfari

It was good to be back on an Iron Age site and good to be back in Wales. On a personal level it meant a lot to me as I had been a student at art college in Cardiff, South Wales, in the early 1980s. My first proper studio as a young artist was in Butetown, in the Cardiff docks, and I was a Gold Medal prize winner in Fine Art at the National Eisteddfod in 1986. This particular part of North Wales occupies a significant place in British art history. The Welsh painter Richard Wilson (1714–82), who is recognized as one of the first artists to use landscape as a subject in its own right, had lived at Llanferres, eight miles south of Bodfari. He was an important influence on a young JMW Turner, whose first independent painting trip, at the age of seventeen, took him up through Wales in 1792. Conditions on Moel-y-Gaer were close to perfect for working in the landscape. From the top of the hill unobscured views lead the eye ten miles north to the Irish Sea, to the south along the Clwydian Hills and west over the Denbigh Moors to Snowdonia on the horizon line. Standing on the hill and looking out, it is possible, with a slight tilt of the head, to relate the features of the hill fort to the surrounding landscape. This way of looking mirrors an important aspect of the painting process: where attention to detail must always be held in balance with an awareness of its relationship to the whole. The cultural and geographical features of this area of North Wales created an ideal context to challenge the conventions of landscape-based painting.

I always found the seasonal nature of the university excavations worked really well with the rhythm of the art-making process. The excavation period is intense and it is the right moment to produce as much material as possible without being too critical. This is followed by a long period back in the studio to think it all through and to begin to make work in a controlled environment before going back on site the following season. This pattern had worked well on previous digs but I was now ambitious to close the gap between the site and the studio. I wanted to be as direct as I could. I wanted to align the painting process as closely as possible with the excavation process

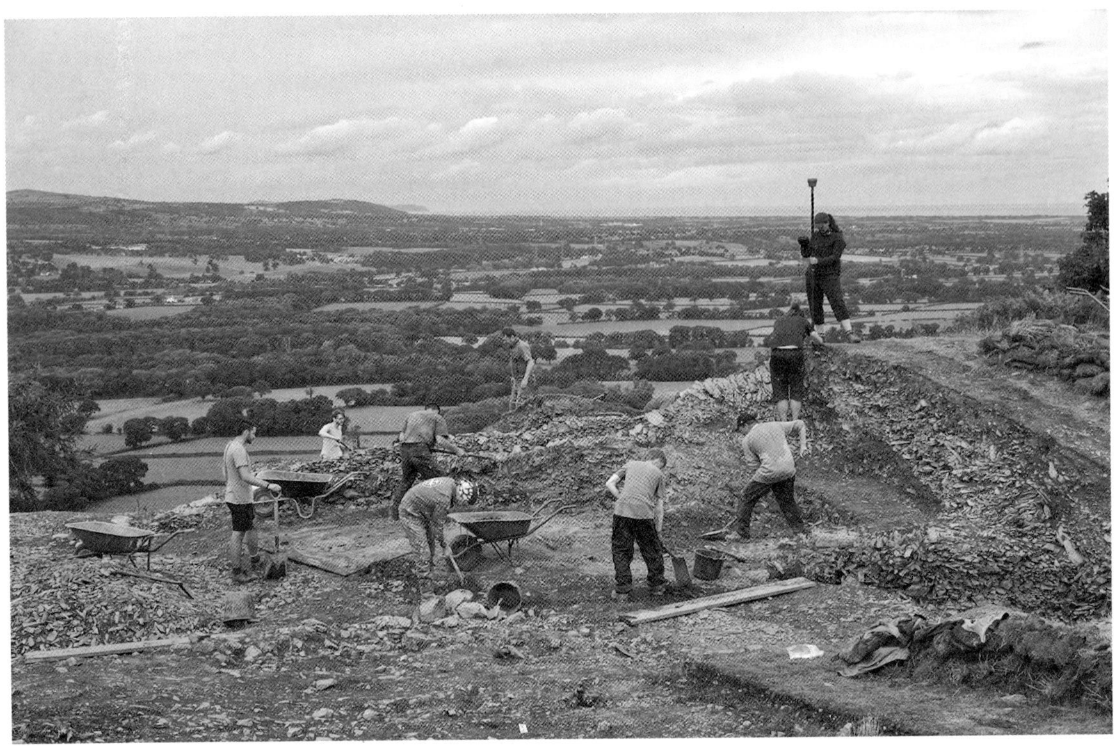

10.1 *Moel-y-Gaer, Bodfari. Excavation site. 2018.*

and to produce paintings under the same conditions as the diggers as they worked. These were some of the new ideas for the Bodfari dig, which I wanted to combine with others from a previous project.

Stonehenge Riverside Project

A few years earlier in 2008 I had been involved in the *Art + Archaeology, Stonehenge Riverside Project*, organized by Helen Wickstead. I was one of a number of artists in residence during the excavations at Stonehenge led by Mike Parker Pearson. We had limited access to the monument itself so we based ourselves above it by the cursus on Lark Hill, next to trenches supervised by Julian Thomas. From here we had a view onto the processional avenue and the rise in the land up to the stone circle. The resulting works were the first paintings I made with unstretched canvas and with an internal space. They were made in response to the experience of walking amongst the stones, which are set out in a sequence of alternating mass and void. The paintings present a solid and blocklike front face which dissolves away as you move across them to the side to look inside. The dimensions I used for these paintings were derived from architectural principles of a later date, Le Corbusier's Modulor, a scale of proportions based on the human body. I produced three large-scale paintings; *Wiltshire Modulor (small)*, *Wiltshire Modulor* and *Wiltshire Modulor Double Void*. I had begun to question some of the conventional physical elements of painting by removing

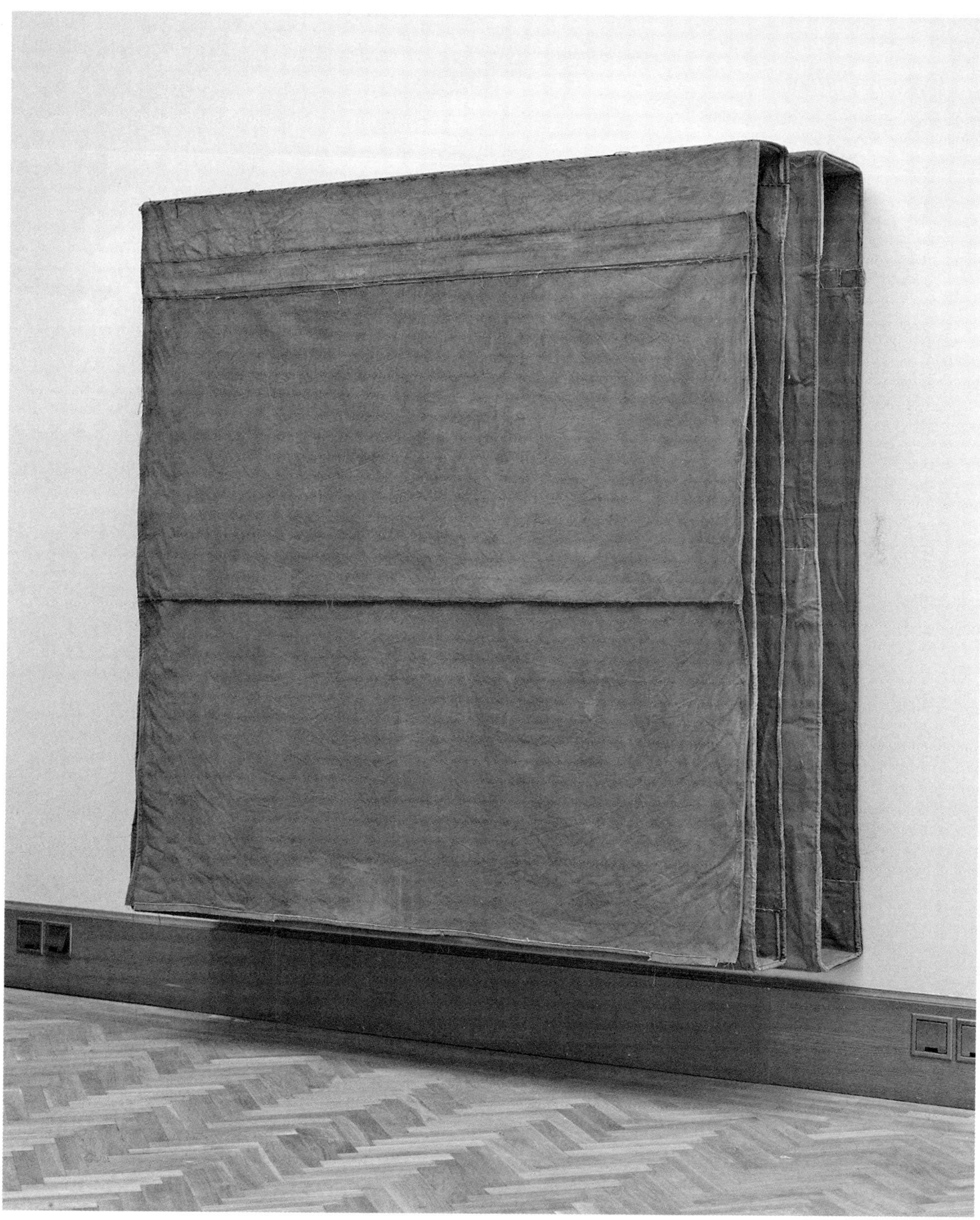

10.2 *Simon Callery. Wiltshire Modulor. 2010–13. Distemper, canvas, wood, thread, cord and steel brackets. 240 x 240 x 60 cm.*

the wooden stretcher and by constructing an internal space. I wanted to develop some of these ideas at Bodfari but this time in closer proximity to the archaeological surfaces, something I was unable to do at Stonehenge.

Preparing the materials

In preparation for the first season, I cut a fifty-metre roll of cotton duck canvas into three-metre lengths. I washed it all to rinse out the starch and to soften the fabric. A three-metre length is the maximum I can handle when it comes to the distemper painting process and the maximum practical length for carrying about in the landscape. I filled a box with 2 kg bags of dry pigments; mars black, mars yellow, caput mortuum, burnt umber, red oxide, and a 10 kg bag of rabbit skin glue as the binder for the paint. For practicality, which is a major concern when working outside the studio, I decided to limit the range of pigment to iron-based earths only. Restricting materials does not always imply a restriction on what can be achieved creatively. I knew that this particular choice of earths, when mixed, would give me a wide range of greens, yellows, and reds. In another box, I packed all the other painting equipment: sponges, brushes, knives, scissors, buckets, and my drawing kit.

Looking for clues

By the time I got to Bodfari, I had already worked on many other sites. I had come to understand an archaeological excavation site as an emphatically physical and ever-changing sculptural environment, created by a team of field archaeologists. Sites are rich in form, colour, texture, material, and the excavation processes; field drawings and recording methods, are fascinating for an artist. These are places where time and material (central concerns for the painter) come together most convincingly with past and present human activity. Although I was familiar with excavation sites, it did not make it any easier to know what to do, when working on a new one. Each site has its own individual characteristics and it is essential to allow them to shape the work as much as possible.

Once the turf and topsoil had been removed, the diggers worked in a line trowelling down to the archaeological surface before focusing on individual features. The exposed iron-rich colour of the soils and the sub-soils at Bodfari guided my first move. I mixed up buckets of coloured distemper, which I sponged into the lengths of canvas laid out in a field at the bottom of the hill. I was not trying to reproduce the colour of these soils precisely. I was trying to get close to its intensity, to get the painting process up and running and to open a connection with the site through colour. I established a pattern of work. I would colour the canvases close to where we were camping and while they were drying I would come up the hill and hover about the trenches listening to the diggers discussing the archaeology and the excavation process and sit with them during breaks to learn more. I used the camera to document the activities and walked the site from trench to trench, getting to know the terrain. Once the canvases had dried, I would roll them and carry them up the hill. At the end of each working day, when it was quiet, I started to lay them

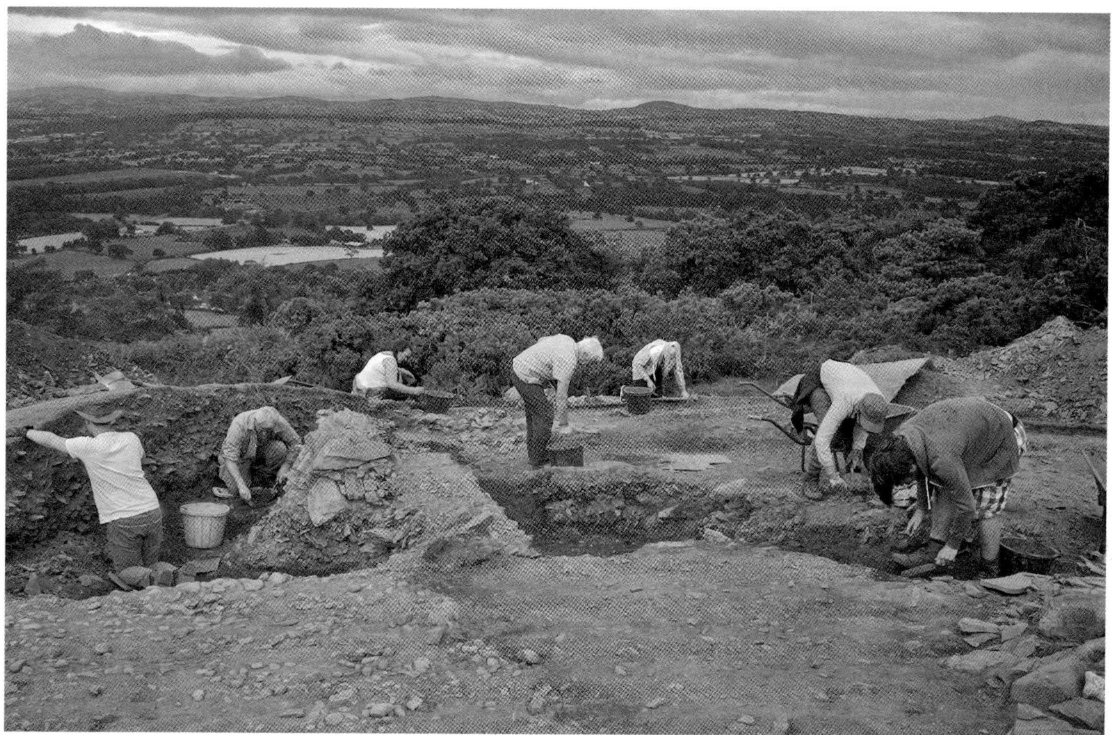

10.3 *Moel-y-Gaer, Bodfari. Excavation site. 2018.*

out on the trenches to figure out ideas for the dimensions and proportions for paintings. This seemed to be a step in the right direction. Once I had put a canvas on a trench it became clear to me that they should be worked there.

Finding a way to be direct

My intention was to find a way to be as direct as I could. I was not interested in making an image of this place. I want to work with it physically and find another way to record it. I was now convinced that the paintings had to be made from canvases marked in contact with the surfaces of the trenches. During the early phases of the dig, I was constantly on the lookout for trenches that I could work on. There were some trenches I would never get on as they would be under excavation season after season. Others were inaccessible, as they were on the steep slope of the ditch rising up to and through the stone rampart, with delicate and unstable surfaces. The most promising ones were on the relatively flat land within the hill fort enclosure, placed there to investigate evidence of occupation. Those trenches suited my purposes best and they contained a wide range of features and surfaces.

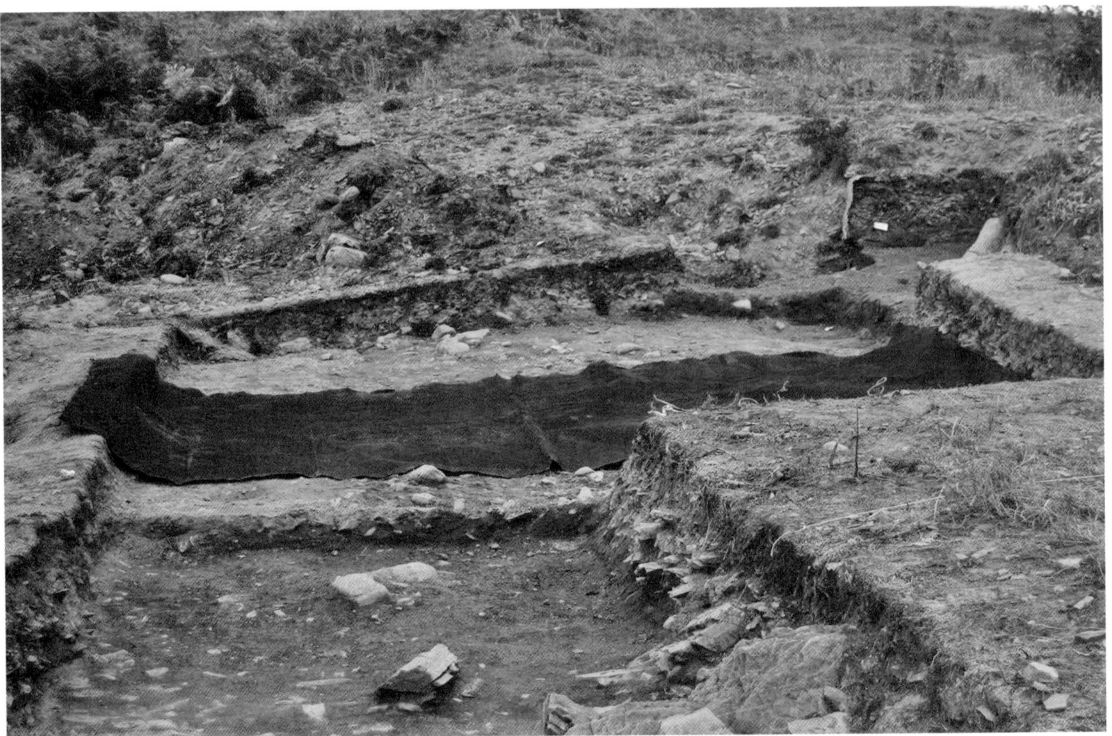

10.4 *Working process; canvas laid on trench. Moel-y-Gaer, Bodfari. 2015.*

Archaeological trench as framing device

To a painter, an archaeological trench appears quite familiar. It behaves as a rectangular framing device or a window onto the surfaces and archaeological features it contains. Visually it operates in a similar way to a stretched canvas supporting and framing the painted marks. What is unfamiliar is the spatial complexity of the excavated surface and the realization that the impressions and voids left by the material that had been removed are of equal importance to what remains. As I watched the diggers at work, I was beginning to think how to find a way to incorporate those less-familiar elements in the painting.

Working on paintings in excavated trenches

As soon as a trench had been excavated and recorded, I had my opportunity. I would throw down a length of my coloured canvas. Crawling across the sheet on my hands and knees with graphite, scissors, and knife, I marked, punctured, and cut the fabric where I could feel a contact with the surface underneath. It could be the edges of an excavated feature or where a section had been dug to a deeper level or stones from the ramparts, tree throws, roots, or loose shattered rock accumulating on the bedrock. If I encountered a large feature, I would draw and cut around the circumference and then throw the detached piece of canvas to one side. As I worked my way across the canvas I concentrated on my left hand as it moved over the cloth scouting out the forms to register, then onto my right hand marking the cloth, first with the graphite and then puncturing it with the knife. Once I had a puncture hole, I could then get the point of the scissors into the fabric to cut it more. It felt strangely collaborative, as if the archaeological surface was offering me material to record, through the medium of the canvas sheet.

The process was direct and of the moment. I worked fast and with urgency. In that situation, the quality of the marks depended on being efficient and expedient. The aesthetic of the cuts and marks are a by-product of getting this balance right. I found that if I paused for a second to consider the aesthetic of the mark I was making, then I risked my chances of getting what I wanted. Although I worked at pace, I never ripped the canvas. A rip would destroy the quality of the drawn line or the precision and placement of a cut hole. Speed had become a useful tool for the creative process. From my point of view, the faster the better, as it impacted my decision making and made me work in new ways. The weather was always a factor. If it started to rain or got windy, I sped up. I chose to carry out this work at the end of the working day when all the diggers had left the site. I needed to be alone and completely focused. I would not stop until I got all the way across the sheet.

One part of a trench might have been excavated more deeply than another. In a fully excavated trench, you may have many different levels ranging from a feature completely dug out and down to the natural next to an undug area where there is no archaeology at all. Formally, it appears to be a geometry or pattern working itself out. I see it in terms of a composition, and I relate the details to the whole. I am interested in how an archaeologist manages such a surface. For a painter, this has meaning, because a painter needs to manage and organize surfaces. A surface needs to be broken down into manageable parts. When I worked in a trench with clear signs of internal divisions, I would make a decision straight away and cut my large sheet down immediately.

Moel-y-Gaer was on private land so at the end of each marking and cutting session I could leave my canvases out on site. There was no need to carry the pile down at the end of the day. I would roll it up or fold it. Overnight water would get inside and puddle there along with a variety of molluscs and insects, who had also found a way in. The distemper would dissolve away in those patches. This was a factor I could not control, and it worried me. All sorts of unpredictable things could happen. One evening inquisitive cattle got through a break in the fence and onto the hill fort. The next day I found my canvas had been trampled. I began to realize that working outside meant that my work would get wet and would be blown about by the wind and end up in the gorse bushes. Contact with the elements had to be accommodated. Once I had accepted this, it was not such a big step to recognize how the weather could be useful and do some of the work for you, in particular, with the softening of the canvas. If you compare a studio-based painting to a painting made outside the studio in the landscape the difference is evident; they might be from the same family but they have completely different characters.

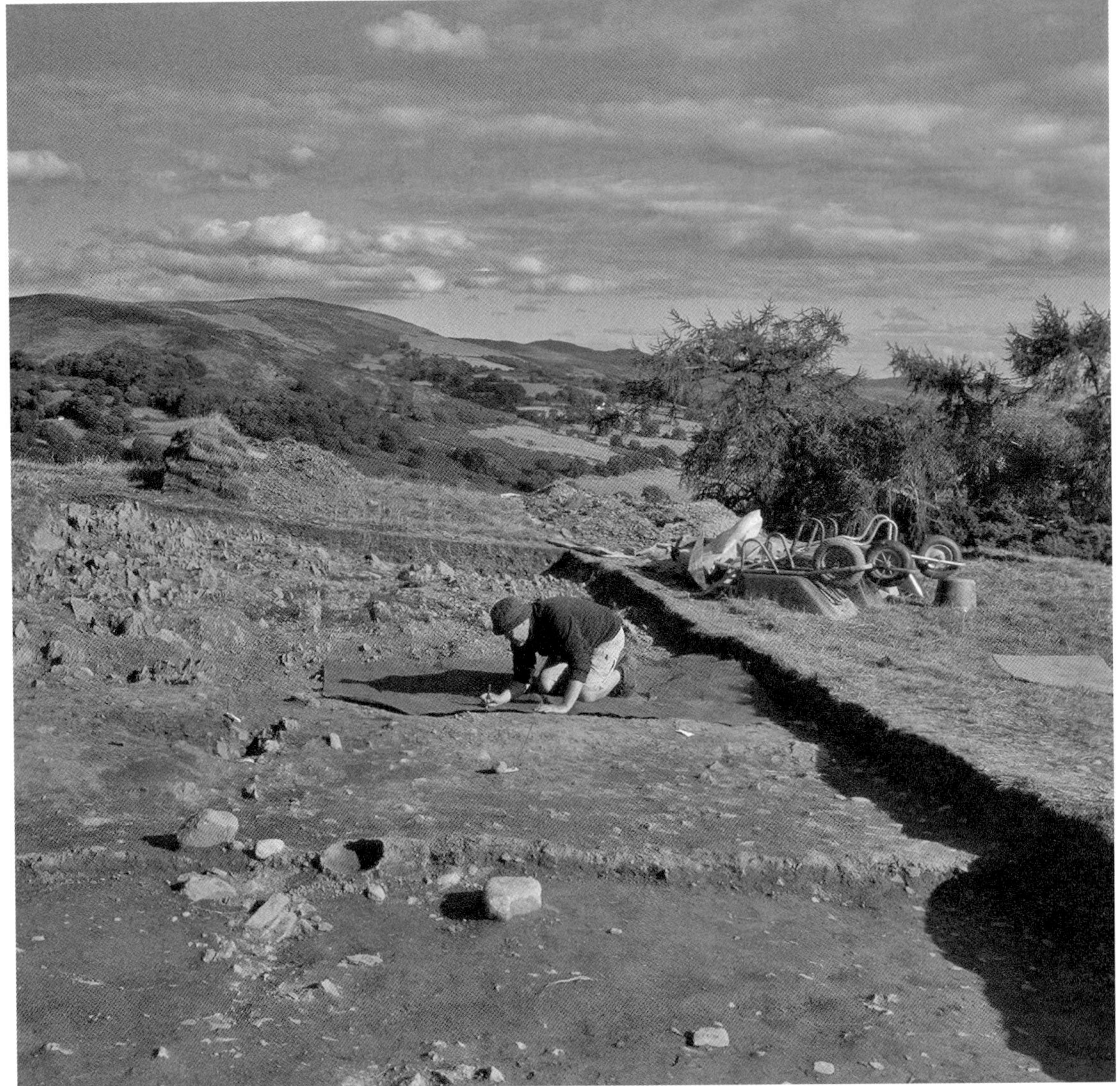

10.5 *Marking and cutting on site painting process. Moel-y-Gaer, Bodfari. 2015.*

Extended trenches and extended paintings

Archaeological trenches can be extended at any point during the excavation process if necessary. They are not fixed. This encouraged me to think that the dimensions and the proportions of a painting could also be extended or altered at any point during their making process. They need not be fixed either. On Moel-y-Gaer, Trench 3B had been extended to Trench 3F. The point where the newly opened Trench 3F met the original Trench 3B lay on an uneven bit of land. This caused an intriguing dislocation in the smooth transition from one trench to the other. It was of no significance whatsoever to the archaeology, but it had a physical and sculptural quality that I could not ignore.

My interest in this relatively trivial detail brought up the issue of my role as artist-in-residence on an excavation site. Was I there to serve archaeology, or landscape-based painting, or maybe both? It was my sole responsibility to define my role in response to what happened during the excavation process and not beforehand. I was supported in this experimental approach by the enlightened director of the dig, who gave me access to all the activity on site and all the conversation without imposing any conditions. I was a witness to all aspects of fieldwork and able to respond to what was important on my terms. This was a privileged position. I was the only one on site free to get things wrong, to misinterpret the archaeology, to see where that might lead. As I understood it, archaeological interpretation seems to be about limiting connections whereas art can benefit through misinterpretation. Doors can open onto new areas by not getting it right.

I wanted the flexibility to change the form of the painting at any point and I also wanted the paintings to have an interior space similar to the Wiltshire Modulor paintings from the Stonehenge residency. This led me to continue to reject the traditional stretcher: the rigid structure that determines and fixes the dimensions and the depth of the painting. I also wanted to continue to work with loose and unstretched sheets of canvas. Slowly, I found ways to replace many of the traditional painting processes with a physical equivalent: for line, I make a cut; for the illusion of depth, I construct an actual space; and for narrative, I leave evidence of how the work has been constructed. I was determined to find a physical equivalent to the established language of mark-making in painting.

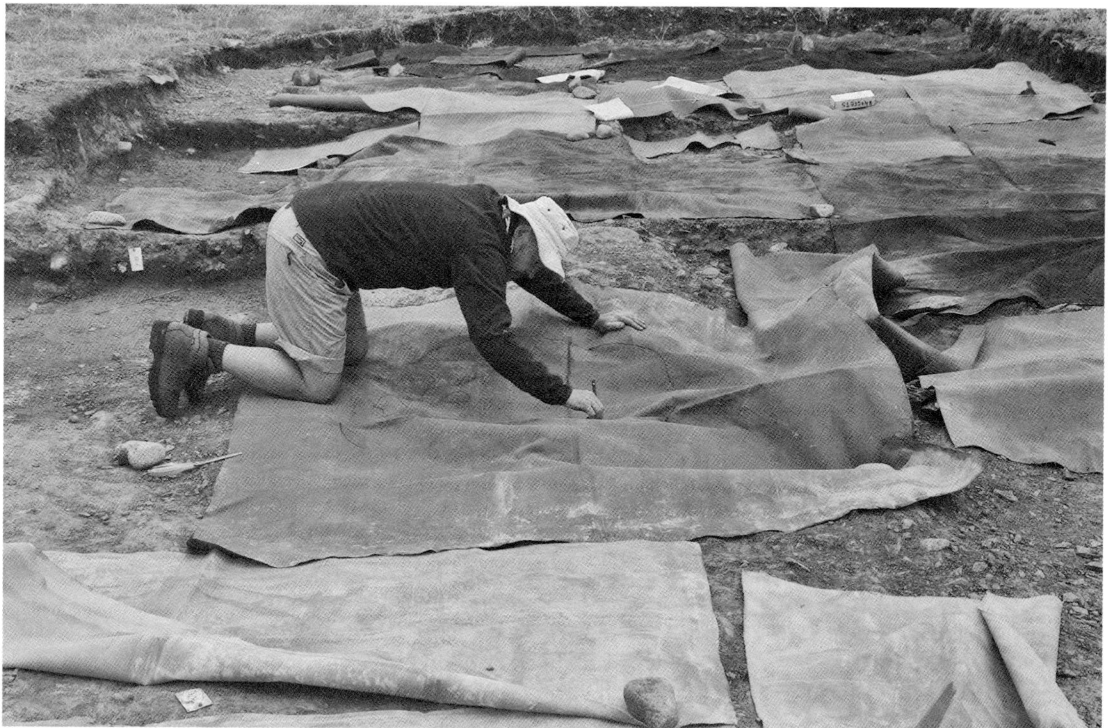

10.6 *Marking and cutting on site painting process. Moel-y-Gaer, Bodfari. 2017.*

Constructing the first Bodfari painting

At the end of each season, I collected all the canvas together and took it back to the studio in London, to add to the growing pile. This is where I was able to stitch the canvas together to construct the painting, using an industrial sewing machine. It is the part of the process I could not carry out on site. Over a total of six, two-week seasons of excavation at Bodfari, I produced enough material to make seven related large-scale paintings. The first work I completed is called *Flat Painting Bodfari 14/15 Ferrous*. This was the painting that established the new working method.

In an attempt to soften and unify the canvas elements I rewashed some parts of it in a domestic washing machine I have at the studio. The spinning function of the machine loosens the threads around the cuts in the fabric, and lengths of it unravel, break loose from the weave to collect as tangled clumps. Rewashing diluted the colour and it lost intensity. I reworked the colour with a weak distemper solution of rabbit skin size, with the intention of retaining the canvas softness and intensifying the colour. I was looking for a balance of these two qualities. There was a lot of rewashing, drying, and recolouring to get it right. While this was going on I could turn my attention to constructing the body of the painting and the front face.

The front face is assembled from a number of parts stitched together. It is at this stage that I am looking for material connections that give it a purpose and a logic. My decisions might be led by the colour relationships, by the scale of the holes in the fabric, or by line. As I worked, I cut into the fabric again or unpicked a section I had already sewn in order to attach another. All this contributes another layer to the accumulating material narrative: the evidence of the working process. I make no attempt to hide the adjustments and they are visible in the finished work. Working in this way is cyclical because all actions are reversible and any canvas parts that are rejected and thrown aside at one point can be picked up and reincorporated at another. Once I have a front face on the go, I stitch on a flat top section. It is similar to a wide sleeve with a slot for the wood flats to be inserted. This top section is in turn sewn to the rear face of the painting. I sew another section with another sleeve to the bottom of this rear face. Finally, this is attached to the bottom edge of the front face. This creates a closed loop. I insert the flat wood elements into the sleeves top and bottom. These flat rigid inserts hold the canvas loop open forming an internal space or body.

Country Register

The largest of the Bodfari paintings is called *Country Register*. This painting was made in 2018, the final year of the excavation. This painting is just over 5 metres long and 2.5 metres high. It is constructed from numerous canvas parts that have been stitched together. Most of the Bodfari paintings are predominantly red oxide but *Country Register* was made from all the green and yellow sheets: mixtures of mars yellow and mars black pigments. The paler sheets have a high yellow pigment to black pigment ratio. They have a golden hue while the ones with a more equal yellow to black ratio are a saturated dark green. There are also a number of canvas elements where I had added burnt umber, so the range of colour across the painting is varied.

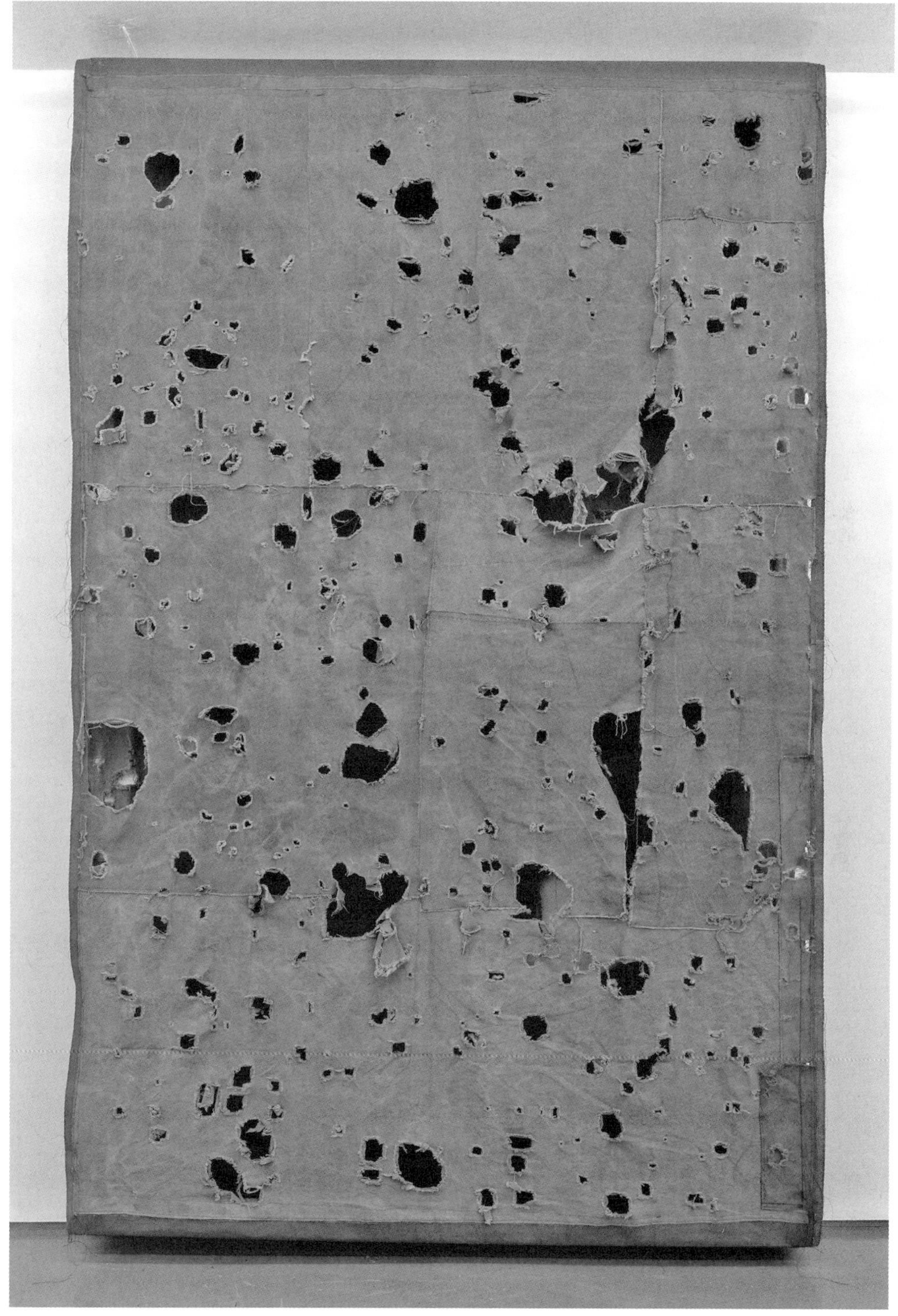

10.7 *Simon Callery. Flat Painting Bodfari 14/15 Ferrous. 2014–15. Canvas, distemper, thread, wood, aluminium. 293 x 182 x 19 cm.*

I laid out all the canvas I had on the studio floor and began to group them according to colour, or by type of mark or cut. Once I had a rough idea of the amount of material available for the work, I taped out a rectangle on the studio floor as an accurate guide to the overall dimensions. I was not thinking about the excavation site anymore. The reference to the site would have to come back in the finished work only if the painting worked well on its own terms. My focus was now totally on the language of painting: on building a unified and convincing surface where all the marks, punctures, and textures find their place. This is another point where aesthetic decision making and practicality overlap. The elements are pinned together on the floor before being taken to the sewing machine for stitching. The stitches are short and linear, and the cut threads are long. The painting is slowly constructed in this way. To begin with it is a fairly straightforward and satisfying process. It became increasingly demanding physically as the sheets got larger and heavier and more difficult to get under the sewing machine arm. Accuracy at this stage, both aesthetic and practical, is a priority. The overall form of the painting and the relationships between one part to another must be precise and intentional.

Generally, the paintings only go up onto the studio wall when they are close to completion and the supports for hanging them are built. This is an exciting moment as the scale of the work is tangible for the first time. The supports are an essential part of the painting, and they are not hidden or disguised. They function to reveal exactly how the work is attached to the wall as an element of the material narrative. The kind of support I use depends on the physical depth of the painting and how far it will come out from the wall. I use aluminium right-angle brackets for

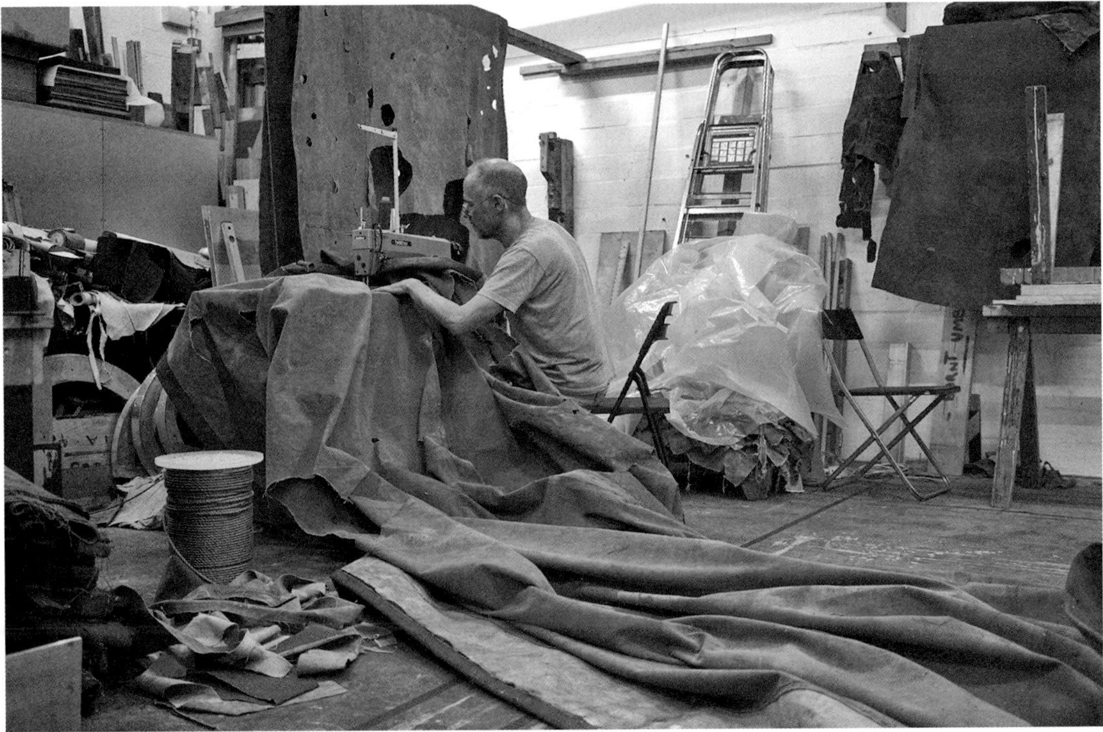

10.8 *Working on* Country Register *in studio. 2018.*

paintings with relatively shallow internal spaces. The paintings hang underneath these aluminium brackets and are bolted to it from above. The brackets hold the top edges of the painting tightly against the metal and they are absolutely straight and rigid. Other supports are made of wood, and the canvas drapes over them. Wood supports tend to give works a softer quality. As a consequence, the traditional relationship between the painting and its support, both in terms of the canvas as well as the hanging method, has changed. The painting can now be considered the entire physical structure. I have recast the functions of the traditional materials of the painting (the paint, canvas, glue size, wood) to different roles. The purpose of all these counteractions is to establish a language for painting based on materiality.

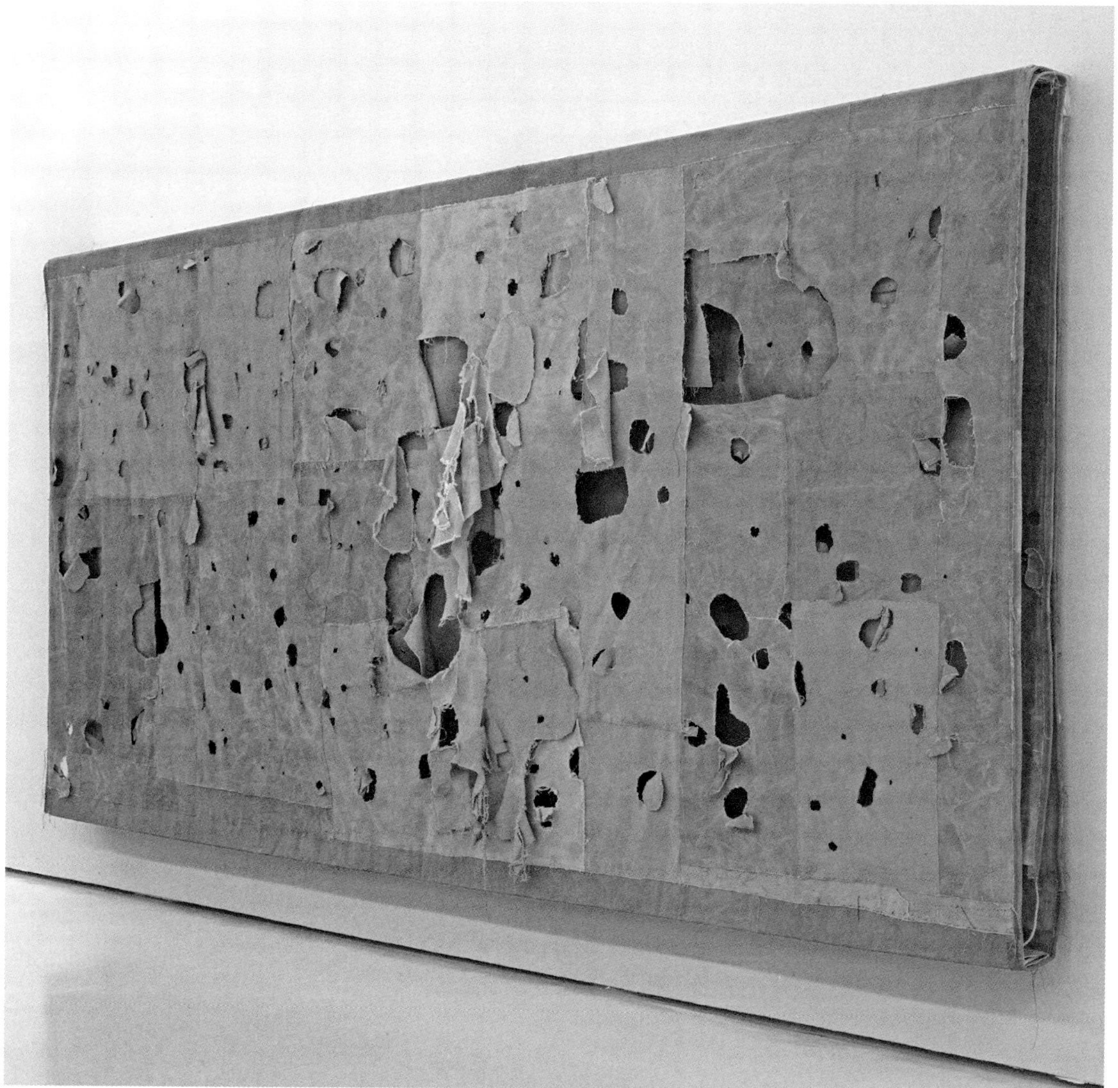

10.9 *Simon Callery.* Country Register. *2018. Canvas, distemper, thread, wood, aluminium rail and steel bolts. 250 x 503 x 22 cm. Collection: Caja de Burgos. Spain.*

The front face of *Country Register* has many punctures and apertures, both large and small, revealing yet another set of punctured and cut canvases hanging inside. The canvas is very soft. There are a number of loose canvas elements sewn onto the front face of the painting. Some of these are used to obscure or partly obscure what lies behind, and others serve to emphasize the softness and tactile quality of the fabric. The right hand and left hand sides of the painting are open and the secondary canvas hanging inside is visible. I use the large scale of this painting to encourage viewers to move across the front face, to 'walk the work' and to experience it in motion. The painting does not operate a static and single viewing point. This work hangs under an aluminium right-angle bracket which gives the canvas a clearly defined, straight, top edge as well as holding it open at the sides to reveal the internal void. The bracket supports the full weight of the painting and allows the fabric and all the attachments to fall and find their position under gravity. *Country Register* has a connection with the British landscape painting tradition, but its purpose has been reassigned to be a register of contact with the physical surface of the landscape, rather than being a topographical record or depiction of it. I think of this work and all the others from Bodfari as contact paintings.

The impact of archaeological excavation on painting

An archaeological excavation site provides access to the physical body of the landscape. If we have serious questions about our relationship with the landscape, then relying on what we can see does not take us very far. Other senses must come into the equation. I had seen the diggers close their eyes when running the trowel over surfaces concentrated on detecting the subtle difference between one material and another. The ears serve to alert them to subtle changes in the material as the trowel runs over and through it. Vibration through the trowel sends a direct physical indicator of changes in qualities of soils, fills, or the natural that the eye cannot always detect, especially in changing light. A deeper connection with the physical landscape calls for an involvement of all the senses. I see this as a clue for what painting should also aim to do. It strengthens my gut feeling that the stress on the visual in the visual arts, as made evident by the very term, establishes the parameters of what can be communicated and sets limits to what can be gained. For art (and archaeology) to really communicate a sense of place it must engage the attention of all our senses or it will risk limiting the range of what can be expressed. I consider the viewers of my paintings as fully sentient, and I try to make paintings for the body as much as for the eye. I have said many times that I work to give painting its body back and, as a consequence, a better awareness of our own.

Although all the Bodfari paintings were made in the landscape and worked on alongside archaeologists, it was never my intention to make the work about archaeology. My intention was more experimental and aimed to reveal, more than anything else, the impact on painting of working on an archaeological excavation site in the landscape. The physicality of the site is embedded in these canvases. I am fully aware of the genre of British landscape painting, but to continue with its picturesque traditions would be a mistake. This would not take into account the materiality of an excavation or the relationship of a site to temporality. These paintings are intended to bring a viewer closer to an equivalent experience of a place, specific to painting, than to a depiction of landscape.

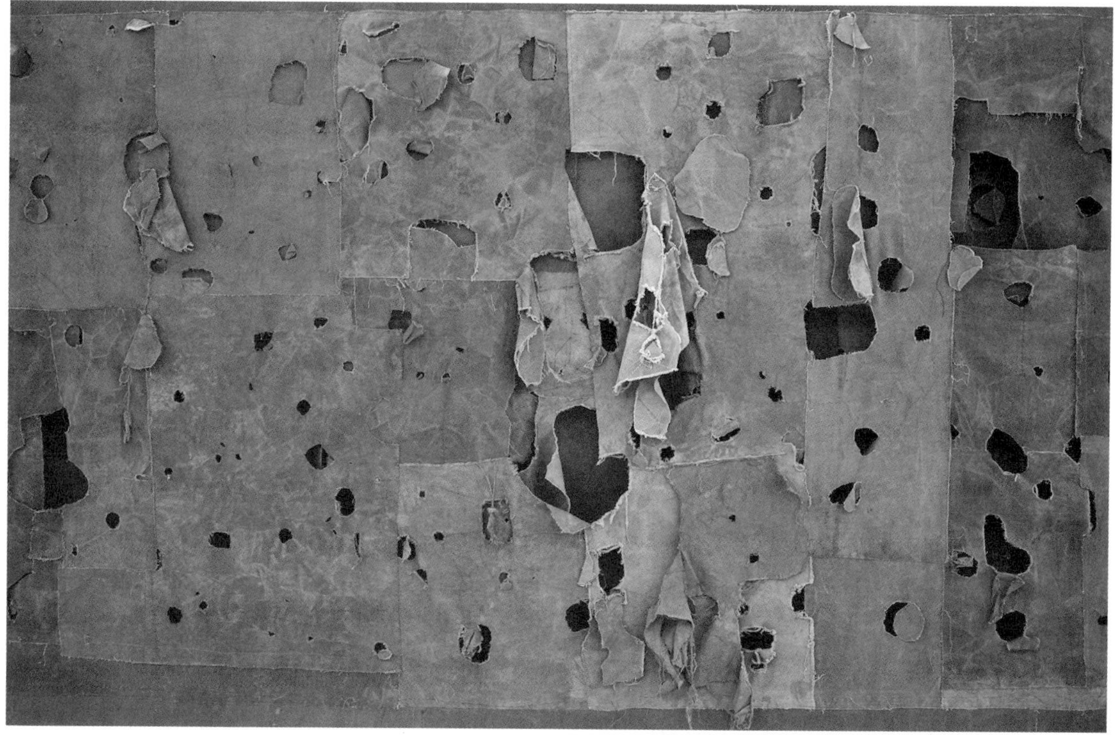

10.10 *Simon Callery.* Country Register *(detail). 2018. Collection: Caja de Burgos. Spain.*

The paintings contain evidence of working in a particular place. Here, I use the word 'place' intentionally rather than 'landscape' to make an important distinction. This word is useful when questioning the purpose of contemporary painting: where is the place for painting today, and where is the place for the viewer? One of the most important jobs of contemporary painters is to continue to question the form and function of painting if they want to keep it alive and relevant.

An encounter with a painting

'Cultivate the mute aspects of painting', wrote the American painter Richard Diebenkorn.[1] I think I understand what he means. Painting exists in a world of silence, and this is a quality of sound, not an absence of it. If we are attentive in this quiet world, then the non-verbal language of painting draws you in slowly. There is looking involved: careful looking. Then there is an engagement of the other senses, a connection is made which is non-visual, and motion, moving back and forward to measure the scale of the work with our own personal dimensions. We are drawn in incrementally: at first visually, then bodily, and then emotionally. The very best painting is not coercive and does not cry out for attention. It is an experience that can engage us completely. This is a description of an encounter with painting which I recognize as a mirror of my experience on archaeological excavation sites. What I felt and what I learnt in those extraordinary places has provided me with a model for what I want my painting to do and a structure for how I want the paintings to do it.

11

Disruption: Changing art and transforming archaeology

Introduction

Doug and Simon's work disrupts their disciplines. Both work on the outer limits of their specialist areas. By breaking down boundaries and moving across borders, they work in experimental ways.

Simon Callery: against painting

Outside of the art world there are some fairly rigid expectations about what a painting is and what it is intended to do. In Western art these ideas are based on definitions established in Europe during the Italian Renaissance. It is not inaccurate to say that these definitions have not changed much since then and we are in fact still working within a Renaissance idiom. A painting is a representation, a depiction, or an image. The physical structure of a painting is a wood stretcher with a primed canvas or linen support for the painted picture. It is designed to communicate its message to the viewer in the most direct way possible. In general, we can expect a painting to be rectangular, flat, and presented on a wall at eye level. A frame hides the edges of the stretcher, separates the painting from the wall it is hung on, and concentrates all attention on the floating picture plane. As soon as a painting does not conform to these requirements, its definition as a painting is in doubt.

Within the art world and amongst the progressive painters, the idea that the function and form of a painting are permanent and fixed has always been in doubt. Changes to the discipline have come from the painters who challenge the established conventions, in order to find ways for it to stay relevant and to reflect its time better. Typically, the upcoming young artists reject the work of their immediate predecessors. It is almost an art world convention that the only way to go forward is to push aside what came before. The irony, which is clear to see, is that the young artists, once they achieve recognition, are themselves the target for the next generation waiting in the wings. Art history proceeds in this manner. Having said this and after much change, there still remain certain features in contemporary painting that precisely mirror what was set in place in the past. A contemporary painter could sit at the table with a Renaissance painter and despite a 500-year difference, they would have much in common to talk about.

In contemporary urban life we are surrounded by images. We are constantly exposed to images and almost everyone is capable of creating a digital image. For Simon, any anxiety around what to paint or why was never about choosing to work with images or not. Since everyone could create images there was no need for a painter to make yet another one. Rather than celebrating this massive expansion of image production and distribution, the artist began to ask questions. We are all now visually sophisticated, though the consequence of such a stress on the visual is that the other senses are disengaged and left out of the equation. Something is missing and we are out of balance. Painting is historically implicated in the development of picture making and as a result it could be the best placed medium to critique what we are doing with it now. Not all artists have issues with the growth of a dominant visual culture. To some extent, from an art world point of view, you could see it as the triumph of Pop culture: the visual language of advertising proliferating in every aspect of life. By the late 1990s when Simon first started to work with archaeologists, there was very little sign of the art world proposing much of an alternative to this situation.

Simon's conception of painting as a unique language and means of expression implies that it is his job to steer clear of working with material already fully absorbed into mainstream culture. The question was how to make paintings that could offer an alternative or counterbalance to what was already in play. When he was asked, this situation encouraged him to grab the opportunity to turn away from the urban environment and towards the landscape to work alongside field archaeologists. Witness to the visceral physicality of the excavation sites but not wanting to make images of them, it became increasingly evident that it was the emphasis on the visual in the visual arts that sets a limit on what could be expressed. As the artist spent more time working in dialogue with archaeologists and informed by the process of excavation, the impact of these places began to exert itself on the resulting work. One group of works called pit paintings, made in response to sites in the Thames Gateway, were circular, multi-part, contained spatial depth, and tipped out from the wall on which they were hung. Since these works were not depictions, the structure of the paintings did not conform to the conventional structure designed for image-based works. These paintings rejected many of the attributes of conventional painting in order to elevate materiality rather than image as the central characteristic. These paintings were designed for the body. The act of turning against painting and challenging its traditions revealed itself to be one of the key elements that sustain and extend the discipline.

Doug Bailey: against archaeology

At the simplest level, Doug creates the work that he makes and designs because it satisfies his desire to explore uncharted territories beyond the boundaries of archaeology. Part of this pleasure he derives from being an iconoclast, from questioning traditional standards and offering alternatives. When he starts to explore new concepts or media, unexpected connections come into being, and unanticipated possibilities take form. Most recently, this occurred with the Releasing the Archive project (see Chapter 12) and just before that with his Ineligible Project.[1] Doug doesn't have a clear understanding of what happens when these projects begin to find their shape, or what might cause them to move in particular directions, but he knows when it starts to happen, because he can feel it within him. When he smashed an amphora at the TAG conference in Syracuse,[2] Doug knew that he was entering dangerous territory; he was excited to enter it, though he had no clear sense of what would result or where the debate that would result would end up.

These projects were not wholly casual wanderings, however; they started in specific, well-defined places with the standard materials of archaeology and historic, ancient, or prehistoric material culture. Beyond that starting point though, there existed only unmapped, and uncharted territories to explore. In Doug's work, a common inspiration is a sense that most current work in archaeology is self-limiting and inward looking, that the assumptions that underlie its practices and processes have not faced sufficient rigorous scrutiny. While there are exceptions, such as high-level philosophical discussions that occupy small groups of theoreticians (primarily focused in northwestern Europe, though in North America as well), the everyday work of archaeologists in the field, the laboratory, and the library, remains grounded in standard, descriptive analytical aims, techniques, and results. By making the work that he does, Doug tries to stretch our understandings and uses of the past in ways that many colleagues find uncomfortable, unethical even. While some may feel that his work is an attack on his archaeological colleagues and their more traditional work as they practice it in a more standard way, Doug's intention is not to assault them or disregard or disrespect their work. The goal is to offer well-worked-through experiments in alternative engagements of the past and its remains.

There is no single, best, way to engage the past, and great is the danger that comes from claims that one particular method, that one specific theoretical stance is most accurate, or that one school of thought or method offers a best way to process objects of the past. In his work, Doug is laying another plate at the archaeological table, and on that plate, he is serving a different meal. More accurately, perhaps, he is putting the plate on the floor or, better still, on the ceiling (and the inconceivability of that is precisely the point). His work offers something else for others to try, to chew on, to digest, or just to spit out. If no one wants to taste what he puts on that plate, then that's fine. There is no ego-driven desire to change a discipline and then lay claim to that change with a stream of graduate students and colloquia. To do so would be to retreat into the standard reputation-driven academic metrics of tenure, promotion, and a career-based economy. The alternative offered in Doug's work is to move outside of that metric-driven way of valuing the work of archaeologists and other academics in the social sciences and humanities.

However, and to continue the metaphor, that alternative dinner plate and its contents have to be in the dining room with other people sharing the meal. The efforts of alternative, iconoclastic work only make sense when they are consumed in that room and at that shared table. To have impact, the new, unsettling work must retain a connection to what it seeks to disrupt. Doug's art/archaeology is still an 'archaeology'. It makes itself known in the archaeological media of publications and conference meetings. It has traction, and it causes (often strong) reaction and response only when it maintains a tension with the standard, traditional ways of archaeological practice and production. On the other hand, art/archaeology violates enough of the core principles of archaeology (preservation, conservation, the belief in an objective past), that it creates degrees of separation (out on the periphery, not part of the main-stream) large enough to allow space for the accommodation of new conversations and practices. These new spaces remain within sight of standard tradition, yet distant enough to be disruptive and subversive. One step farther (outside of that room with its table laden with plates of archaeological meals) and no connection would remain with anything at all archaeological. That would be a step too far, and the resulting work would lack the power of reactive opposition.

In the Ineligible Project, *for example, the instructions were to disarticulate archaeological artefacts and to break their cultural, chronological, or aesthetic connections with the past. Even here though, in those objects (and remaining in the dust or liquid or fragments into which those artists transformed those objects) remained deeper, essential, metaphysical essences of being-of-the-past: an unbreakable connection through which ran the resulting artwork's power and the success of the exhibition curated. The power of each object and of the* Ineligible *exhibition surged at the moment of the viewer's (often traumatic) realization of the destructive actions required for the creator to make the finished work. Therefore, while art/archaeology makes explicit the act of disarticulating work from the past, it only succeeds because there remains an underlying connection to that past. Because of this, art/archaeology is not just art, but also it is not just archaeology; it is something else, and that something else is original, creative, and disruptive.*

Simon and Doug's work are at home in neither of their worlds, traditionally defined. Doug does not make archaeological interpretation; Simon does not make conventional paintings. But there is more to it than this. Both rebel against their colleagues and the longer histories of work in their disciplines. At first sight, there is nothing new about this. The aim of much archaeology (especially academic archaeology) in most intellectual regions of the world is to create new understandings of the past.

Doug's work questions the assumptions that the archaeological approach to the past (and the objects and buildings and ruins and bodies of that past) is the best (and only) way for us to relate to materials that we classify as artefacts and that make up an entity that we call the past. It asks an existential question: why has modern western society archaeologized our relationship to the past? One answer is that one of the sources of archaeological action is a lustful yearning: desires for knowledge, but also for appropriation, possession, control, hoarding, and consumption of pieces (artefacts) and places (sites) of the past. This desire is evident both in individuals' longings to collect, register, and regulate ancient and prehistoric objects, as well as in institutions' desires to control historic landscapes and nations' proto-communities. In this, an erotics of desire mixes potently with the geopolitical greed of nation-states and colonizing communities. The results are acquisitive claims for the past. In its position as an objective, accredited methodology of actions, archaeology remains the primary aider and abettor for satisfying these desires.

In his work, Doug prefers to explore alternative territories, where the intent of his practices and products disrupt and confront existing ways to collect and colonize the past. In these alien zones, he prefers to practice art/archaeology in ways that make trouble, and overturn thought, thinking, and thinkers. The project opposes salvaging, conserving, and reconstituting the past, and its peoples, objects, and places. Uncomfortably, it questions the deeply held assumptions about how (and more vitally why) we value the past and its material objects in the ways that we do. The goal is to shift the tectonic plates under our scientific and intellectual feet. As such, art/archaeology is an existential challenge to archaeology as a practice, a vocation, and a tool for cultural and political players.

Making change and making new work

There are other people making work today and there have been people in the past who have been interested in the idea of how you change the discipline of painting. The question becomes, why does it happen? Where does the impulse come from? It's not an invention. It's a genuine need and it happens on the level of the individual. Different groups of artists will be working on similar projects without even knowing that other ones are actually working on them in another city in another part of the world. It appears in different cities, and it becomes a ground swell. It's only at certain points you recognize it, usually when you travel and meet people. Today, that happens online and through the access to other artists' work on screen. In all of this, the art world itself, so to speak, is not putting these things together. Artists do that. It's complex. It's about what happens on the studio floor.

Similar things happen in archaeology, though it is more likely to happen in the lecture hall of a university or, much more likely, in the seminar room of a conference, or the pages of an academic journal. The role played by the studio floor and the artist working in one place is not mirrored by the excavation trench and the person digging in another. Beyond experiments in methodology, perhaps, change in archaeology comes at a less physical or tactile level. One result of this is the unhelpful dichotomy of field archaeologist and theoretician or synthesizer: the former is held to be a labourer uncovering and explaining the past; the latter as the cognitor and conductor of the broader symphony that emerges and is broadcast to the academic and general public. Archaeology is highly structured and disciplined in this way, and as a result change is more controlled.

Unlike archaeology, and more similar to artistic practice, fundamental, informed change comes from putting your hands into the process: into the dirt, into the pigment. Otherwise, the result is never anything other than theoretical positioning or external topologizing. The majority (perhaps all) of the claims for change and disciplinary disruption in archaeology takes place in an intellectual (and not manual) place. With few exceptions, such as work on the roles of the senses in thinking about the past, archaeology looks to academic argument (and publication) for its change. Most often this happens when an archaeological scholar (and not a fieldworker) discovers and adapts a philosophical or theoretical position from a non-archaeological discipline: sociology, social theory, critical theory, political theory, economic theory, philosophy, and a range of other social sciences and humanistic fields.

Both Simon and Doug's work comes from their experiences and not from theoretical borrowings. Simon's painting would not have changed if he had not been physically present at excavation. There would have been no need to make the new work that became his pit paintings or contact paintings. It was only by experiencing those excavations as processes of change in the landscape that provoked the need for change within his own work. Doug's work releasing artefacts and images through disarticulation and dissolution followed the same path: taking risks in violation with the professional ethics of his discipline. He spent a year on sabbatical diving deep into the land and environmental art of the 1960s and 1970s as well as the Dada and Surrealist creators of the 1920s and 1930s. He submerged himself into the works (and writings) of artists who disrupted the ways that art creation was defined (and shown and purchased) in those two periods. When he got back to his 'studio' (read 'excavation' or 'lecture hall') nothing looked the same; he could no longer write the academic papers or books in the ways that he had successfully been doing. A first result was a risky argument for not interpreting or explaining houses and buildings in prehistoric Europe.[3] He felt a second, more substantial response, when he was next in the field, directing an excavation in Romania; and the results of that discomfort led him to unleash artists onto the village community where his project was based, as discussed in detail in Chapter 4. None of it felt right anymore. It all looked very different. What were they doing there, trying to answer standard archaeological questions about the origins of sedentism? Why were they digging holes in the ground in their attempts to find out?

Embracing failure is a clear path to change and disruption, as failure is defined as not meeting the stated expectations of a movement or discipline. Valuing misinterpretation is another: to knowingly misinterpret or mis-construct in order to produce other ways of thinking and making.

12

Releasing the Archive
(Doug Bailey, 2020)

In a gallery of the International Museum of Contemporary Sculpture in Portugal, six videos run in loops on wall-mounted monitors. To begin, each fades-in from black to the image of a 35mm transparency, its mount made of silver cardboard bearing hand-written notes: labels (e.g., 'Keltic', 'Armenoid', 'Mongoloid Mexico'); numbers for cataloguing, projection sequencing or dating (e.g., 8361; '85; 1/20); or otherwise abstract markings (e.g., a slash, a red dot). Almost immediately after the black fade clears, viewers see a light yellowish liquid being poured down from the upper left corner of the image, and they realize that the transparency is in a clear plastic tank, and that its top edge has been clipped onto a holder so that it stands upright.

In one video (no. 164), the image on the transparency is of a man photographed in profile. With short, light, reddish-blond hair, he looks to the right. His shoulders, and what the viewer can see of his chest, are bare. On the video-monitor's screen, around this image, the viewer watches as the level of the liquid pouring in rises up beyond the top of the transparency and out of shot at the top of the screen. In the liquid, for a second or two, air bubbles swirl up and away; minute specks of dust settle to the bottom.

Then, nothing.

After ten or twelve seconds, sheets of smaller, white, and clear bubbles start to rush to the surface of the liquid, like a miniature snowstorm falling in reverse, towards the sky. In appearance like the other air bubbles, these only flow from the centre of the image, from the man's face: not from the mount or the bottom of the container.

As more bubbles release from the image, the blond-haired man's face starts to lose its contrast. He starts to disappear, dissolving into the air bubbles. On the right edge, where the transparency image meets the mount, the viewer can see some of the strip of black film-sprocket holes from the photographer's roll of film. From this strip, a stream of black material now shoots up, like liquid smoke from a fire. Sixty seconds into the video, the man's image has vanished completely, or maybe just a bare ghost of it remains. Ten seconds later, the black sprocket-strip along the side has disappeared as well. On the left side, where the image meets the cardboard mount, silver bubbles start to race to the surface. From the space where the man's face once was, another, finer set of bubbles rises. Then, nothing of the image, ghost or otherwise, is left. The video fades to black.

In the five other videos of the Santo Tirso installation, the same sequence occurs: fade-in, liquid covers the transparency, the image of a person's face releases and disappears, fade-to-black. None of the six videos are synched with each other: each installed to run in its own time, fading-in and

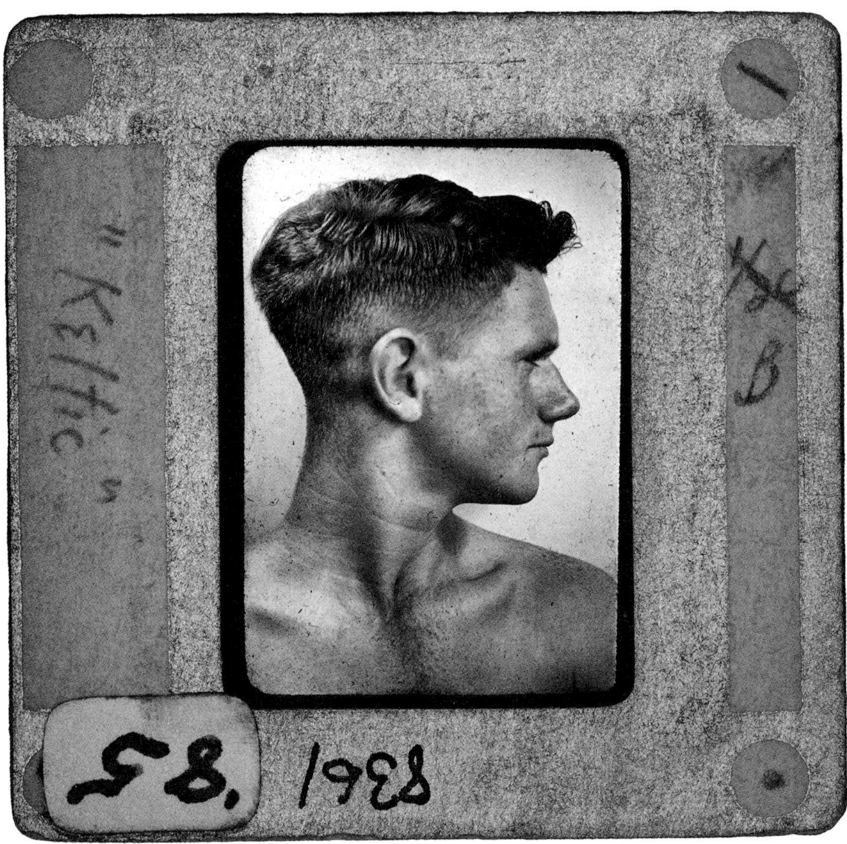

12.1 Releasing the Archive: *transparency no. 164.*

fading-out without correlation to the others. In all of them, the barest soundtrack can be heard: the sploshing of the liquid as it pours into the container, rises up, and covers the transparency.

Variation among the videos rests in the subjects of the images and in the notes written on the mounts. Each of the six videos presents a different transparency. All bear images of men, all bare-chested: in one image, a tanned man, maybe in his late teens or twenties, with dark hair, faces the viewer; in another, a dark-haired man, maybe in his thirties looks directly at the viewer; in the third, yet another dark-haired man, photographed in profile, looks to the right, his nose touching the edge of the image area, his neck slightly bowed; in a fourth video, a man with a bald (or shaven) head looks to the left; and in the fifth, another dark-haired man, in his thirties or early forties, looks to the right, his long, thin neck accentuated by the profile view.

All images in the videos are of men, all bare-chested, some in profile, with the profiles of their noses in image-centre, and hair cut up and away to leave a clear view of the shape of the ear. No face holds any expression beyond static stillness. The men who look out at the viewers meet their gazes in disturbing ways, locking onto them. Some may want to look away and perhaps need to, but they do not. The notations on the transparency mounts range in content, but a common theme

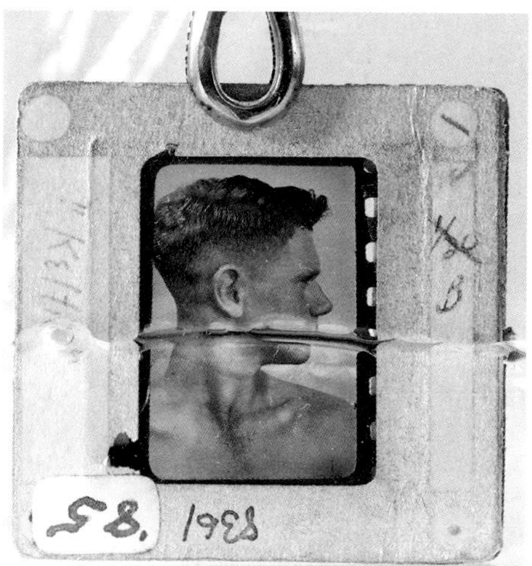

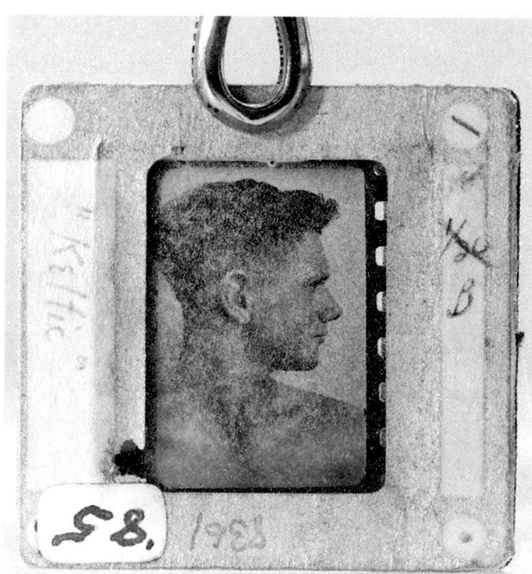

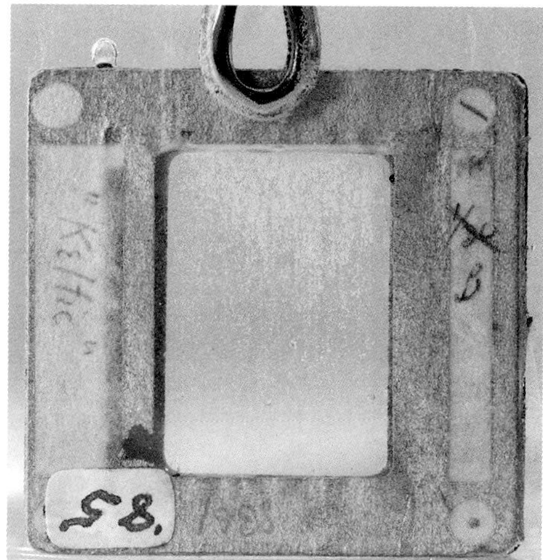

12.2 a–c Releasing the Archive: *transparency no. 164, three moments of dissolving.*

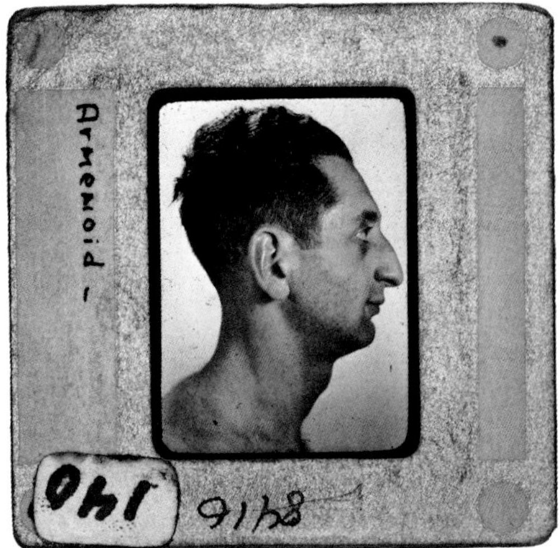
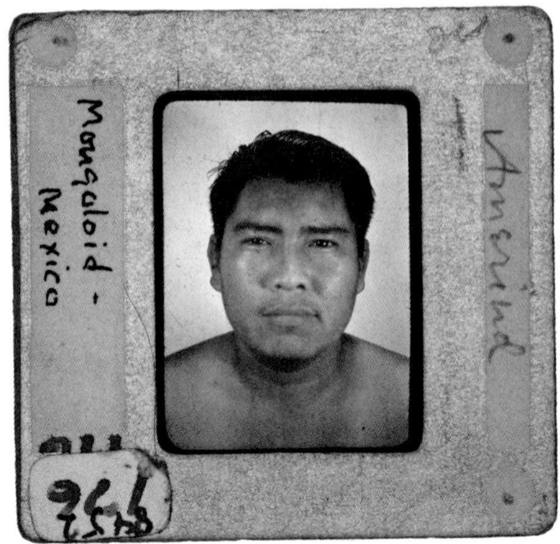
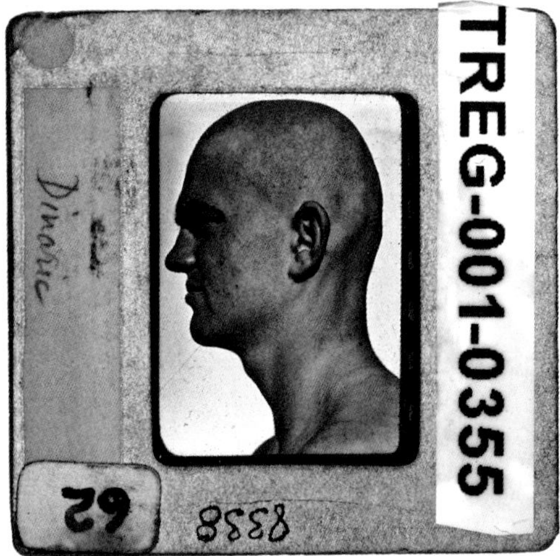
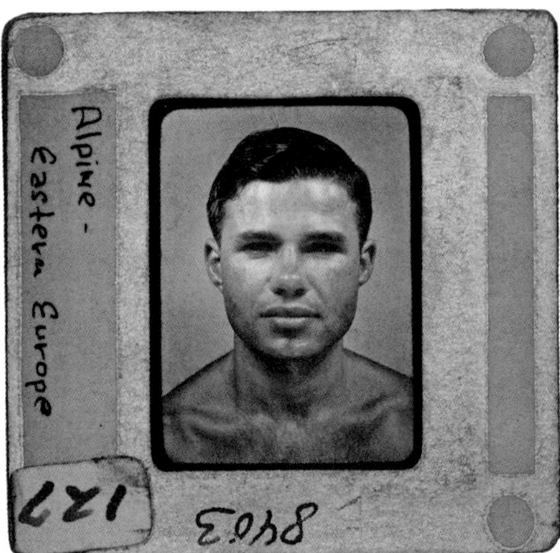

12.3 Releasing the Archive: *grid of four faces, undissolved.*

is clear: 'Keltic'; 'Dinaric Western Asia + eastern Med.'; 'Armenoid'; 'Dinaric'; '~~Dinaric — European~~ Iranian Plateau' [sic]. Each label identifies a specific ethnic group.

The project

These six videos were the final stage of a longer project and experiment, which resulted in two exhibitions in Portugal in 2020 and 2021.[1] In those exhibitions, the videos were installed with 18 giant enlargements of the transparencies (some 100 x 100, others 200 x 200 cm), and a live analogue projection of similar transparencies cycling through a carousel projector. At the core of both exhibitions, the videos were the result of an unexpected performative outcome of the chemical act of releasing the emulsions and dyes from the plastic surfaces of the transparencies. I developed the method through trial, error (and failure) in 2017 while I was a research fellow at the Centre for Advanced Studies at the Norwegian Academy of Sciences in Oslo.

I had started with an unformed idea about making these images unviewable. The transparencies were part of a museum archive from my home institution in San Francisco, and I had made the decision that the transparencies should not be kept in that archive. In normal museological circumstances, our institution would have tried to return the images to the subjects depicted in them, a standard, ethical process of visual repatriation. The people these faces belonged to, however, were untraceable. Further, it was clear to me that the images were the product of unethical study and use that relied on (constructed and repeated, even) ethnic and racial profiling, and that retaining them in the archive further victimized their nameless subjects. I decided that I should liberate the images by physically releasing them, though I was conflicted about doing this and about what the best way (if there even was a best way) to do that might be.

Experimentation

Some years earlier, I had been struck by reading about how Roy Stryker had tried to negate negatives that did not fit the shooting scripts of the Farm Security Administration, the Information Division of which he led in the 1930s. When Stryker came across an image that did not fit into the 'poor-but-happy' vision that the FSA wanted to project for Americans suffering during the Great Depression, he would make the image unusable by perforating the negative with an ordinary stationery hole-punch. Would this work for my purposes? I didn't know. I wanted to try.

The archive of transparencies that I was working with included the images of these bare-chested men in their silver cardboard mounts, but it also included other sets of images: casts of the fossil-remains of our earliest human prehistoric ancestors; non-human primates such as baboons and chimpanzees; subjects for study by medical anthropological analysis; stages of human reproduction; general human anatomy; archaeological objects; and the human subjects from ethnographic fieldwork. The archive had been part of a research and teaching collection assembled and used by series of professors and students over several decades.

As I started my experimentation in Oslo, I took one of the transparencies (it was from the reproductive health series), found a hole-puncher in the Centre's supply closet, and perforated the slide. I punched six holes in it: three through the image's plastic and three through the cardboard mount. These actions were violent and destructive; it didn't seem right, though I couldn't define what 'right' might have meant.

I tried something else. I went back to the stationery closet and found a pair of scissors. I took a transparency from another series (of non-human primates) and cut it into eleven pieces, and as I did, the transparency fell apart, plastic film separating from the mount. I had the same sensation: destruction and material violence. Disturbing, wasteful even.

The next week I was in Sweden, where I had been invited to give a lecture about my visual archaeology work at the Museum of Antiquities of the University of Gothenburg. For that lecture, to make an unrelated point about the sensory and perceptual experience of projecting 35mm

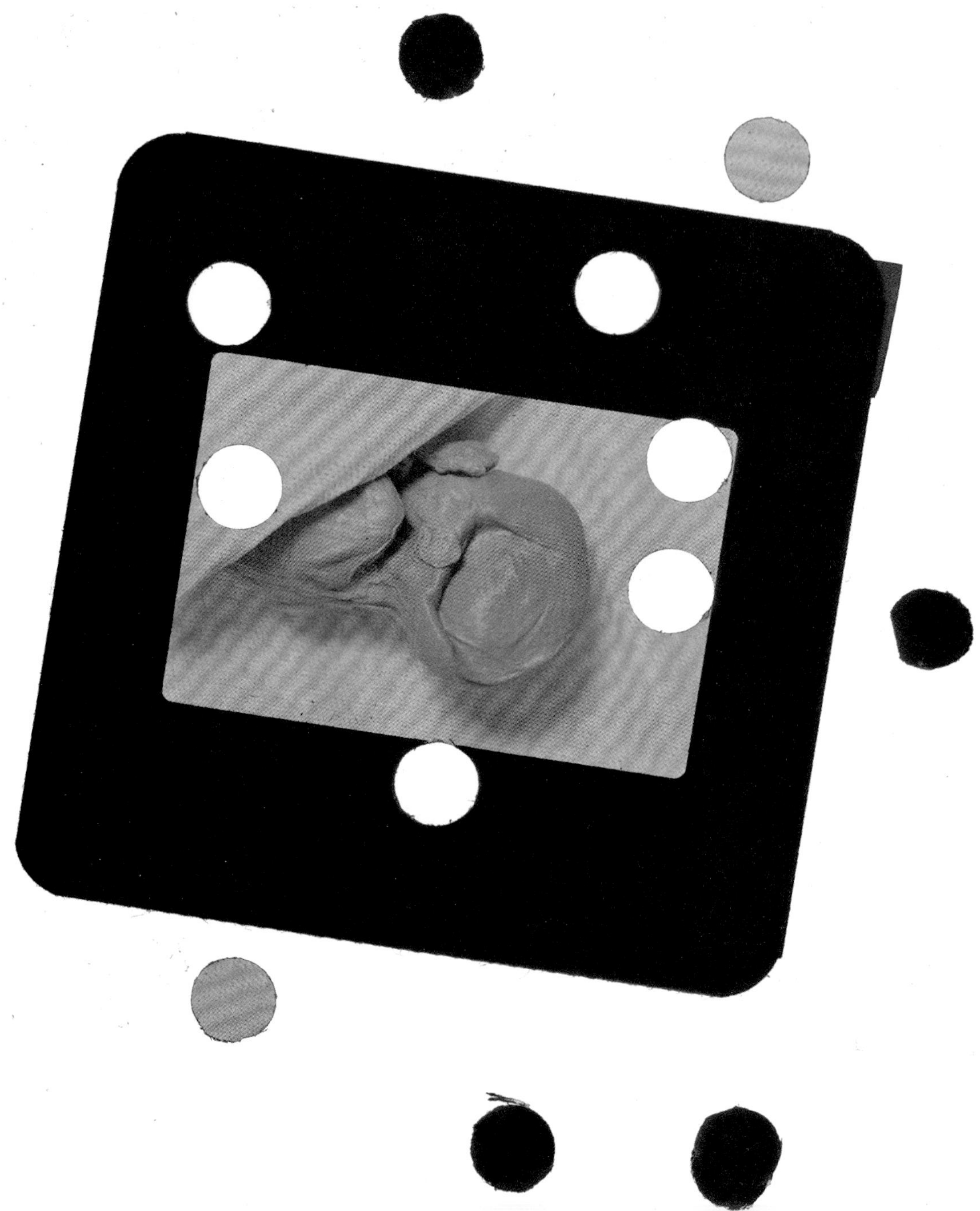

12.4 Releasing the Archive: *hole-punched transparency.*

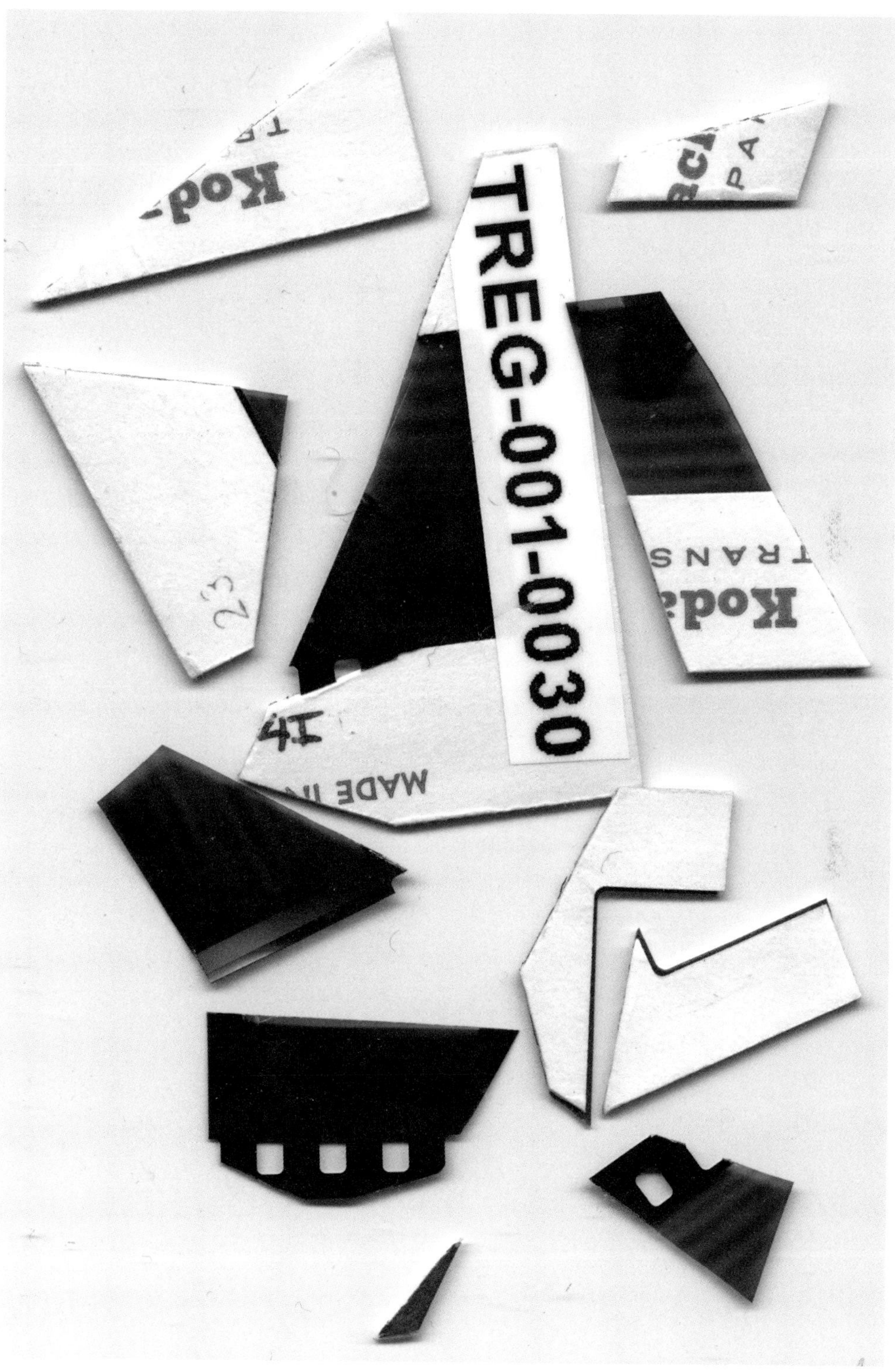

12.5 Releasing the Archive: *cut transparency.*

slides on large screens, I had set up a Kodak slide projector, and loaded a carousel with transparencies from the archive. As I set up the projector, arranged my notes and a glass of water for the talk, I noticed a couple of candles in holders on the table at the front of the lecture hall. What if I set one of the transparencies on fire?

The lecture started. I began by projecting the transparencies, and explained their museum origins and the conundrum I faced. I asked the audience, 'What should we do with this archive?' While they made their suggestions, I picked up a box of matches, and lit one of the candles. I walked over to the projector, pulled out the transparency that had just been on the screen, and walked back to the candle. The room went very still. People stopped taking notes. I held the transparency over the flame. Quickly, wisps of smoke rose from the plastic. In the middle of the image that I was holding above the flame (it was a photograph of the x-ray of a woman's pelvis at eight months of pregnancy), a hole appeared in the plastic as the film deformed, melted, and started to burn. Smoke curled towards the ceiling. I pulled the transparency away, shook it to stop the fire, and turned to the audience. Most were shocked. Some grinned. My host was holding a fire extinguisher.

Destructive and violent as had been my use of the hole-punch and the scissors, my melting and burning the transparency in Gothenburg had shifted my approach to the material and my own reaction to my efforts. Thinking about it later, the sensation that remained was the way that the plastic had started to melt and burn, especially how the smoke had risen from the transparency, as if the subject of the image had been transformed out of the pigment and dye and into vapour and barest essence, which, in turn, had risen up as smoke and dissipated into the air currents of the room and, eventually, had escaped the room and the building and dispersed in the breezes of Gothenburg. It was as if I had released the image and its subject from being trapped both in the transparency and in the larger teaching collection of the archive. The violence and destruction of the earlier experiments had been replaced by a liberation of release.

Later that month, I was scheduled to give a talk on the same topic back at the Centre for Advanced Study in Oslo. Several days before I was to speak, I asked the seminar organizer about using a candle to melt and burn another transparency. My colleagues (usually supportive in every way) said No. Rule learned: never ask permission to do something experimental or controversial. The idea that some experimenter (me) was going to burn something in the seminar room in a

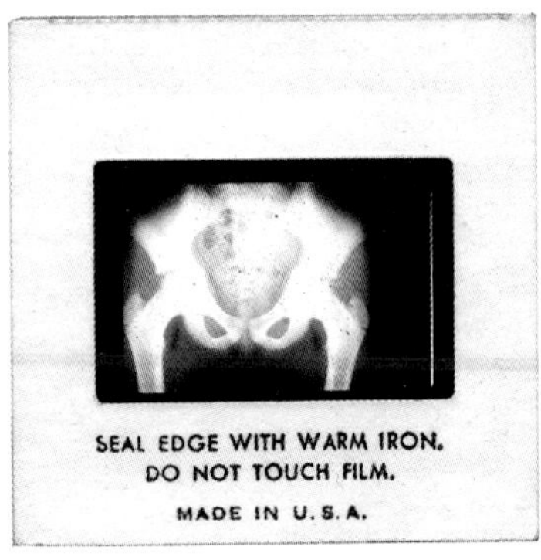

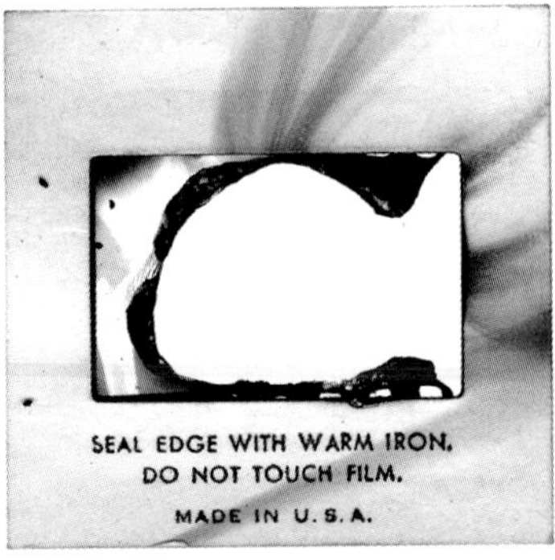

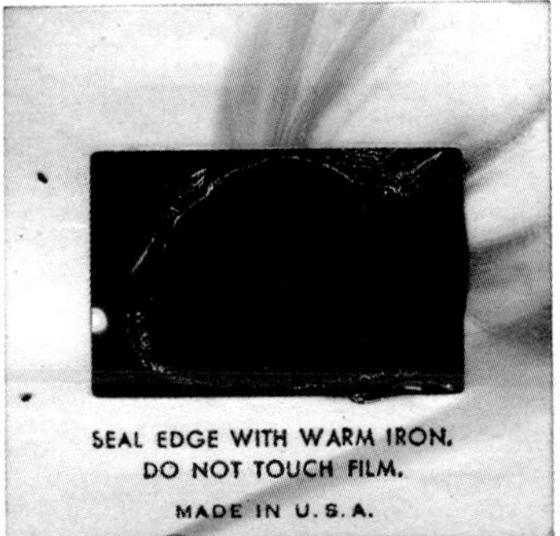

12.6 Releasing the Archive: *burnt transparency.*

centuries-old, mainly wooden building in Oslo was not received positively. The Academy of Sciences was housed in a wood-framed building, commissioned in the late nineteenth century by then Minister of Labour Hans Rasmus Astrup, as his family residence. Designed by the architect Herman Major Backer and built in 1887, the structure was protected as a cultural monument and registered on Oslo's heritage Yellow List. Fire or even the open flame of a single candle was not an option. What to do? How was I to explore and present my emerging idea about the release of trapped subjects from the archive?

Dissolving

The day before the talk, I was making a coffee in the Centre's basement kitchen. I needed to wash out my cup, so I looked under the sink for a cloth. I opened the cupboard door, and I saw a big blue plastic bottle: beach. What would happen if I poured bleach over a transparency? I grabbed a soup bowl from the shelf above, took a fork from the drawer, and unscrewed the bottle of bleach. I put one of the transparencies (this one from the series of ethnographic fieldwork subjects) into the bowl. It lay flat on the bottom of the bowl. I poured in half an inch of bleach. With the fork, I pushed the transparency down under the bleach. Nothing happened. I waited. Nothing. The bleach had no effect on the image or the mount.

I wasn't wearing rubber gloves and I didn't want to put my hands in the bleach to take out the transparency, so I picked up the fork and put the tines under the transparency to lift it out. The slide slipped off the fork at an angle, and as it did, a sludge of bright yellow dye slid off the image. I pulled the fork out and watched as the yellow dye swirled in the liquid bleach. I stirred the transparency with the fork and then flipped it over in the bowl. As I flipped it, blue dye ran off of the image, and I watched it mix, like a cloud, with the yellow. I teased the transparency with the fork, agitating it as I might do when developing a print in the darkroom. More dye dissolved from the image and mingled in the bleach with the others. I pushed the slide down to the bottom of the bowl and held it there with the fork; the last dyes left the image surface and rose in smokey streams to the surface of the liquid. After another minute or so, no image remained. With the fork, I fished out the now blank transparency. I had found my fire-replacement.

In the seminar the next day, I used a video of the bleach experiment in lieu of the candle burning. The effect was the same, both for my purposes, but also for the audience. One woman (a photographer and the partner of a good friend and colleague) wiped away tears as she watched the transparency dissolve in the bleach. The discussion and debate were vigorous. In the following months, I experimented with beaching transparencies. I went to the hardware store down the street, and asked for the strongest bleach that they had. I went to a homeware shop and bought several clear plastic containers, the sort of thing that you might store cereal in. I found a stationery shop and bought bull-dog clips and rubber bands.

In my office at the Centre, I attempted one combination and then another, trying to manufacture a tank in which I could treat the transparencies with bleach, but also in which I could hold the images upright, so that I could make videos with my little digital Leica as the images released. Once I had built the tank, I experimented dissolving transparencies. Not all transparencies reacted to the bleach in the same way. Different types and vintages of transparency material responded in different ways. Some resisted dissolving altogether, particularly if the film was mounted between two pieces of glass. The cardboard-mounted Kodak Ektachrome transparencies worked best. In most cases, when I poured in the bleach, there was a pause (maybe ten or twenty seconds), and then the dyes would be released from the plastic and stream up to the surface of the bleach, as if escaping captivity. For another fifteen seconds or so, clouds of different coloured dyes would swirl in the bleach, mixing with each other, then slowly thinning until there remained no trace of them (and, thus, of the original image or of its subject). What remained was nothing more than light yellowish liquid. After I removed each newly blank slide, I placed it to dry on paper towels that I had spread on my desk.

The prints

Before I had started my experiments in releasing, I had scanned all of the transparencies. At that point in the project, while I wasn't quite sure where I was headed, my archaeological training told me to create a digital record of the archive. Thus, as I moved forward, I had digital images of the transparencies made before the releasing process, and now I had a growing pile of newly bleached blanks. I found a cardboard shoe box and started to fill it with the dried blank transparencies. As I was doing this, however, I stopped and held up one of the blanks to the early spring sunlight coming through my office window.

The slide was not, in fact, blank. During the drying process, something had appeared on the surfaces where the now dissolved image had once been. Though almost invisible, there was still something there. I set up a scanner in my office, cabled it to my laptop, fixed the transparency into a plastic attachment for holding slides, and pressed the scan button.

Even in the scan-preview function, I could see that far from being blank, the transparency still held an image, though it bore no resemblance to the original subject. I adjusted the resolution, image-size, and colour settings, and ran a full, high-resolution scan of all the released slides. Still, whatever was there was not yet clear. I still couldn't make out what it was. Next, I opened all of the scanned images in Photoshop. With the first file that opened, I was amazed and disturbed. I opened up all of the scans. Bright colours: mostly yellows or light greens, but also purples. Skeins of dots appeared as if racing across the images. Groupings of black spots. Sweeps of small and larger specks concentrated in the middle of one image, distributed towards the edge of another. No clear shapes that resembled the human head, none of the colours or gradations of tone from the original images of bare-chested men. One resembled a shattered window with shards of glass, strangely misshaped and bent. Another, pale purple covered with many thousands of black specks, but with an unrecognizable shadow of an amorphous shape lurking in the upper right corner. Yet another with slow undulations of dark lines running up from the bottom and over from the side of the image. A strange dark figure, almost but not human-shaped drifting off to the left of another transparency.

The blank surfaces were not blank at all, but fully alive with forms and waves and glimpses of something, somehow always just out of focus, of bare traces of what had been there once, but which had, now liberated, left only spiritual essences.

My comparison of each transparency, as it had looked before releasing, with how it looked afterwards spoke to this transformation. I noticed that though each image (and its subject) had been transformed, the hand-written notation on the mounts had remained. While the image (and

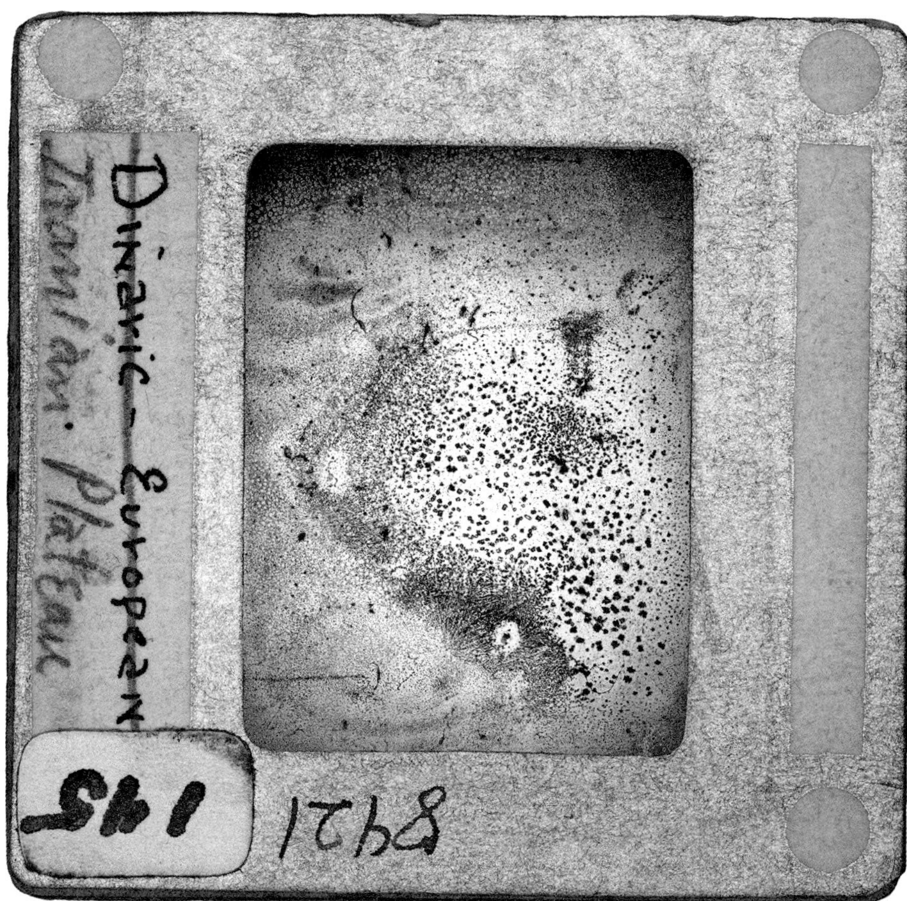

12.7 Releasing the Archive: *ghost slide*.

perhaps thus the human subject of that image) had been released by the bleach, up into the liquid, and then out into the sewage system of the Centre and eventually into the Oslo Fjord (I had flushed the bleach and dye mixtures down the office toilet), the evidence of the ethnic profiling remained unchanged. The system remained, but the subjects had been freed.

When planning the first exhibition of this work (in Santo Tirso, in northern Portugal), we designed the show so that the videos would run on monitors placed on one of the walls of a long thin gallery, with prints of the before-and-after dissolving images running down the opposite wall. These prints were large, disturbingly so: 100 x 100 cm prints, side-by-side, in pairs of images of the transparencies and the mount before bleach and the same after dissolving. Two, even larger prints (200 x 200 cm enlargements) of the forward-facing bare-chested men, again of image and mount combined, met visitors face-on when they entered the gallery. The dramatic increase in size boosted the impact that the images made. From a visual object that is tiny (5 x 5 cm, mount included) and which requires a light table or a special viewer for the interested observer to see it, we inflated the object to monumental proportions, to the extent that the once tiny head, now mounted on the wall was larger than life-size, especially the life-size of the people who came to see the show.

Projection

Transparencies, however, are most often viewed as projections made onto a screen, often in a lecture hall or classroom. To add this visual experience to the Santo Tirso show and to introduce the relationship of spectator-watching to subject-being-viewed, we set up a carousel projector at the far end of the gallery, loaded a tray with the remaining transparencies, and set the projector to run on a loop, without any introduction or obvious starting or ending points. Unexpectedly, one of the most powerful sensations thus created was the constant sound of the projector running: the fan whirring, the click-chunk of a transparency falling from the tray into the projection window in front of the bulb, the motor of the lens as it auto-focused, the ratchet of the metal arm lifting it back into the tray when its five seconds of appearance was over. Even less expected were the occasional drifts of dust that sprinkled or danced through the cone of projected light shining towards the screen. What was in this dust? Perhaps some other being (insect or animal) that had been released from its living form by some other process? What is dust anyway? What origin might it have had? And the brief moment of darkness when one transparency lifted out before another one dropped in; the dust in the cone of light never looked the same from one to the next. What had happened? How had it changed?

Connecting with the audience: Carpintarias

Releasing the Archive was installed, sequentially, in two Portuguese venues: first, as described above, in the spring and summer of 2020, in Santo Tirso, northern Portugal, at the International Centre for Contemporary Sculpture; the second was in the spring and summer of 2021, in Lisbon, at the Carpintarias de São Lázaro cultural centre. Both installations used the same core components: photographs, videos, and projected transparencies; both were accompanied by public lectures or debate.

Three innovations made the Carpintarias show in Lisbon distinct in ways that drew exhibition visitors further into the processes, methods, and themes that were central to the project. Some of these Lisbon alterations came from adapting the videos, prints, and carousel projections to the specifics of the Carpintarias' physical layout: a single, larger space all of which was dedicated to *Releasing*. The team in Lisbon added additional elements, a larger wall text introducing the show, and a set of questions for visitors to consider as they walked through the show; the texts of these questions were projected (in looping sequences) from the ceiling down and onto the floor, so that people could not avoid walking on and reading them.

Another addition was a public debate involving regular visitors to Carpintarias and invited members of the Lisbon-based museum collections and government archives. The latter spoke about their reactions to the transparency releasing project, the exhibition in terms of their own work in the professional world of managing collections and maintaining archives. Not

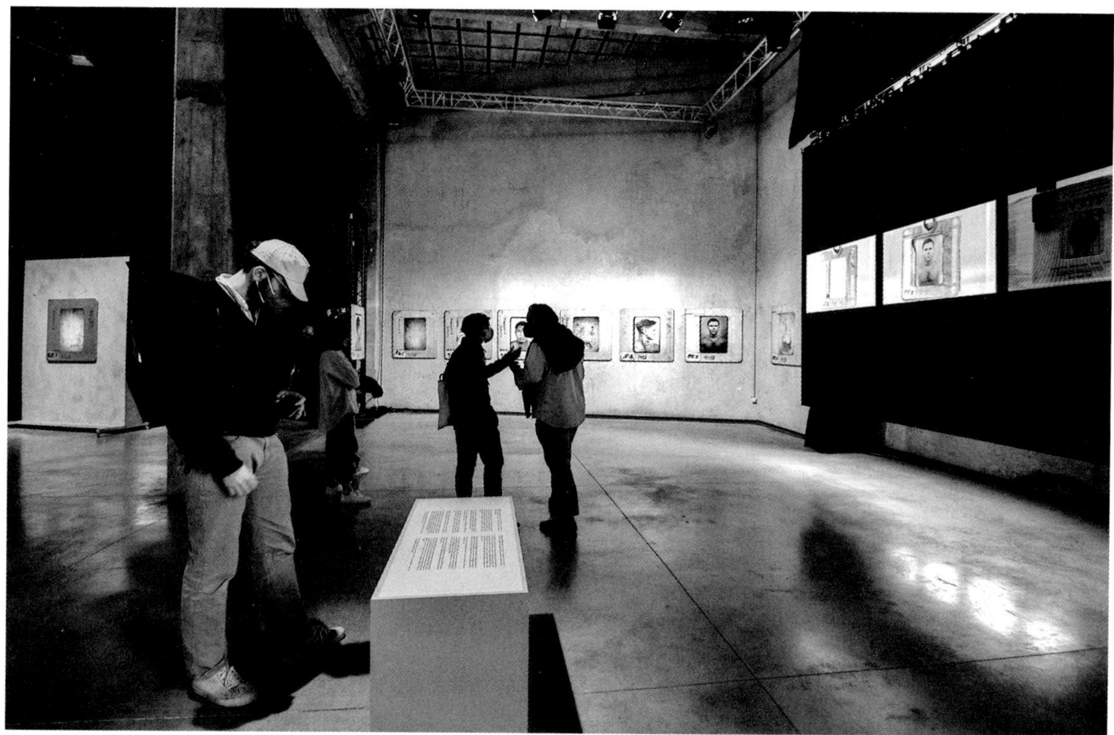

12.8 Releasing the Archive: *exhibition view, Carpintarias de São Lázaro, Lisbon, 2021.*

unexpectedly, that discussion was highly charged, with a rich divergence of opinion not only about the exhibition, but also about the role that archives of people's images (from facial recognition, government-issued IDs, and closed-circuit television) plays in modern state societies, such as Portugal.

The Carpintarias team added one other innovation: one that energized the show and integrated the visitors in it. After each visitor had purchased their entry ticket, they walked up a short set of stairs leading to the exhibition entrance. At the top was a member of the team, with a Polaroid camera in hand. Visitors were told that in order to enter the show, Carpintarias required that the gallery take a polaroid photo of them. If the visitor declined, then their entry fee was refunded, and they were directed towards the exit. Few declined. Their Polaroid photos in hand, visitors then entered the exhibition, read the introductory text, and wandered through the gallery space looking at the enlarged photos of the transparencies, the videos, the carousel projections, and the questions projected on the floor.

At the end of the visit, each person stood in front of a table on which sat two Perspex boxes, of equal size, side-by-side; the top of each box had a narrow postcard-sized slot cut into it. On the wall behind the boxes was a text instructing the visitor to make a decision about the destiny of their Polaroid. Visitors could either place their picture in the box on the left (the clear Perspex of which had been blacked out with paper and tape) which was labelled 'Archive'. Polaroids deposited in this box would be kept in the collection of Carpintarias, to be used and stored as the Centre saw fit and

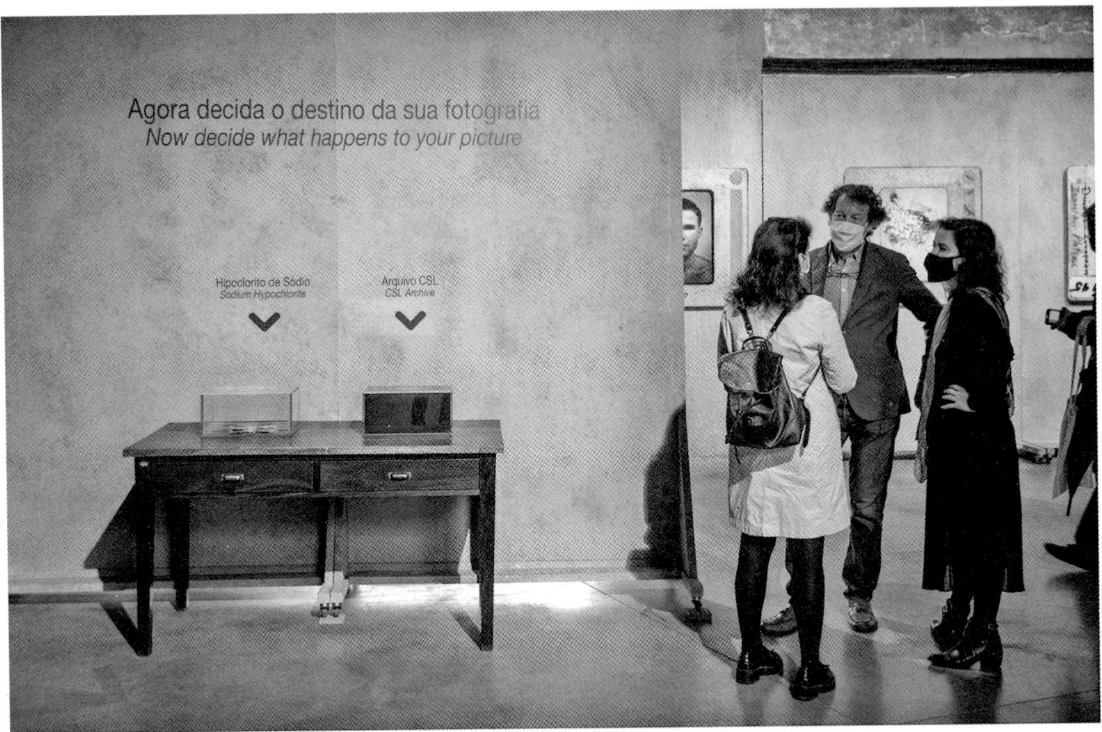

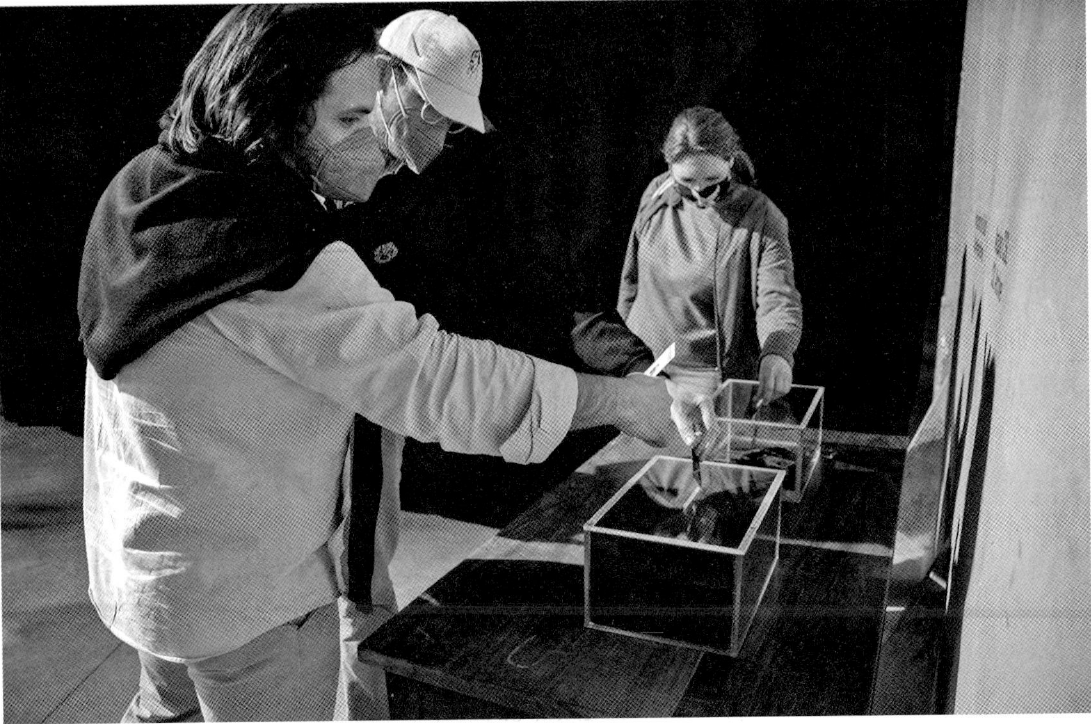

12.9 Releasing the Archive: *decision boxes at Carpintarias de São Lázaro, Lisbon, 2021.*

beyond the control of the visitor. The other box was clear plastic and had an inch or two of clear liquid in it: Polaroids placed in this box dissolved in the liquid.

The archive/dissolving decision created animated debate and discussion. Friends disagreed. Couples argued. Many agreed. Some hesitated. Others made their decision, almost casually, without delay. Some tried to smuggle their images out of the gallery when they left. Roughly equal numbers of people left their Polaroids in the liquid as in the archive box.

Both the Santo Tirso and the Carpintarias installations of *Releasing* raised significant issues that are central to the ways that we think about archives and institutional collections. These themes and debates have solid history within the social sciences and humanities, and one could do much worse than starting a review of that history with a re-reading of the French sociologist and philosopher Jacques Derrida's seminal book *Archive Fever* published in 1995.[2]

To take that path, however, would be to remain in the standard tradition of academic thought. Peer-reviewed journal articles would result, perhaps even a monograph or an edited volume focused on the topic. Those texts, of course of value, would never find the traction, generate the reactions (of disgust and of wonder), or reach the range of the size of the audiences that the two Portuguese shows obtained. In distinction and counterpoint to that standard tradition of academic discourse about artefact, archive, conservation, and preservation, the *Releasing the Archive* project, through its videos and photographs, but even more pointedly, in the chemical actions of dissolving and release, constitutes a work about the past and our engagement with it that sits well beyond the boundaries and limitations of the current practices of archive and collections management, archaeology and heritage practices.

Notes

1 Two journeys, three voices

1 Bailey 2005a.
2 Clifford 1981.
3 Leiris 1934.
4 Bailey 2008.
5 Bailey 2014a.
6 See also Bailey et al. 2010.
7 Bailey 2018b.
8 Bailey and Simpkin 2015.
9 Bailey 2013.
10 Bailey 2024.
11 Bailey 2014b.
12 Renfrew 2003.

3 Authorship

1 Bender et al. 2008.
2 Dural 2007.

4 *Twenty Minutes Inside Out*

1 Bailey et. al. 2010; https://vimeo.com/manage/videos/1078042338.
2 Project participants: Peter Biella, Cătălina Dănilă, Iván Drufovka, Paul Evans, Claude Heath, Michaël Jasmin, Judy and Mark Macklin, Steve Mills, Pavel Mirea, Simon Thorne and Angela Walker. See Mills 2011 for details of all work completed.
3 The Cardiff side of the project was co-directed by Dr Steve Mills of the School of History, Archaeology and Religion at Cardiff University; in Romania, Dr Pavel Mirea of the Teleorman Regional Historical Museum took the lead role as collaborative director of the work. The project's success is the result of Steve and Pavel's dedication and work.
4 Bailey et al. 2010.
5 Heath 2011.
6 Thorne 2011a.
7 Thorne 2011b, 2011c.
8 Jasmin 2011a, b.

9 Bailey 2021.

10 https://www.dwbphotography.org/romania.

11 Biella and Drufovka 2010, 2011.

12 Bailey and Simpkin 2015.

13 Van Dyke and Bernbeck 2015.

14 Diller and Scofidio 1992.

5 Creating original work

1 Bailey 2018a.

2 Bailey 2000.

3 Bailey 2005a.

4 Bailey 2017a, 2017b and 2018a: 1–40.

7 Different times

1 Von Uexküll 1940, 1957, 2010.

2 Bailey 2018b.

8 *Which Ruins do we Valorize*

1 Olsen and Pétursdóttir 2014.

2 Bailey 2014b.

3 McLucas 2000.

4 Bailey 2000.

9 Avoiding meaning

1 Heisenberg 1927.

10 *Country Register*

1 Diebenkorn 1966–76.

11 Disruption

1 See Bailey 2020a, Bailey et al. 2020a, 2020b: 28–50, 64–97.

2 See Bailey 2023.

3 Bailey 2005b.

12 *Releasing the Archive*

1 See Bailey et al. 2020a; Carpintarias 2021.

2 Derrida 1995.

Bibliography

Bailey, D. W. 2000. *Balkan Prehistory: Incorporation, Exclusion, and Identity.* London: Routledge.

Bailey, D. W. 2005a. *Prehistoric Figurines: Representation and Corporeality in the Neolithic.* London: Routledge.

Bailey, D. W. 2005b. Beyond the meaning of Neolithic houses: specific objects and serial repetition. In D. W. Bailey, A. Whittle and V. Cummings (eds), *(un)settling the Neolithic*, pp. 95–106. Oxford: Oxbow.

Bailey, D. W. 2008. Art to archaeology to art to archaeology. University College Dublin, Scholarcast (http://www.ucd.ie/scholarcast/scholarcast9.html). Accessed September 1, 2024.

Bailey, D. W. 2013. Cutting the earth / cutting the body. In A. Alfredo González-Ruibal (ed.), *Reclaiming Archaeology: Beyond the Tropes of Modernity*, pp. 337–45. London: Routledge.

Bailey, D. W. 2014a. Art//archaeology//art: letting-go beyond. In I. Russell and A. Cochrane (eds), *Art and Archaeology: Collaborations, Conversations, Criticisms*, pp. 231–50. New York: Springer.

Bailey, D. W. 2014b. Which ruins do we valorize? A new calibration curve for the Balkan past. In B. Olsen and Þóra Pétursdóttir (eds), *Ruin Memories: Materiality, Aesthetics and the Archaeology of the Recent Past*, pp. 215–29. London: Routledge.

Bailey, D. W. 2017a. Art/Archaeology: what value artistic-archaeological collaboration? *Journal of Contemporary Archaeology* 4(2): 246–56.

Bailey, D. W. 2017b. Disarticulate – repurpose – disrupt: art/archaeology. *Cambridge Archaeological Journal* 27(4): 691–701.

Bailey, D. W. 2018a. *Breaking the Surface: An Art/archaeology of Prehistoric Architecture.* Oxford: Oxford University Press.

Bailey, D. W. 2018b. The Uexküll calibration: chronology and critical flicker fusion frequency. In S. Souvatzi, A. Baysal and E. Baysal (eds), *Time and History in Prehistory*, pp. 31–41. London: Routledge.

Bailey, D. W. 2020a. Art/archaeology: the Ineligible Project. In D. W. Bailey, S. Navarro, and Á. Moreira (eds), *Ineligible: A Disruption of Artefacts and Artistic Practice of Art*, pp. 13–28. Santo Tirso: International Museum of Contemporary Sculpture.

Bailey, D. W. 2020b. Releasing the visual archive: on the ethics of destruction. In B. Olsen, M. Burstrøm, C. DeSilvey, and Þ. Pétursdóttir (eds), *After Discourse: Things, Affects, Ethics*, pp. 232–56. London: Routledge.

Bailey, D. W. 2021. *Walking in Place: A Romanian Village.* San Francisco, CA: Blurb.

Bailey, D. W. 2023. The Syracuse Amphora Project: on violence against artifacts. In C. Watts and C. Knappett (eds), *Ancient Art Revisited: Global Perspectives from Archaeology and Art History*, pp. 112–24. New York Routledge.

Bailey, D. W. 2024. Beyond archaeology: death and the erotics of things past. In H. Bjerck, M. Burström, Þ. Pétursdóttir, and A Svestad (eds), *For Love of Archaeology*, pp. 20–9. Tromsø: Tromsø Museum Press.

Bailey, D. W. and Simpkin, M. 2015. Eleven minutes and forty seconds in the Neolithic: underneath archaeological time. In R. Van Dyke and R. Bernbeck (eds), *Subjects and Narratives in Archaeology*, pp. 187–213. Boulder, CO: University Press of Colorado.

Bailey, D. W. (with P. Biella and I. Druvofka), 2010. *Twenty Minutes Inside Out: Landscape Transformation in Neolithic Southeastern Romania.* 20 minute video. https://vimeo.com/manage/videos/534525094.

Bailey, D. W., A. Cochrane, and J. Zambelli, 2010. *Unearthed: A Comparative Study of Jōmon Dogū and Neolithic Figurines.* Norwich: Sainsbury Centre for Visual Arts.

Bailey, D. W., S. Navarro, and Á. Moreira (eds), 2020a. *Ineligible: A Disruption of Artefacts and Artistic Practice.* Santo Tirso: International Museum of Contemporary Sculpture.

Bailey, D. W., S. Navarro, and Á. Moreira (eds), 2020b. *Creative (un)makings: Disruptions in Art/ Archaeology.* Exhibition catalogue. Santo Tirso: International Museum of Contemporary Sculpture.

Bender, B., S. Hamilton, and C. Tilley, 2008. *Stone Worlds: Narrative and Reflexivity in Landscape Archaeology.* New York: Routledge.

Biella, P. and I. Drufovka, 2010. *Eternity was Born in the Village.* Video. [USA]. San Francisco State University.

Biella, P. and I. Drufovka, 2011. Lost in eternity. In S. Mills (ed.), *Interventions: Măgura Past and Present*, pp. 75–92. Bucureşti: Renaissance.

Carpintarias de São Lázaro, 2021. *Releasing The Archive: Exposição a Partir da Investigação e Criação Visual de Doug Bailey* [*Exhibition Based on the Research and Visual Creation of Doug Bailey*]. Lisbon: Carpintarias de São Lázaro.

Clifford, J. 1981. On ethnographic surrealism. *Comparative Studies in Society and History* 23(04): 539–64.

Derrida, J. 1995. *Archive Fever: A Freudian Impression* (trans. Eric Prenowitz). Chicago, IL: University of Chicago Press.

Diebenkorn, R. 1966–76. Studio note. Reproduced in Jane Livingston and Andrea Liguori (eds), *Richard Diebenkorn: The Catalogue Raisonné, Volume 1*, p. 201. New Haven, CT and London: Yale University Press.

Diller, E. and R. Scofidio, 1992. Case no. 00-17163. In J. Crary and S. Kwinter (eds), *Zone 6: Incorporations,* pp. 344–61. New York: Zone Books.

Dural, S. 2007. *Protecting Çatalhöyük Memoir of an Archaeological Site Guard.* Walnut Creek, CA: Left Coast Press.

Heath, C. 2011. Unsighted tactile drawings of prehistoric archaeological objects. In S. Mills (ed.), *Interventions: Măgura Past and Present*, pp. 185–202. Bucureşti: Renaissance.

Heisenberg, W. 1927. Über den anschaulichen Inhalt der quantentheoretischen Kinematik und Mechanik [The actual content of quantum theoretical kinematics and mechanics]. *Zeitschrift fur Physik* 43: 172–98.

Jasmin, M. 2011a. The grid in context. In S. Mills (ed.), *Interventions: Măgura Past and Present*, pp. 217–36. Bucureşti: Renaissance.

Jasmin, M. 2011b. *The Brain of the Archaeologist: An Art and Archaeology Dialogue.* Grenoble: Deux Points.

Leiris, M. 1934. *L'Afrique Fantôme* [*Phantom Africa*]. Paris: Gallimard.

McLucas, C. 2000. Ten feet and three quarters of an inch of theatre. In N. Kaye (ed.), *Site-Specific Art: Performance, Place and Documentation*, pp. 125–38. London: Routledge.

Mills, S. (ed.), 2011. *Măgura: Past and Present.* Cardiff: Cardiff University Press

Olsen, B. and Þ. Pétursdóttir (eds), 2014. *Ruin Memories: Materiality, Aesthetics and the Archaeology of the Recent Past.* London: Routledge

Pearson, M. and M. Shanks, 2001. *Theatre/Archaeology.* London: Routledge.

Renfrew, A. C. 2003. *Figuring It Out: The Parallel Visions of Artists and Archaeologists.* London: Thames and Hudson.

Thorne, S. 2011a. Sounds like nothing. In S. Mills (ed.), *Interventions: Măgura Past and Present*, pp. 93–118. Bucureşti: Renaissance.

Thorne, S. 2011b. *Some Spaces.* CD. Cardiff: Simon Thorne Music.

Thorne, S. 2011c. *Măgura: Romanian Village Soundscape.* CD. Cardiff: Simon Thorne Music.

Van Dyke, R. and R. Bernbeck (eds), 2015. *Subjects and Narratives in Archaeology.* Boulder, CO: University Press of Colorado.

Von Uexküll, J. 1940. *Bedeutungslehre* [*The Theory of Meaning*]. Leipzig: J. A. Barth.

Von Uexküll, J. 1957. A stroll through the worlds of animals and men (trans. Claire Schiller). In Claire H. Schiller (ed.), *Instinctive Behavior: The Development of a Modern Concept*, pp. 5–80. New York, NY: International Universities Press.
Von Uexküll, J. 2010. *A Foray into the Worlds of Animals and Humans With a Theory of Meaning* (trans. Joseph D. O'Neil). Minneapolis, MN: University of Minnesota Press.

Index